Re-Orienting Fashion

Dress, Body, Culture

Series Editor **Joanne B. Eicher**, *Regents' Professor, University of Minnesota*

Books in this provocative series seek to articulate the connections between culture and dress which is defined here in its broadest possible sense as any modification or supplement to the body. Interdisciplinary in approach, the series highlights the dialogue between identity and dress, cosmetics, coiffure, and body alterations as manifested in practices as varied as plastic surgery, tattooing, and ritual scarification. The series aims, in particular, to analyze the meaning of dress in relation to popular culture and gender issues and will include works grounded in anthropology, sociology, history, art history, literature, and folklore.

ISSN: 1360-466X

Previously published titles in the Series

Helen Bradley Foster, *"New Raiments of Self": African American Clothing in the Antebellum South*

Claudine Griggs, *S/he: Changing Sex and Changing Clothes*

Michaele Thurgood Haynes, *Dressing Up Debutantes: Pageantry and Glitz in Texas*

Anne Brydon and Sandra Niesson, *Consuming Fashion: Adorning the Transnational Body*

Dani Cavallaro and Alexandra Warwick, *Fashioning the Frame: Boundaries, Dress and the Body*

Judith Perani and Norma H. Wolff, *Cloth, Dress and Art Patronage in Africa*

Linda B. Arthur, *Religion, Dress and the Body*

Paul Jobling, *Fashion Spreads: Word and Image in Fashion Photography*

Fadwa El-Guindi, *Veil: Modesty, Privacy and Resistance*

Thomas S. Abler, *Hinterland Warriors and Military Dress: European Empires and Exotic Uniforms*

Linda Welters, *Folk Dress in Europe and Anatolia: Beliefs about Protection and Fertility*

Kim K.P. Johnson and Sharron J. Lennon, *Appearance and Power*

Barbara Burman, *The Culture of Sewing*

Annette Lynch, *Dress, Gender and Cultural Change*

Antonia Young, *Women Who Become Men*

David Muggleton, *Inside Subculture: The Postmodern Meaning of Style*

Nicola White, *Reconstructing Italian Fashion: America and the Development of the Italian Fashion Industry*

Brian J. McVeigh, *Wearing Ideology: The Uniformity of Self-Presentation in Japan*

Shaun Cole, *Don We Now Our Gay Apparel: Gay Men's Dress in the Twentieth Century*

Kate Ince, *Orlan: Millennial Female*

Nicola White and Ian Griffiths, *The Fashion Business: Theory, Practice, Image*

Ali Guy, Eileen Green and Maura Banim, *Through the Wardrobe: Women's Relationships with their Clothes*

Linda B. Arthur, *Undressing Religion: Commitment and Conversion from a Cross-Cultural Perspective*

William J.F. Keenan, *Dressed to Impress: Looking the Part*

Joanne Entwistle and Elizabeth Wilson, *Body Dressing*

Leigh Summers, *Bound to Please: A History of the Victorian Corset*

Paul Hodkinson, *Goth: Identity, Style and Subculture*

DRESS, BODY, CULTURE

Re-Orienting Fashion

The Globalization of Asian Dress

Edited by

*Sandra Niessen, Ann Marie Leshkowich
and Carla Jones*

Oxford • New York

First published in 2003 by
Berg
Editorial offices:
1st Floor, Angel Court, 81 St Clements Street, Oxford, OX4 1AW, UK
838 Broadway, Third Floor, New York, NY 10003-4812, USA

Berg is an imprint of Oxford International Publishers Ltd.

Library of Congress Cataloging-in-Publication Data
Re-orienting fashion : the globalization of Asian dress / edited by
Sandra Niessen, Ann Marie Leshkowich, and Carla Jones.
        p. cm. -- (Dress, body, culture, ISSN 1360-466X)
Includes bibliographical references and index.
    ISBN 1-85973-534-7
    1. Costume--Asia. 2. Fashion--Asia. 3. Clothing and
dress--Cross-cultural studies. I. Niessen, S. A. II. Leshkowich, Ann
Marie. III. Jones, Carla. IV. Series.

GT1370.R4 2003
391'.0095--dc21

                                                              2002155875

British Library Cataloguing-in-Publication Data
A catalogue record for this book is available from the British Library.

ISBN   1 85973 534 7 (Cloth)
       1 85973 539 8 (Paper)

Typeset by JS Typesetting Ltd, Wellingborough, Northants.
Printed in the United Kingdom by Biddles Ltd, Guildford and King's Lynn.

Contents

Notes on Contributors

Parminder Bhachu is Professor in the Department of Sociology at Clark University (USA), where she held the Henry R. Luce Professorship in Cultural Identities and Global Processes from 1991–2000. She has monitored the salwaar-kameez economy professionally for over a decade. Her current interest in how women create new economic spaces in global markets has developed from her long-term research on women's cultural and commercial entrepreneurship. She examines the impact women are making as economic and cultural agents using racialized, political, and cultural aesthetics while they assert their agendas in new capitalist economies. Her latest book, *Dangerous Designs*, is in press with Routledge (2003).

Carla Jones is a Postdoctoral Fellow in the Vernacular Modernities Program of the Department of Anthropology, Emory University (USA). She is an anthropologist whose research focuses on the intersection of new class and gender subjectivities in urban Indonesia. Her current book project, based on her dissertation research in Jakarta and Yogyakarta, investigates how visions of development mediate notions of self-improvement and discipline held by women in the Indonesian middle class.

Hjorleifur R. Jonsson is Assistant Professor in the Anthropology Department at Arizona State University (USA). He has done research in Thailand, Cambodia, and Vietnam, primarily among ethnic minority populations in the hinterlands. His research interests include the politics of culture and identity, and ideologies of environments. His current research focuses on the projection of national and minority identity in museums, and the role of sports in the reworking of minority identity. He has written "Serious Fun: Minority Cultural Dynamics and National Integration in Thailand" (American Ethnologist, 2001), and "Does the House Hold? History and the Shape of Mien (Yao) Society" (Ethnohistory 48, 2001). His article, "French Natural in the Vietnamese Highlands: Nostalgia and Erasure in Montagnard Identity," appeared in *Of Vietnam: Identities in Dialogue*, edited by Jane Winston and Leakthina Ollier (2001).

Ann Marie Leshkowich is Assistant Professor of Anthropology in the Department of Sociology and Anthropology at College of the Holy Cross (USA). Her research focuses on gender, economic development, life-history narratives, markets, and fashion in Vietnam. She is currently working on a manuscript based on her doctoral dissertation exploring the intersections between economics, kinship, politics, and agency in the lives of female cloth and clothing traders in Ho Chi Minh City.

Sandra Niessen is Associate Professor in the Department of Human Ecology, University of Alberta (Canada). Her research focuses on indigenous weavers and handwoven textile production in Indonesia. She has recently completed a book manuscript entitled *The Batak Textile Repertory: Design, Technique, Nomenclature*, the final of three volumes that explore the meaning and history of Batak clothing and textiles. Together with Anne Brydon, she co-edited *Consuming Fashion: Adorning the Transnational Body* (Berg Publishers, 1998).

Rebecca N. Ruhlen is a Doctoral candidate in the Department of Anthropology at the University of Washington (USA). Her research focuses on the progressive women's movement in South Korea, particularly organizations that deal with violence against women.

Lise Skov is a post-doctoral research fellow in the Department of Sociology, Copenhagen University (Denmark). She is co-editor, with Brian Moeran, of the ConsumAsiaN Book Series. Her book, based on her doctoral dissertation on the cultural production of fashion in Hong Kong in a global perspective, is forthcoming.

Nora A. Taylor is Assistant Professor in the Interdisciplinary Humanities Program and the Department of Art History at Arizona State University (USA). An art historian specializing in Southeast Asian Art History, she has published widely on Vietnamese painting from a variety of angles including nationalist politics, forgeries, gender in art, art in the era of globalization, and perceptions of Hanoi in Western eyes. She has recently completed a book manuscript entitled, *Painters in Hanoi: From Colonial Subjects to Global Objects*, in press with the University of Hawaii Press.

Acknowledgments

The present collection of essays was prompted by two professional panels highlighting the social and political roles of clothing in Asia. The first, entitled "Designing Women: The Use of Fashion to Construct International Modernity, National Tradition, and Gender in Indonesia, Vietnam, and within the South Asian Diaspora" was organized by Carla Jones and Ann Marie Leshkowich for the Association for Asian Studies (Boston, 14 March 1999). The second, "Wearing the Nation: Fashioning Citizens in Twentieth-Century East Asia," was put together by Rebecca N. Ruhlen and Perri Strawn for the American Anthropological Association (Chicago, 17 November 1999). All of this volume's contributing authors participated in those panels. In addition, the panels benefited from the participation of Penny van Esterik, Linda Angst, and Perri Strawn.

Joanne Eicher, the Dress, Body, Culture Series Editor, encouraged us to develop the presentations for publication, and she and our anonymous reviewer offered useful suggestions on how to improve our first draft. We are grateful for their insightful assistance. The final submission was greatly improved by Elizabeth Muller's sharp eye and tactful suggestions about grammar, style, and usage. We are also grateful to Damaris Dodds for compiling the index to the volume. Emory University and the College of the Holy Cross generously provided funds to defray editing and publication costs.

In addition to all of those whom our individual contributors have acknowledged in their essays, we would like to thank Pete Loud for providing the maps for the volume as a whole. Mark Lewis patiently advised us in our search for and refinement of the images for this volume, particularly the cover. Han Feng, of Han Feng Collections, generously donated our cover image.

Finally, Berg Publishers have made this publishing experience a very pleasant one. We happily acknowledge our efficient and always gracious contacts there: Kathryn Earle, Kathleen May, Sara Everett, Samantha Jackson, Jennifer Howell, and Emma Farley.

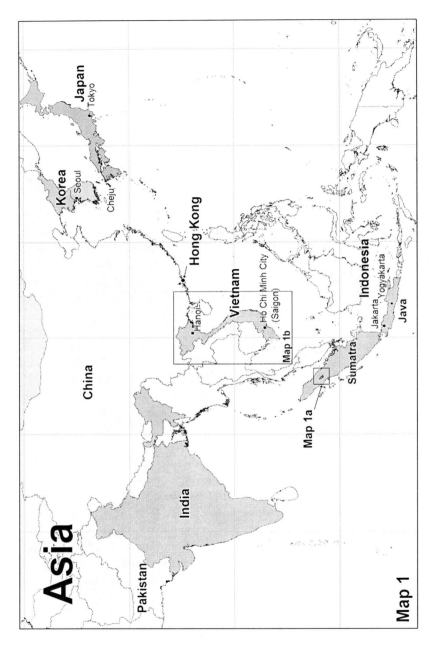

Map 1 Asia (Map credit: Pete Loud)

Map 1

x

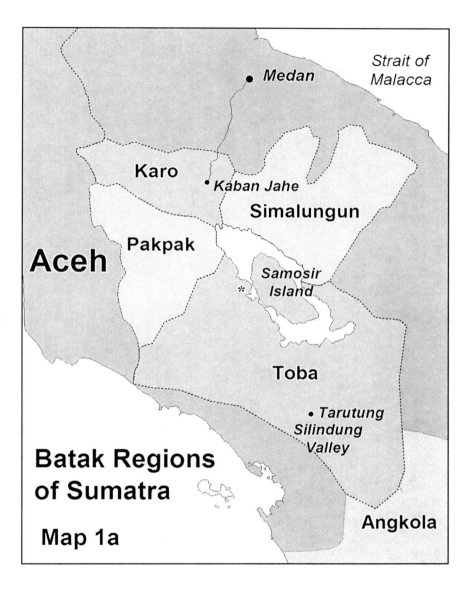

Medan

Strait of
Malacca

Karo

Kaban Jahe

Simalungun

Aceh

Pakpak

Samosir
Island

Toba

Tarutung
Silindung
Valley

Batak Regions
of Sumatra

Map 1a

Angkola

Map 1a Northern Batak Regions of Sumatra (Map credit: Pete Loud)

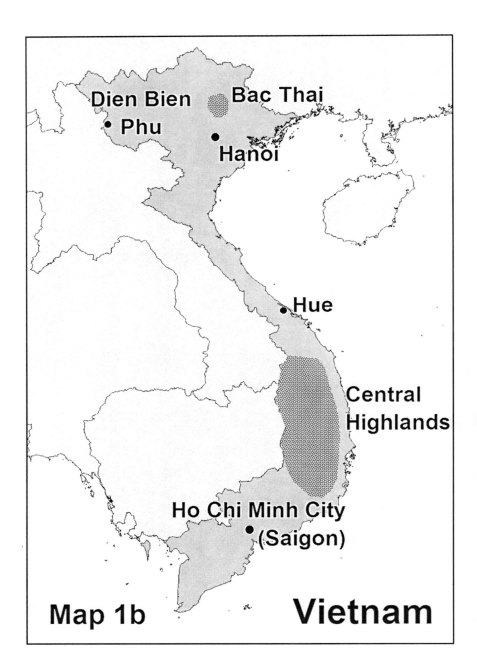

Map 1b Vietnam (Map credit: Pete Loud)

Introduction: The Globalization of Asian Dress: Re-Orienting Fashion or Re-Orientalizing Asia?

Carla Jones and Ann Marie Leshkowich[1]

Fashion icon Princess Diana wears a *salwaar-kameez*, or Punjabi suit, as flashing cameras record her latest fashion statement. A *New York Times* fashion spread heralds the arrival of "Indo-chic," a haute couture interpretation of Vietnamese peasant and elite clothing. A savvy entrepreneur in Jakarta commissions rural Batak weavers to make items that will be marketed as "ethnic chic" in high-end boutiques in Indonesia and abroad.

Meanwhile, an Indonesian professional woman wonders whether her custom-made power suit will make the right impression at an interview. A Hong Kong designer wants to experiment with traditional styles, but worries, quite rightly, that the international fashion press will dismiss him as merely a Chinese designer. Korean feminists don *hanbok* in an impromptu fashion show for their colleagues at an international women's conference. And Vietnamese state propaganda posters include colorfully dressed ethnic minority women as signs of the modern nation's diversity and liberal acceptance of different traditions.

During the 1990s, Asian fashion became a noticeable global trend, changing the way that people inside and outside Asia think about and practice dress.[2] Taken from the chapters in this volume, the vignettes above capture three phenomena that together constitute the globalization of Asian dress. First and most visibly, fashion elites and celebrities on the global stage embraced particular elements of Asian style for the world to see. Although present throughout the 1990s, the passion for so-called Asian chic occurred in waves. An initial peak in 1992/93 coincided with the release of high-grossing Asian or Asian-themed films, such as *M. Butterfly*, *Indochine*, *Heaven and Earth*, and *The Wedding*

Banquet. Janet Jackson and Madonna produced music videos inspired by Asian images, a Chinese nightclub for the former, and what director Mark Romanek described as a "Zenned-out minimalism" for the latter (Corliss 1993: 69). A second peak occurred in 1997/98, a period in which David Tang held a splashy opening for his Shanghai Tang boutique on New York's Madison Avenue, *Memoirs of a Geisha* topped best-seller lists, and the Dalai Lama became a celebrated pop-culture figure heralded at star-studded benefit concerts to Free Tibet. Throughout the decade, stylistic inspirations and cultural practices from Asia were so prevalent that they had become mainstream, even as they retained an exotic flair. As one American fashion columnist describes the trend, "Now everybody and his mom are 'into' acupuncture, organic vegetables and yoga. Meanwhile . . . sarong skirts and kimono jackets have become part of the working vocabulary of American fashion designers. The Tweeds catalog touts 'the pristine appeal of yoga pants' and Eddie Bauer calls attention to 'the unique mandarin collar' on a white cotton shirt" (McLaughlin 1998).

Second, while North Americans and Europeans explored the exotic yet familiar allure of mandarin collars, Asian men and women confronted the mundane, but increasingly complicated, dilemma of what clothes to make, sell, buy, and wear. As Asian economies flourished, then crashed and began to recover, Asians of different classes, ethnicities, and genders faced the decision of whether they should wear Western or Asian clothing. The former offered a neutrality of appearance and the hope that one might become an unmarked member of a modern international community in which Western suits, pants, shirts, skirts, and dresses are standard fare, but at the possible price of a loss of individual or ethnic identity. The latter seemed to celebrate that identity, while at the same time marking the wearer as Other, as not fully at home in the centers of power and normative Western fashion, even as those norms appeared to embrace Asian aesthetics. In between these two poles lay myriad options for combining, reinterpreting, and adapting clothing to make more particular statements about the wearer's identity and position, with each possibility carrying both costs and benefits.

Third, these decisions were reinterpreted by Asian states seeking to craft visions of national unity for domestic and international audiences by juxtaposing stylized images of modernity, gender, and ethnicity, often in ambivalent or contradictory ways. States such as Singapore, Vietnam, China, and Indonesia touted versions of Asian modernity in which economic prosperity could coexist with, or even be achieved through, commitment to traditional values. Tourist posters echoed this juxtaposition by luring travelers with images of colorful customs, pristine religions, and unique sites, all conveniently accessible through modern cities and airports. In most cases, women clad in traditional dress visually symbolized this timeless, exotic Asian-ness.

Figure I.1 Princess Diana in salwaar-kameez in Pakistan, May 1997. Photo by Graham Tim/Corbis Sygma.

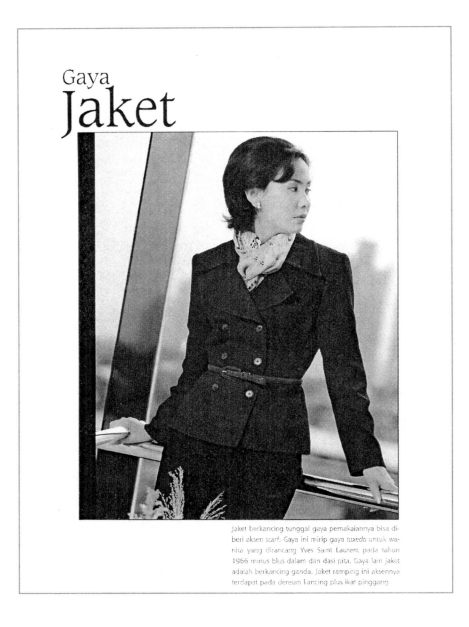

Gaya
Jaket

Jaket berkancing tunggal gaya pemakaiannya bisa di-
beri aksen scarf. Gaya ini mirip gaya tuxedo untuk wanita yang dirancang Yves Saint Laurent pada tahun
1966 minus blus dalam dan dasi pita. Gaya lain jaket
adalah berkancing ganda. Jaket ramping ini aksennya
terdapat pada deretan kancing plus ikat pinggang.

Figure I.2 Indonesian fashion magazine promoting "Jacket Style" to readers, with text instructing the reader on ways to wear such a jacket, May 1997. Courtesy of *Femina* magazine.

Far from being separate, these three aspects of the globalization of Asian dress are intimately linked and interdependent. Princess Diana's donning of the salwaar-kameez (Figure I.1) was possible because the garment, worn by South Asian migrants, had become a visible presence on London streets. In wearing this outfit, Diana valorized it as an element of international fashion, and this in turn made fashion-conscious South Asian British women, both elite and middle-class, even more eager to be seen in it. The Indonesian woman choosing a power suit turned to a national fashion press for advice about what international looks were "in" (Figure I.2). She also, however, took care to adapt these styles in accordance with local informal and personal standards of what was then considered appropriate and attractive. In both cases, the supposedly global and local in Asian dress are intertwined, interdependent, and mutually determining. This book is about these connections: their specific contours, their significance for Asians, and their implications for contemporary global understandings of "Asia" and "fashion."

The chapters in this volume document the extent to which Asian dress has been globalized. On the one hand, variations of Western clothing are the standard fare throughout much of Asia. On the other hand, the so-called traditional costumes of many Asian countries – garments such as the South Asian sari and salwaar-kameez, Japanese kimono, Chinese cheongsam, Korean hanbok, and Vietnamese *ao dai* – are experiencing a revival in those countries and their diasporic communities. They have also become familiar in style, if not in name, around the globe and serve as muses to inspire European and North American designers.

While the global interest in Asian dress might seem to open new democratic forms of cross-cultural exchange, the chapters in this volume also highlight a disturbing side to these developments: the processes through which Asian dress has been globalized and celebrated within and outside Asia are also profoundly Orientalizing and feminizing. Even as the cross-fertilization of Asian and Western styles is changing the way people throughout the world think about and practice dress, the dress styles and dress practices associated with Asia and Asians have been consistently reworked through processes that might be called "homogenized heterogeneity": their differences are identified, assessed, and appropriated, purportedly with the goal of deciding where Asian dress fits into the global pantheon of clothing configurations. The result, however, is that no matter what form these fashions may take and no matter how praised they may be by fashion elites located in the centers of power, they get defined as somehow lesser than, somehow Other to, and somehow more feminized than their perennial Western foil. As our title, "*Re-Orienting Fashion*" suggests, Asian styles may be reorienting global fashion, but the very same globalization processes that have garnered international attention for Asian dress are re-Orientalizing Asia and Asians.

In this introduction, we establish the theoretical backdrop for the book by weaving together the connections between globalization, Orientalism, gender, and fashion that led to and resulted from the explosion of Asian dress onto the world scene in the 1990s, the period in which the contributors to this volume conducted much of their research. We begin by exploring how Orientalism emerged in the colonial era as a mode of knowledge production that defined "the Orient" as fundamentally Other, feminine, and perpetually inferior to the West in ways that supported colonial domination. The contours of Orientalism are particularly complex when one considers fashion, for colonial dress became enmeshed in struggles over race, gender, tradition, and imitation. As a result, the daily sartorial decisions that Asians made became politically charged tools in contests over identity, status, and power.

We then turn to contemporary contexts to explore how globalization has perpetuated the Orientalist legacy. The tenets of Orientalism have been reworked, challenged, and reinscribed to characterize certain types of people, activities, and items as lesser members of the global family by defining them as Other, local, traditional, and feminine. We find the link between feminization and marginalization of particular significance, for it can be seen not just on the concrete level of economic and cultural experiences, but also on the abstract level of globalization theory. By exploring a specific example of how globalization has been analyzed by one noted anthropologist, we argue that a masculinist bias has diverted scholars' attention from the issue of how the fundamental processes of globalization – the increased movement of people, things, capital, and ideas around the world at an ever-accelerating rate – are profoundly gendered and gendering. By not exposing and critiquing these gendered dynamics, the knowledge generated by contemporary theory risks discursively naturalizing and reinforcing the material, social, and cultural inequities emerging through globalization.

It is a central contention of this volume that globalization as an Orientalizing and gendering phenomenon becomes apparent through an ethnographic focus on dress practices. Understood in its experiential complexity, what people wear is the most visible and sensitive social register illuminating key points of articulation between the broader and more intimate processes of contemporary globalization. By exploring how people dress at different moments, we can reveal the relationship between individual choices, themselves subject to varying degrees of constraint or agency, and larger interests, such as nations, corporations, and markets, that are invested in individuals performing in particular ways. These processes are especially interesting for their effects on people who get caught in the middle because of their class, race, and gender identity or their economic, social, and cultural practices. In this way, the anthropological focus on real people making real decisions connects us to the discursive work of Orientalism.

6

The use of dress as a means to perform identity is further complicated by the highly competitive, status-conscious, and exclusive world of international fashion. Sandra Niessen documents (Afterword, this volume) how fashion has long retained its power by operating as a definitional system. Fashion leaders possess the ability to name certain groups, typically Western elites, as having "fashion" (changing style trends over time) or being fashionable (dressing in ways consistent with or in the vanguard of those trends). They also define large groups of Others: those in the West who pay little attention to fashion (the unfashionable) or who dress in opposition to dominant fashion (the practitioners of anti-fashion), and those in societies deemed not to have fashion at all (the wearers of "traditional" or "ethnic" dress). Since the colonial era, the fashion industry has spread its production and distribution functions around the world. Cross-fertilization between Western and non-Western fashion systems has been so extensive as to make a distinction between the two no longer tenable. Meanwhile, fashion's definitional apparatus continues to grind, locating those who are deemed to have or not to have fashion in ways that produce new global class differences. In the Afterword, Sandra Niessen considers how this volume's focus on Asian dress practices sheds light on the ways the globalization of fashion, as both an industry and a conceptual mode for characterizing dress, challenges us to develop new understandings of what fashion is, how it operates, who controls it, and what stakes are involved in participating in it.

Our task here is to highlight a different, but complementary, set of questions: Does global interaction with Asia as a form of style allow privileged consumers who know little about Asian people and places to avoid seriously engaging with the cultural substance of those styles? Does performing Asian style mask or enable practices that produce new kinds of global material and cultural differences? How do the Orientalizing and gendering processes propelling the globalization of Asian dress affect the daily decisions that Asians make about clothing? What is the significance of these decisions, both for the wearer and for our conceptions of globalization, Asia, and Asian-ness?

Considered as a whole, the chapters in this volume imply a theoretical framework for approaching these problems that combines insights from performance theory and practice theory. Performance theory, particularly as developed by Butler (1990), highlights the possibilities for agentive creation of identity through the manipulation of appearance. Practice theory (Bourdieu 1977 [1972], 1984; de Certeau 1984), in contrast, emphasizes the ways in which tastes are shaped by and constitutive of social positioning through such factors as class, educational level, race, ethnicity, or gender. Combining the two by focusing on *performance practices* allows us to see how, within a constrained and treacherous field of already constituted identities, people nonetheless have room to maneuver by fashioning themselves. These self-fashionings, however,

7

Carla Jones and Ann Marie Leshkowich

always risk reinscribing preexisting negative characterizations, such as the ones created through gender and Orientalism upon which we focus.

Within a global context in which Asia and Asian-ness are already saturated with constraining significations, self-Orientalizing and internal Orientalizing become understandable, but fraught, strategies for the performative construction of identity. The extent to which Asian dress is reorienting fashion versus re-Orientalizing Asia rests fundamentally on the factors of who is performing, with what intentions, under what circumstances, and before what audience. We suggest that studying the ways in which mid-level actors decide to make, wear, buy, or sell clothing in different Asian contexts can defy the Orientalist stereotypes of Asian style as passive and traditional, even as those actions are often made invisible in global cultural, rhetorical, and material practices that feminize Asia and the fashion world.

Dressing, Gendering, and Orientalizing the Colonial Subject

What are the conditions that have positioned dress, both in Asia and as read by outsiders, as marked Other or feminine? What factors shape current interpretations of how Asians choose to dress, and of styles that appear to be Asian in global cities, be they Jakarta or New York? Addressing these questions requires a historical perspective. Although only two contributors to this volume directly discuss colonialism, we find that colonial discourse and domination linked dress to specific kinds of meanings, meanings that continue to circulate in the contemporary era. Edward Said's analysis of Orientalism (1994 [1978]) provides a compelling frame for understanding these dynamics. Said argues that imperialism created ideologies and representations of fundamental opposition between groups labeled East and West. This enterprise entailed defining and categorizing what the Orient was, a feat of knowledge production accomplished through scholarly research, "exotic travels," and mass-mediated images such as postcards and exhibitions.[3] When combined with direct military force, colonial-era Orientalism as a way of seeing and knowing facilitated domination by Othering and feminizing colonized peoples, casting them as timeless, exotic, passive, or oppressed, but always fundamentally different from and inferior to those in the West. Orientalist discourse sometimes established Western superiority by baldly defining Others as unrepentant savages or backward races. At other times, however, Said finds that the discourse operated more subtly. For example, Orientalist scholars, including archaeologists, historians, and ethnographers, conducted extensive research to identify the charming or valuable aspects of a group's heritage. Their "discoveries" were then celebrated in ways that suggested that the people to whom these traditions belonged were ignorant of their worth and hence in need of Western masters to teach them about themselves.

Building on Said, we argue in this section that the effects of the creation of Orientalist categories and modes of discernment are particularly striking for matters of style in Asia. Through Orientalism, differences in appearance and clothing were often read by the colonizers as indexes of deeper differences, even as the colonizers' discursive categories created the reality they supposedly described. Knowing what styles were fashionable in the metropole, collecting items from natives who were unaware of the value of their own cultural charms, enforcing dress codes among settlers, or critiquing native dress styles as imitative of the West or backwardly bare all served to make style an important terrain for negotiations over power. While some European colonial powers in Asia were met with forms of undress that they read as charmingly simple or disturbingly exposed, others were presented with sophisticated forms of civilization and appearances that took considerable discursive work to critique.[4] Reducing these varied forms of difference to simply bad or excessive style attempted to contain the threat of moral and political conflict. While we do not suggest that all forms of colonial rule were uniform or monolithic, we are interested in how a shared concern with matters of culture, and by extension matters of appearance and dress, served to cement apparently natural differences between colonizer and colonized. These discourses continue to shape readings of dress practices today, so that even when Asian dress is celebrated, such moves perpetuate a script of a dominant, knowledgeable West and an inferior, ignorant Orient. Four themes – race, gender, tradition, and imitation – show particularly well how ideas about dress and difference in several Asian colonial-era contexts were reworked, dropped, and picked up again in ways that made these ideas seem natural.

First, racial difference was read from dress practices under conditions of rule, both in the colonies and in Europe. For example, Emma Tarlo's research argues that British colonial rule, and Indian nationalism later, relied on strategic uses of masculine dress (1996). Tarlo describes how British colonials saw the Indian dhoti as emblematic of the savage and effeminate Indian male: savage because the item left the torso and lower legs unclad, and effeminate because the draped fabric more closely resembled the voluminous shirring of European women's dress than the more tailored straight lines of men's suits.[5] That the dhoti could be so associated with racial inferiority shaped later nationalist rhetoric such that, as Partha Chatterjee has argued, Indian men seeking an alternatively modern Indian national culture felt they had no choice but to wear the European-style suit (1993).

Not all critiques of racial inferiority were made on the basis of bodily exposure or simplicity of fabric. Elaborate and luxurious garments could similarly be read as morally suspect forms. A striking example is that of Chinese silks. Early European explorers described Chinese court culture and trade in silks as impressively civilized. The silk trade from multiple Chinese dynasties to Rome and later to Northern and Western Europe was the result of the greater Chinese ability to produce fine fabrics, and of the European desire for a luxurious textile, for both men and women. Yet the drape and sheen of silk also eventually took on an effeminacy associated with the perceived decadence of Chinese culture. As a result, by the beginning of the eighteenth century, Europeans no longer found silk an appropriately masculine fabric for men's clothes (Honour 1961: 31; Steele and Major 1999: 71). Precisely because of such distinctions between morally upright, utilitarian Western dress and sumptuous, decadent native clothing, Asian elites sometimes held on to elaborate styles or developed even more luxurious ones. This could serve as a silent protest against colonial attempts to usurp their power or as an attempt literally to fashion themselves as still possessing that power. According to Jean Gelman Taylor, this was the case in the Dutch East Indies during the mid- to late nineteenth century (1997). As aristocratic and royal families' material power decreased, males donned increasingly elaborate clothing. Aristocratic women were likewise important elements symbolizing this now fading power, as they were photographed in ever more restrictive and sumptuous clothing associated with "tradition," such as the wrapped sarong.[6]

Second, and linked to this, we see that native women were deemed needy of rescue from native culture and native men precisely because of their supposed connection to tradition. Colonial discourse found in native women a particularly attractive symbol for justifying rule, thereby making gender a salient factor in debating cultural differences. Colonialism in its Orientalist form inscribed privilege as masculine, and masculinity as European. The European male was young, virile, clean and fully clothed, often in a suit (cf. Smith 1995; Tarlo 1996; Wilson 1985). In turn, the colonized male was dehumanized, represented as either brutishly male or effeminate. In this struggle over political power, native women served as particularly fertile symbolic terrain. In some versions of Orientalist logic, proof of the native male's backwardness could be found in his treatment of native women, as measured against a universal index of civilizations. As Frantz Fanon argued about colonial fascination with the veil in Algeria, the struggle over women's appearance had high stakes, "wrenching her free from her status . . . shaking up the [native] man" (1965: 39). Much of the rhetoric justifying colonial conquest rested in the liberation of native women from the tyranny of native men. In colonial India, Partha Chatterjee argues that the civilizing mission of British conquest was based on eradicating "barbarism" evidenced by a whole canon of "traditions" which oppressed Indian womanhood (1993: 118).[7] Bound feet provided a similar rationale for expanding Western presence in China. This "curious erotic custom" (Levy 1966) served nicely as evidence that Chinese elite culture was actually barbarism masquerading as sophistication (Fan 1997; Steele and Major 1999; Wang 2000).

Third, colonial relations configured dress and gender in ways that affected nationalist movements and subsequent postcolonial states, through claims to "tradition." This process began before actual independence in many cases. To continue with examples from Chatterjee's research, once "tradition" was linked to women in colonial rhetoric, an indigenous bourgeoisie that was in large part the invention of colonial policies had little choice but to resist subjugation on the same terms, that is, over the treatment of women. Women became the boundary for marking colonizer from colonized. As a result, they came to stand for two highly stylized senses of the nation: the traditional essence requiring defense from outside contamination, and the internally different Other, the one that made the nation aware of itself. An imagined middle-class native woman was recast, not as evidence of Indian backwardness, but as the repository of a superior Indian "tradition." For example, Bengali men, acting in the outer material world of business and politics, had little choice but to wear European-style clothing. However, Bengali women were increasingly encouraged by Bengali men to preserve and present local culture through the use of "traditional" dress, i.e., the sari. Bengali women were therefore charged with upholding tradition through avoiding adoption of European manners or styles "such as the blouse, the petticoat, and shoes" (Chatterjee 1993: 122).

Fourth, and finally, even though new nationalist movements found it necessary to adopt forms of European style while seeking political legitimacy, they nonetheless sought to distinguish themselves from direct mimicry of European styles. Consistent with the Orientalist narrative, however, "native" attempts at approximating and reworking colonizers' styles could never fully succeed, no matter how hard one strove. Such attempts typically failed on two levels: first, in the eyes of the fellow colonized and, second, in those of the colonizers. Emma Tarlo describes how Indian men who chose to wear a European-style suit were initially ridiculed by their fellow class and ethnic peers. Similarly, Vicente Rafael documents how Filipino elites who dressed in European suits to participate in the American census were branded traitors in nationalist plays (2000). To colonizers, such attempts appeared as failed imitations, proof that natives were incapable of originality.[8] Racial difference not only endured in spite of one's dress, clothing made it even more evident. Yet as Homi Bhabha argues (1997), mimicry is never complete, it is never a direct reinscription of the dominant narrative. For example, Dipesh Chakrabarty has suggested that while colonial Indian women's magazines promoted companionate marriage and orderly, clean homes, which might appear to imitate European styles, they nonetheless did not wholly endorse colonial models of ideal womanhood (1992).[9] Rather, such magazines profiled women who did imitate European women (such as by wearing a blouse and skirt, or by playing tennis) as comical, absurd or tragic. In fact, new forms of national femininity were seen as selectively rejecting European femininities as hypersexual, consumerist, and inappropriate to newly forming national cultures.[10]

While the themes of race, gender, tradition, and imitation emerged and were elaborated upon in different configurations in particular historical settings, all colonial Orientalisms shared key features. First, they were the result of unequal and sometimes violent contact between colonizing and local populations. Second, they rested on a constant script of difference and superiority. Viewing the world as having distinct and opposing cultures, evident in part by the unique and perhaps antithetical ways that people dressed, was an appealing frame for interpreting social, political, and stylistic encounters in the colonial era. The fact that conditions of colonial subjugation and domination not only facilitated but required the success of such dominant discourses may make them seem irrelevant to the current era, in which the world is supposedly being brought closer together under global exchanges of ideas and money. Yet, the very same Orientalist logic that cast Asia as feminine or women's dress as traditional in the colonial era continues to have salience today, under the apparently new guise of globalization.

Globalization and the Production of Feminized Locals

On the surface, colonial Orientalism and contemporary globalization seem quite different. The former drew its authority from the careful study and institutionalization of difference in order to compartmentalize the world into discrete and unequal regions. The latter, with its increase in the frequency, quantity, and importance of flows of people, things, capital, and ideas around the globe, seems to rest on breaking down barriers to draw us into common channels of communication and community.[11] Looking deeper, however, scholars began in the 1990s to suggest that globalization is as productive of difference as it is of similarity. In addition, we find that these differences depend on many of the same discursive tropes of race, gender, tradition, and imitation that were previously deployed in colonial contexts. To explore the construction and effects of such rhetoric, we consider in detail one example of gender stereotypes: an image of women as timeless exemplars of localized tradition marginal to global processes. Not only is such a description empirically inaccurate, but its continued prevalence in both popular culture and scholarly accounts suggests that globalization itself needs to be explored as a gendered process producing and reproducing conceptions of a feminized, local Other.

When anthropologists first began considering globalization in the 1970s and 1980s, their foremost concern was to determine whether these processes were hurting or helping the supposedly local producers of local cultural traditions that had constituted their traditional object of study. The first round of evidence fueled critiques of globalization as neo-imperialist processes that incorporated people, often forcibly, into international capitalist structures. Images of a world drinking Coca-Cola and donning Levi's jeans encapsulated the threat of homogenization: an erasure of local distinctions and conformity in cultural practices in which people would look the same, act the same, and use the same goods. Although scholars concerned about homogenization sought to liberate peoples around the globe from colonial and neo-colonial domination, they shared the colonial-era supposition that the adoption of Western products or styles by non-Western peoples was an unreflexive, uncritical, and problematic form of imitation involving a rejection of their traditional cultures. Whether those traditional cultures were being derided by colonials as backward or lauded by leftist scholars as authentic expressions of ethnic identity and history, "culture" in both views seemed an essential feature bequeathed to a group as a racial or genetic inheritance that they could abandon only at their peril.[12]

By the 1990s, anthropologists and other scholars of globalization found reason to be optimistic about the fate of cultural heterogeneity. First, as part of a broader turn toward the study of consumption practices,[13] many noted that when products are used in different contexts, even products as synonymous with American corporate capitalism as Levi's jeans (Ong 1987), Coca-Cola (Miller 1997), and McDonald's (Watson 1997), their meanings are transformed.[14] Second, in the 1990s, the growing desire among Euro-American populations for clothing and other items of "ethnic chic," a development with which we began this introduction, suggested that globalization allowed for multidirectional cultural exchange. Young Malaysian girls working in electronics factories may be discarding sarongs in favor of jeans (Ong 1987), but trendsetters within the society where the jeans originated were now freely experimenting with those sarongs. Far from dying or fading away, diversity under globalization seemed to be more mobile and hence more widely appreciated.

Rather than the either/or paradigm of homogeneity versus heterogeneity, a rich assortment of studies focusing on cross-cultural consumption now suggests that globalization is producing what David Howes refers to as a "multiplicity of possible local–global articulations" (Howes 1996: 6).[15] Such studies also argue that these articulations are the result of encounters negotiated on unequal terrain. What we have, then, is what might be described as *homogenized heterogeneity*. Difference is appreciated, but it is also characterized and commodified globally through flows of knowledge, money, and people structured in accordance with relations of power.[16] In the process, difference is transformed. Its edges are smoothed and its contours are flattened so that it fits more neatly into its assigned pigeonhole in the global display of culture. Certain groups and activities thus come to embody "tradition" more than others, a move that seems to reflect appreciation for diversity, but that can also position the groups in question as Other to global modernity.

Just as colonial Orientalisms depended on the discursive work of ruling classes and scholars, the contemporary production of homogenized heterogeneity rests on the definitional work of new kinds of global economic, social, and cultural elites. Ulf Hannerz (1996) has described one such elite class: the relatively well-off, educated, and globally sophisticated "cosmopolitans" whose passionate pursuit of the new and diverse drives the creation of global culture.[17] At the opposite end of the spectrum are locals: those whose orientation remains rooted in everyday experiences and local frames of reference.[18]

While being a cosmopolitan or local may seem an empirical affair, these statuses in fact depend as much on ideological orientations for apprehending the world as on concrete, measurable factors such as income, education, or consumption preferences. According to Hannerz, cosmopolitans may move around the world in clearly transnational projects, but they can also remain at home and consume the diversity of food, clothing, movies, art, etc. that global processes bring to their doors. Meanwhile, locals can travel and yet retain a fundamentally local perspective. Determining which passengers on an international jet flight or which diners at a local "ethnic" restaurant are or are not cosmopolitan thus rests on trying to fathom the intentions and perspectives motivating their actions. This feat is often accomplished through associative logic in which intention is ascribed based on the observed or presumed tendencies of others with whom one appears to share characteristics, most commonly gender, race, ethnicity, class, place of residence, religion, and education. Unfortunately, such an endeavor is prone to stereotyping. Ulf Hannerz's discussion of locals is instructive in this regard. He is noteworthy among prominent theorists of globalization for his attention to the concrete details of human actors' experiences. Nevertheless, in trying to characterize those experiences, he risks reproducing stereotypes about the local and traditional – stereotypes that in this case have much to do with gender.

As an example of a transnationally mobile local, Hannerz cites a 1985 *International Herald Tribune* article describing Nigerian market women's regular travels between Lagos and London (Harden 1985).[19] By wearing loose-fitting clothes, they were able to smuggle products in both directions: outbound, they strapped dried fish to their thighs and upper arms; on the return flight, they carried frozen fish sticks, dehydrated milk, and baby clothes. Hannerz characterizes such acts as not cosmopolitan: "The shopping trips of Lagosian traders and smugglers hardly go beyond the horizons of urban Nigerian culture, as it now is. The fish sticks and baby clothes hardly alter structures of meaning more than marginally" (103). No matter where they go – and these particular traders go quite far – locals retain a fundamentally insular perspective.

The example of Nigerian traders caught our attention, primarily because their gender and the gendered nature of the commodities they carried (baby clothes, milk, and fish used in meal preparation) leapt off the page in what was otherwise a gender-neutral discussion of how people locate themselves as privileged cosmopolitans. Why, we wondered, did these internationally mobile women and their imported goods seem so obviously local? What further meanings were deployed by categorizing people and their activities in this way? What does this suggest about globalization as a gendered and gendering process?

An initial answer may be that associations between women, the traditional, and the local seem obvious. Indeed, in societies around the world, women *are* often held up as the bearers of tradition, as inculcators of cultural values through their roles in childrearing, and hence as somehow more connected to the space of home. As described above, many of these ideologies were explicitly deployed by colonial regimes and anticolonial nationalist movements. The problem is that anthropologists, since Sherry Ortner (1974) and others (Collier 1974; Rosaldo 1974) explored the question of whether and why women appear to be universally subordinated, have tended to treat these characterizations, not as concrete and accurate descriptions of fact, but as discourses, as symbolic representations of the world and how it is gendered. By assuming the meaning of gendered activities, we not only miss the opportunity to interrogate how globalization processes construct gender, but risk further reproducing and naturalizing problematic gender stereotypes that a priori dismiss certain types of people, activities, and positions as insignificant.

How might an analysis of globalization as gendered and gendering complicate the claim that Nigerian women traders are not cosmopolitan? To start, it requires looking beyond stereotypes of women, domesticity, and locality to explore the broader context shaping the Lagos–London baby clothes trade. The newspaper article cited by Hannerz provides rich detail about this: how short-lived affluence during the 1970s oil boom, subsequent hard-currency shortages, government import restrictions, an overvalued exchange rate, and price controls on airline tickets combined to create strong Nigerian demand for imported goods and the opportunity to acquire them through extralegal measures (Harden 1985). The vibrant trade that resulted involved not just women, but men, many of them well-connected bureaucrats, and not just baby clothes and foodstuffs, but electronics, parrots, automotive parts, cosmetics, and consumer electronics. As for the baby clothes, they might be seen in Nigeria as the height of modern style, in large part because they come from a place as powerful and exotic as London. Smugglers thus may be crucial mediators through which elites and others in Lagos acquire the material goods literally to fashion themselves (and, in this case, their children) as cosmopolitans conversant with global heterogeneity.[20] Dehydrated milk might carry the same sort of associations; we know, for example, that much to the dismay of public health officials who promote the nutritional and hygienic superiority of breast milk, dehydrated milk and baby formula have spread quickly around the world precisely because of their mass appeal as emblems of modernity.

Within this broader context, it becomes hard not to see Nigerian traders and the items in which they traffic as intimately implicated in processes of globalization. The only way to know for sure what the items carried by the traders represent is to trace these items, their histories, and their meanings, and to look at who creates, transports, sells, and consumes them, and why. That this may not seem necessary reflects just how taken-for-granted are the associations between women, the local, and the traditional.

We have focused on one example because we find it to be illustrative of what feminist scholars have critiqued as a widespread "masculinist" tendency in studies of globalization in which women are either entirely absent or assumed to occupy subordinate positions. Aihwa Ong (1999), Kamala Visweswaran (1994), Dorinne Kondo (1997), and Carla Freeman (2001) have noted similar problems in the work of Arjun Appadurai (1996, 1990) and David Harvey (1989). The critiques tend to focus on the authors' abstraction of global processes so that they become unmarked and ungendered. This amounts to an erasure of how gender and other factors unequally shape access to processes of cultural production and material accumulation. In different ways, these critiques suggest that, far from being a statement of fact or essential identity, whether one is mobile, global, and transnational, or nonmobile and local is a historical development, emerging through the particularities of political economy, social stratification, and gender roles and ideologies.[21] To put it succinctly, whether one is male or female, with all that may imply in a given cultural context, shapes how one experiences and participates in globalization.

While critiquing theories of globalization for not paying sufficient attention to women is significant, we find that this risks distracting us from the potentially radical implications of gender analysis. Simply looking at women is not enough. Rather, we must focus on processes of gendering that, as Gayle Rubin (1975) has argued, divide the world so that spheres of human activity and knowledge become conceived of as masculine and feminine in ways that valorize or constrain that activity. Citing female traders as an example of the local in an increasingly global world not only erases these particular women from globalization, but replicates gendered categories that define the local as feminine and Other to globalization processes. What's more, it is not just women who get assigned to the feminized local realm, but all who traffic in what can be defined as locally meaningful goods.

This discursive move should seem familiar to students of Orientalism: a realm of the world gets defined as feminine and Other to a more masculine and powerful subject in ways that confirm that subject's mastery of or superiority to the Other. Through such gendering processes, globalization reworks and perpetuates the Orientalist philosophies developed with colonialism. To the extent that theorists of globalization do not explicitly unpack these associations, they reproduce and legitimate them, much as Said claims an earlier generation of Orientalist scholars defined their object of study in ways that confirmed this region's Otherness and lent credence, however unintended, to colonial domination. When these gendering moves occur today on the global stage within the already feminized realms of fashion and Asian culture, the associations become all the more insidious and powerful. It is to these issues of contemporary Orientalism that we turn below.

Continuing Orientalist Legacies through Fashion

During the 1990s, several prominent and stereotypical images of Asia coexisted comfortably in the cultural landscape of Europe and North America. In terms of style, we saw the proliferation of trendy "Oriental" lifestyle elements described in romantic prose designed to conjure up visions of a timeless, exotic, spiritual, and mysterious land. Geopolitically, there was the specter of a Chinese military apparatus and government actively rejecting Western democracy. Another image was of the Asian businessman, often Japanese or Chinese, wielding a cell phone and briefcase as he traveled the region making the deals that propelled the Asian Economic Miracle. Spending the money generated by that miracle was the brand-conscious female consumer of luxury goods who slavishly followed trends that originated in Europe or the United States. And behind these images was the specter of subservient Asian women, in myriad forms: from uncomplaining yet overworked factory laborers, to demure and subservient geishas, to oppressively veiled Pakistani Muslim women, and hypersexual Thai prostitutes.

These images are rife with contradictions: a spiritual Asia, a superficial Asia focused on consumption, an economically and militarily powerful Asia, an oppressed Asia, a demure Asia, an erotically charged Asia. Why can such dramatically different stereotypes as these comfortably coexist in Western minds? While these images reference particularly modern features of globalization – transnational factories, global fashion, mass consumption, international capitalism, and sex tourism – the assumptions, viewpoints, and discursive moves through which these images are produced are by no means new. Contemporary ways of knowing and representing the Oriental Other as timeless, exotic, untouched, dangerous, passive, inscrutable, or oppressed are the legacies of earlier Orientalist frameworks developed to understand and subjugate Asia. Although much of this occurred under colonial domination, a period that has now ended in its formal sense, these categories of difference continue to have enormous explanatory appeal in the current era of globalization and the uncertainty that it has created about Western political, military, and economic dominance. As Orientalist logics circulate to counter this uncertainty, they are also subtly reworked to take account of new realities and thus produce new contours of difference. We see this as occurring in three ways. First, the masculine threat posed by Asian economic and military strength is reworked to seem androgynous or feminine. Second, diverse Asian cultures and histories are reduced to mere stylistic flourishes and hence feminized as part of the preserve of fashion. Third, Asian women are described as unambiguously oppressed and rendered passive, either by global capital or by their own traditions. As such, they are seen to be in need of rescue by enlightened Westerners.

During the 1990s, the two most threatening images of Asia circulating in North America and Western Europe centered on Asian economic and military prowess. These were usually rendered as a Japanese corporate powerhouse ready to outcompete Euro-American industry and a Chinese military machine capable of rejecting and defeating the forces of Western democracy.[22] Even so, the images provoking such panic contained ready-made possibilities for neutralizing the threat. The Japanese businessman with his suit and cell phone, as Dorinne Kondo points out (1997), was rendered not as hypermasculine, but as anonymous and effeminate. He was no longer a threat to the West, but an unsuccessful mimic of it, either a corporate drone who did what he was told or a duplicitous, unethical competitor. Similarly, Chinese soldiers seemed less men than machines who followed orders and marched in step, not because of an affirmative commitment to country, but because they valued life differently and unquestioningly followed orders. In such ways, even images of a masculine Asia become rhetorically rendered as androgynous, passive, and perhaps even feminine.

The second dimension of contemporary Orientalist discourses of Asia is that of Asia as a source of exotic style. It strikes us as not coincidental that at the same time as the Asian Economic Miracle and Chinese military might sparked Orientalist anxiety in the West, Asian chic became all the rage in international fashion. This version of Asia has been a sort of utopian and euphoric embrace of elements of particular Asian traditions that now have come to stand for an undifferentiated Asia. From haute couture collections such as John Galliano for Christian Dior, which in 1997 featured bright reinterpretations of the Chinese cheongsam, to renditions of rice bowls and chopsticks aimed at the American middle class by mass retailers such as Pottery Barn and Pier One, Asian-ness has been reduced from a potentially threatening and unmanageable Other to a mere fashion statement. This process of glossing certain items as generically Asian alters the meanings and practices associated with them and erases their specific cultural and national origins. Asian chic is something that, while aesthetically appealing to many, is ultimately a trend: something simply to be consumed and then moved beyond.

We are not suggesting that a conspiracy of fashion-industry power brokers negotiated with global political and economic leaders to create a solution to a perception of a Yellow Peril lapping at American shores. But neither would such a conscious collusion have been necessary, for that is the power of discourse. Strikingly, the end to the "miracle" of Asian dominance in the late twentieth century came at the hands of foreign-currency investors as many of the region's currencies collapsed in 1997. Yet just as the painful economic crisis affected more and more Asian countries through 1998 and 1999, so did the cachet of dressing and decorating in an Asian style increase in North America and Europe. Asia is indeed an invented construction, something that says more about an unmarked West than it does about any particular culture or nation in the region called Asia, but it is nonetheless a very real construction. It has become a commodified identity that corporations can define and sell as an invented yet racialized style.

That the threat to Western superiority posed by Asian business, military, and cultural strength was countered by reducing Asia to a style statement on the terrain of fashion – an industry with fascinating gendered connotations – suggests this move to be an emasculating or feminizing one. As a privileged site of production, fashion – particularly "high fashion" or haute couture – is a powerful sphere of cultural production. Nonetheless it is imagined as a feminized world. Its target audience is primarily female. Its constituents are thought to consume excessively and to be uncritically enthusiastic about personal decoration – charges disproportionately leveled at women.[23] The world of fashion appears obsessed with surface appearances over hard, cold realities such as finance.[24] Even though the high-fashion world is populated by men, the most successful designers are assumed to be homosexual (i.e., not fully masculine), and those who do engage in heterosexual relationships are greeted with raised eyebrows as the exceptions that prove the rule.

These impressions continue in spite of the fact that garment industries have been touted as the first step toward globalizing a developing economy, a move whose dependence on a supposedly docile feminine workforce might be seen as implying a contrast to the clearly masculine character of global industry.

Anthropological studies of female factory laborers provide clear support for the ways that industrial regimes consciously draw upon patriarchal ideologies to control their labor force, often colluding with national governments and workers' families to keep young women in line and their appetites, both material and sexual, under control (Mills 1999; Ong 1987; Salaff 1995 [1981]; Wolf 1992). In material and symbolic terms, then, laborers in the fashion industry are subject to a gendered system of production in which they are the passive, feminized mass to be ordered and controlled by what would seem to be gendered as the masculine structure of industrial production.[25] But, material production is different from cultural production, and it is on the discursive level that fashion is feminized.

When the idea of "Oriental" style is added to the already feminized field of fashion, the discursive production of gender becomes all the more complicated and powerful. The striking proliferation of things "Oriental" at the precise moment that Asia appeared to enter global circuits of wealth and power clearly calls for critical analysis for what it reveals about continued Orientalisms in the West. It also raises the much less apparent, but perhaps more provocative, question of what happens when these styles reverberate back to the sites from which they are imagined to have come.

The case of Princess Diana's donning of the salwaar-kameez mentioned above provides a useful example. A garment that had been worn by North Indian and Pakistani women for generations was suddenly deemed "fashion" by British socialites, not just because Princess Diana was a person whose every fashion choice was followed closely but because it made sense in a comfortable Orientalist logic. In this way, a cultural form that had been invisible to Western consumers was made chic through the recognizing and expert eye of an outsider. The garment had to cross a border to become "fashion," in a way that it could never have been while South Asian women wore it, and the only person capable of taking it across that border was a privileged celebrity and outsider. Another effect of the garment's journey was to make it seem newly chic to those very women who had always worn it in their everyday lives. The irony for them, however, was that pride in their garment's new fashionability could be interpreted through Orientalizing logic as a kind of enlightenment, a consciousness about the value of their garment that could only come from the Western fashion establishment telling them what was precious in their cultural heritage and what was not. The effect, then, was that these very women could appear to be imitating Western fashions even as they were said to be wearing their own traditional clothing.

This brings us to the third aspect of Orientalizing discourses about Asia, namely the ways in which notions of Asian style reinforced preexisting images of an essentialized, feminized Oriental Other powerless both at home and on the job. Even as critiques of Orientalism are commonplace within the academy, images of the voiceless, agency-less, victimized Asian woman still hold enormous explanatory power. One such example can be found in anti-globalization movement rhetoric that focuses almost unproblematically on the docility of the Asian female sweatshop worker, reproduced as an often mute symbol for a transnational movement. The campaign has been effective in linking global brand names, like Nike and Reebok, to images of poor underage women working in transnational factories. Such images are based on the material reality of harsh factory-floor working conditions. Yet the extent to which such campaigns have been able to raise general public consciousness about these issues has also been the result of discursive work. Representations of docile factory women, even as they call attention to very real circumstances of exploitation, confirm long-standing Western stereotypes of the subservient Asian woman.

So compelling are discourses of victimization and passivity that they readily explain other Asian women's behavior, even when those behaviors occur in dramatically different contexts or at opposite ends of the class spectrum. Passiveness, and the oppression it implies, thus come to be read as a function of an essential cultural or national identity, rather than as the result of limited material power. A few additional examples will clarify this. In contrast to the docile factory laborer toiling in the trenches of production, it would be tempting to see the image of the consuming wealthy Asian woman as an important corrective. Yet even this stereotype is often read as an expression of a peculiar cultural essence. Although luxury fashion lines in Europe earn a significant portion of their revenues from sales in Asian markets, those consumers are interpreted as blindly following the dictates of a fashion system or obeying mass group tastes. Rather than shopping to articulate a unique personal identity, as Western consumers might sympathetically be read, such women are imagined as selfishly and unreflexively seeking status (or face) through acquisition of Western luxury goods.[26] Similarly, images of oppressed Asian women coexist comfortably in Western media with stereotypes of the savvy but restrained sexuality of the kimono-clad geisha, popularized in Arthur Golden's 1997 Novel *Memoirs of a Geisha*. The geisha was celebrated as nostalgic proof of the gentility and eroticism of Asian femininity, something Western women lack. At the same time, it implied a critique of the brutality of a society that would develop such an institution.

Images of passivity and oppression therefore work not only to erase striking cultural contradictions among various stereotypes, but also to make class differences seem less visible. Asian women's oppression is explained as a function of their being Asian and female – their essential national and cultural identities – not as a function of an often highly limited access to resources that might produce that oppression. It is precisely these problematic stereotypes that the contributions to this volume challenge. They do so by uncovering the practices and meanings surrounding the production, circulation, and consumption of clothing items, both "traditional" and "modern," and by both Asian men and women. In doing so, they expose the Orientalist workings of globalization that have either denied agency to Asians in general and Asian women in particular or consigned them to the realm of tradition. By highlighting the particular positions Asian consumers and producers occupy, the contributors tease out the interconnections between class and identity.

Asian women are thus not simply modern producers or traditional consumers, but a mix of all simultaneously.[27] The very same women who may be oppressed by harsh labor conditions, low pay, and coercive regimes of labor discipline on the factory floor may choose to use part of their wages to purchase fashions through which they craft themselves as members of a new generation less beholden to traditional strictures on feminine decorum. Or, they may use their paychecks to purchase newly chic "traditional" outfits. As liberating as these sartorial statements may be, they can also carry prices: the disapproving scrutiny of others for challenging standards of feminine modesty, the material reality that Third World money spent in mass consumption tends to flow back to First World corporations, or the erasure of agency due to the assumption that wearing kimonos (or salwaar-kameez or sarong or hanbok or cheongsam or ao dai) is just something that Japanese (or South Asian or Indonesian or Korean or Chinese or Vietnamese) women do. Making sense of these choices and their ramifications requires charting how and why particular people are acting through both agency and constraint, and to understand the dialectical relationships between these characteristics. One way to do this, we suggest, lies in combining insights from performance theory and practice theory.

The Practice of Performance

Choosing what clothing to make, sell, or consume are all acts of performance because they provide an opportunity to display oneself to others in ways that can register one's actual or desired identity along a variety of lines – class, occupation, gender, sexual preference, race, ethnicity, religion, age, marital status, educational level, location of residence, etc. As such, performing difference or alliance through dress is simultaneously an act of politics and of self-making. Judith Butler has argued, based on the work of Michel Foucault, that performance is always more than the pure outward expression of an inner, essential self. Rather, such a self does not exist. It is precisely through performing that identities are made under conditions of unequal access to power and resources. As such, it is a constitutive and political act (1990).[28]

The metaphor of performance proliferated in academic circles in the 1990s because it resonated with fantasies of self-making, of rejecting prefabricated identities and challenging constraints by becoming who we want to be. If identity were simply a performance, then recognizing that it was not based on anything material or essential offered the possibility for reinvention.[29] These reinventions could be obvious or, more importantly, quite subtle. Even as people appeared to be performing the roles assigned to them, they might add little touches of irony or parody that could highlight just how constructed, just how much of a charade the whole affair was. If these points could be recognized as such, then the arbitrariness of identity would be exposed in ways that might allow for even more autonomous self-creation through role-play. This was a particularly strong thread in Butler's thinking about sex and gender. As Rosalind Morris claims, "By asserting that the body assumes its sex in the culturally mandated practices of everyday life, the theory of gender performativity offers the possibility of re-styling that body in non-normative and occasionally subversive ways" (Morris 1995: 573). Performativity seemed the newest chapter in scholars' ongoing "romance of resistance" (Abu-Lughod 1990).

It is in the very metaphor of performance, however, that problems with this approach to dress and identity arise. Ironically, theorists who took as their point of departure the constraints and expectations that demand that we behave in certain ways may have underestimated just how constraining this context could be. While performativity emphasizes playing at roles, performance in fact is highly structured work. Performers require costumes, roles, and scripted lines and movements that they then memorize and enact before a critical audience. None of these is created by or dependent solely on the performer. Even improvised performances interact with audience expectations; they may challenge or startle us, but they do so by engaging us through shared understandings. All performances thus depend on preexisting conditions and meanings with which one may be able to play, but not without significant limitations. We may choose to dress in a certain way in an attempt to achieve a more privileged identity, but whether that performance is perceived by other people as believable, as "real," and hence whether we are recognized and validated as the person we wish to be, depends on how we have been previously classified. The task becomes to identify how these internally and externally produced constraints emerge, and how they affect performances.

This is precisely what practice theory has sought to do. One of the main goals of practice theory, as outlined by Bourdieu (1977 [1972], 1984) and de Certeau (1984) is to show how social and cultural structures become translated and enacted through individual daily practices, such as habits of speech, physical mannerisms, or dress, and taste in art, music, or literature. As such, practice theory shares performance theory's emphasis on how abstract social and cultural categories become expressed and reproduced through individual actions. According to Rosalind Morris (1995), it was precisely this shared concern and the already established appeal of practice theory that provided fertile ground for the proliferation of performance theory in the 1990s.

We see in the two theories, however, a crucial difference in the weight they give to preexisting constraints. Intended as a corrective to structuralism that would allow for improvisation, uncertainty, and individuality in social life, practice theory nonetheless seems to depict people as trapped in structures that they helplessly reproduce. For example, Bourdieu (1984) convincingly shows that class is not simply economic, but social and cultural. His discussion of social and cultural capital gained currency mostly because it squared with the fluidity of late twentieth-century life, in which people of the same income may be perceived as having different class status depending on their family backgrounds, education, clothing choices, and preferences for art, music, reading, etc. At the same time, however, practice theory risks making these class distinctions seem static; class status may not be the result simply of income, but it can be calculated, almost arithmetically, by taking account of how education and social connections shape taste. Little room is afforded for individual choice or idiosyncrasy, the very factors that practice theory hoped to address.

We have, then, two theories designed to track how social and cultural forms get reproduced and reworked through individual role-play. One (practice theory) risks reducing people to the sum total of their socially and culturally defined roles. The other (performance theory) overemphasizes the notion of play in "role-play" in an attempt to focus on the artificiality of identity, the agency of the individual performer, and the potential subversiveness of even the most banal practices of dress and self-display. What is needed is a synthesis of the two: an attention to *performance practices* that tracks the constraints shaping and limiting identity creation and subversion. Even if we view the performance of self as stemming from conscious choice, we must recognize that our desire to be a certain way is not entirely self-generated, nor can we determine the outcome. The desire to perform emerges within the concrete circumstances of our existence and the way that existence has been characterized by others, and it is often with those others that the success of the performance, in the eyes of both performer and audience, is debated and determined. As such, even the performance of a desired identity can feel mandatory, and its effects can be ambiguous.

Rebecca N. Ruhlen's study of the Korean hanbok (Chapter 3 of this volume) aptly captures the uncertainty arising from attention to performance practices. Ruhlen's chapter begins with a recollection of her encounter with a senior staff member at a Korean feminist organization. The staff member normally wore Western-style clothing to work, but, on the day she was scheduled to meet with a potential donor, she donned a hanbok instead. Ruhlen's astute analysis of this episode highlights the complicated agency involved in this choice of dress. The woman had clearly *decided* to wear a hanbok, and she chose a particularly fashionable style then considered quite modern. Even a modern hanbok, however, conjures up images of a traditional Korean woman, a fact which Ruhlen claims this particular woman consciously manipulated. She wore a hanbok in order to shroud her potentially threatening feminism in the guise/ garb of the more traditional and properly demure Korean woman. Do we interpret wearing the hanbok as a performance foisted upon the woman that forces her to reenact a demure femininity so as to reinscribe the secondary status that she otherwise seeks to challenge through her activism? Or, do we see it as a conscious display to garner affirmation by an audience, expressed in the concrete form of a donation that will enable her to continue working to change gender relations in Korea? If the performance is conscious in order to manipulate her intended audience, as Ruhlen suggests it is, is it what Rosalind Morris (1995) has identified as a parodic performance, one also intended mimetically to expose how arbitrary the construction of this vision of Korean femininity is? Following in this line, does the parody succeed? It seems not to, for as Ruhlen notes, wearing a hanbok is interpreted, not just by unastute outsiders, but by Korean women themselves as just something that "we Koreans do" (page 134). To turn the wheel even further, then, what might or might not be a conscious performance to reproduce gendered assumptions mimetically in order to achieve a preformulated goal gets interpreted by the audience as an unconscious expression of essentialized gender and national identity. This outcome seems to suit the performer just fine in the short term, but it poses troubling implications for her long-term goal of reworking gender relations in Korea.

Ruhlen's analysis underscores the centrality of concepts of femininity to the practice of performing identity through dress. Being marked as part of the category "female," with all its associations with tradition and domesticity, shapes Korean women's access to modernity. They are nonetheless participating in modernity in ways that might work to their symbolic and material advantage. In doing so, they may also be able to alter the conditions of their gendered marking. The new hanbok is new, but it is also old, and the gender identity associated with it is being reconfigured and reconfirmed. Whether the performance is in fact a reconfiguration or a reconfirmation seems to depend on other factors. What access to capital – social, cultural, and economic – does the performer have? How much attention is the audience going to pay to determining the purpose behind this performance?

Projecting these concerns outward to the international stage, we suggest that by analyzing the articulations of transnational capital and human activity as performance practices, women's actions can be seen as neither the result of a totalizing Orientalist gaze from a Western fashion industry, nor the enacting of postcolonial national scripts, nor the unproblematic expression of self. Yet the extent to which practices of dress performance are intended or received as political or resistant acts depends on the audience(s). Acts that may seem resistant in a local context can take on alternative and less radical meanings in a global context, and vice versa. Given the weighty discursive legacy of Orientalism, its reworking through globalized economic and cultural structures, and the gendering processes associated with both, self-Orientalizing and internal Orientalizing emerge as reasonable, yet highly fraught, modes for individual and state-sponsored performances of gender and national identity on the domestic and international stages.

Internal and Self-Orientalizing as National and Personal Strategies

Ruhlen's research on Korean feminists' use of the hanbok in local and international contexts provides a rich example of how wearing an item of supposedly traditional dress can be seen by the wearers as expressing pride in national identity. Such moments can serve to reify and make all the more natural the comfortable link between nation and gender. At the same time, the specific instances Ruhlen describes raise a complication: what do we make of a feminist, one who in many ways wishes to challenge Korean traditions, wearing an item so associated with tradition?[30]

If the image of a feminist wearing traditional clothing seems contradictory, that may be precisely the point, for it communicates the sense that women are, as Norma Alarcón, Caren Kaplan, and Minoo Moallem have argued, "both of and not of the nation" (Alarcón et al. 1999: 13). Because women are seen as fodder for symbols, they can simultaneously be imagined as essentially maternal and iconic of a national body, yet also different, citizens who must prove their worth through high-stakes performances of identity. The stakes become even higher in a context of globalization and transnational exchange that seems to challenge or at least destabilize that identity. Thus, while transnational exchanges in wealth or ideas appear to facilitate a well-meaning transnational feminism, these representations are still grounded in, and reinscribe, national affiliations. Orientalizing gazes, both across and within national boundaries, can serve local national goals. The feminist clad in traditional garb reinterpreted as a modern fashion statement provides Koreans unsure about their status within a globalized economy with a reassuring image that even as things change, the core of national identity remains in Korean hands.

26

Orientalist rhetoric is therefore co-opted, but also further elaborated, in local Asian contexts in ways that are specific to differences in power and gender, yet also serve the nation. Two forms in particular have been identified by scholars: internal Orientalism and self-Orientalism. Finding ways to interpret how each of these strategies shapes the intentions, context, and effects of Asian women's various dress choices requires that we attend not only to the oppressive institutions that benefit from their choices, but to the self-making and nation-making consequences of those decisions.

Several authors studying postcolonial and nationalist conditions in Asia have described forms of "internal Orientalism." Geraldine Heng and Janandas Devan (1992) describe an "internalized Orientalism" in the patriarchal Singaporean state that identifies those elements *within* the nation that prevent it from fully achieving a state of development that can prove it has "arrived" on the international front. In this case, those segments of the population charged with dragging down national success are consistently classed, raced, and gendered. Through a 1980s "debate" on marriage and reproductive choices, poor women of color were blamed for preventing the national success of Singapore.

Louisa Schein defines a second form of "internal Orientalism" within China. While exoticized Others are often deployed by states as a sort of exotic color that will lure sightseers, the Chinese state, according to Schein, creates a fuller spectrum of exoticized Other that has little to do with international tourism or global politics. Rather, Schein describes how the Chinese state and urban Han Chinese have created a domestic narrative of Otherness about ethnic minorities that casts the Miao ambivalently as both backward and "titillating" (2000: 101). Their proximity to nature is evidence of lack of civilization but also of erotic simplicity. Not surprisingly, the symbol of ethnic identity that serves so malleably as both positive and negative is the ethnic woman, usually dressed in colorful, ethnically identifiable clothing.

In both examples, states seeking to position themselves as civilized, strong, and worldly do so through rhetorics of self-assessment that locate progress disproportionately with certain groups and displace the blame for limitations onto clearly identifiable Others. Much as colonial states justified their rule by defining the problems of the races they sought to control as a natural feature of those races and hence one they were powerless to address themselves, modern Asian nations often identify the Other within. They do so both to rationalize economic, social, or cultural obstacles and to establish the nation, usually dominated by ethnic majority groups, as the appropriate vehicle to address those problems by civilizing the internal Other or, at the very least, constraining it.

This brings us to a second form of Orientalism that has been identified by contemporary scholars of Asia, that of self-Orientalizing. If Orientalism has an ambivalent array of meanings, then claiming control over representations of exoticism can appear to reverse the imbalance of power between the West and the Rest. Just as national discourses of internal Orientalizing allow Asian states to seize control over the process of defining who is Other, so can producing and consuming an exoticized image of one's own cultural identity be a technique for asserting discursive control that can seem to turn the negative narrative of Western Orientalism on its head.

The Asian Values debate in insular Southeast Asia has been a particularly energetic case of such work. One example is that of the Singaporean state, which has invested deeply in creating and embracing a neo-Confucian identity. The campaign, headed by Prime Minister Lee Kuan Yew in the 1980s and picked up by other regional leaders in the 1990s, excavated and celebrated a narrow interpretation of Confucianism as the shared transnational heritage of all successful Asians. Part of the appeal of this rhetoric to leaders and many citizens was that it inverted the colonial-era accusation that Confucian philosophy might prevent full development (e.g., Marx's Asiatic Mode of Production, or Max Weber's argument that Confucianism was too hierarchical to allow flexible change). The Singaporean strategy has been to promote a version of Confucianism that not only instills pride in the Singaporean population for its "tradition" but provides the cultural rationale for a patriarchal state and its tactics in generating a skilled and globally attractive labor force. According to Aihwa Ong (1991, 1997), such self-Orientalist narratives are often told by national male leaders to attract foreign investors by depicting female workers as having a racially and culturally specific ability to do repetitive physical work for long hours. In this way, the now familiar refrain on the docility of Asian women workers is the result, not just of Western stereotyping, but of well-documented official investment rhetoric by Asian governments to perpetuate those stereotypes.

These self-Orientalizing moves highlight the problematic politics through which conditions of domination are resisted, yet reproduced. This can occur even when one consciously intends to combat Orientalisms. Dorinne Kondo (1997) calls such attempts "counter-Orientalisms" and uses this term to describe the ways in which Japanese fashion designers mobilize stereotypes of Asian-ness to question difference. Their efforts, however, rest on a form of self-Orientalizing that ultimately reinscribes difference.[31] Part of Kondo's discussion concerns an ad campaign for the Japanese Suit, a garment produced by Rei Kawakubo's line Comme des Garçons in the late 1980s and marketed especially to Japanese businessmen. The ads, according to Kondo, sought to counter negative global images of Japan and Japanese masculinity, ranging from military defeat in the Second World War to the emasculation of contemporary Japanese men that we described above. The ads do so by evoking emotionally laden images of a particularly Japanese masculinity that is spiritual, harmonious, authentic, and forward-looking, even as it has been marked and Orientalized. All of this is then declared embodied in a Japanese Suit designed to appeal to conservative businessmen who might otherwise be wary of "fashion." Kondo reads the ads as doing two things at once. On the one hand, the ad campaign offers a way for Japanese men to create an affirmative masculinity that arms them against Western dominance. On the other hand, this masculinity is reactive, in that it is established on a terrain in which Japan is perpetually positioned as effeminate and inferior. The campaign plays on this fact, for in attempting to convince potential customers of the very need for such a thing as a Japanese Suit, it reinforces Japanese men's insecurities by implying the unsuitability of the British suit for their racialized bodies and identities. The Japanese Suit is thus intended to counter Orientalist depictions of Japan, at the very same time as its successful evocation of consumer desire rests on and confirms Japanese men's anxieties about being inferior mimics of Western capitalist powers.

Internal and self-Orientalizing are never simply unidirectional moves by elites against the disempowered. Just as indigenous bourgeoisies used selective strategies of "tradition" and "modernity" to resist colonial identities, so too are postcolonial populations selectively embracing elements of exoticism that serve their own purposes of self-orienting. Gender can figure centrally in this regard around questions of both masculinity and femininity. While Kondo focuses on images of Japanese manhood, the complicated conditions of who is Orientalizing whom and why similarly preclude easy interpretations of victimization or domination in representations of Asian women. Women's choices to attempt counter-Orientalisms by playing with images that might otherwise be seen as if one were Orientalizing oneself contrast with stereotypes of passive, docile Asian women, while nonetheless still reinscribing difference. It is here that this volume's dual focus – first, on Asian states' internal Orientalizing practices through images of clothed women; and, second, on mid-level, feminized Asian actors' self- and counter-Orientalizing dress practices – becomes particularly instructive.

The Chapters: Asian Dress as Re-Orienting and Re-Orientalizing

It has been our aim in this introduction to demonstrate how dress has been a primary tool in representing and deploying national and gender differences, from the days of colonial Orientalisms to the equally Orientalist context of contemporary globalization that simultaneously promotes Asian chic, national costumes, and Western fashion. It should not be surprising that it is primarily through the feminized arena of dress that Asian nations respond by constructing internal Others so as to imagine themselves as masculine agents directing civilizing processes of economic development. It should also not be surprising that it is through dress that Asian women as consumers, marketers, and producers perform self-Orientalizing displays that contain the possibility for the kinds of counter-Orientalisms Kondo identified. As powerful and as telling as dress may be for performing alterity and resistance, it is highly limited. Just as Dick Hebdige (1979) observed about the potential for political resistance through subcultural style, styles are vulnerable to manipulation by commodity capitalism and the dominant cultural order precisely because they are so plastic and open to multiple interpretations and reinterpretations. Far from being a liberatory space of personal expression or a frivolous pastime, Asian dress has become a profound site of contestation, a source of global fascination, and a space for national debate. This makes the dress choices that Asians themselves make all the more significant.

Ultimately, we need to find some way to confront the complexity, ambiguity, and ambivalence that surround the dress decisions Asians make and the dress representations of Asia and Asians that circulate within Asia and around the world. Looked at together, the chapters in *Re-Orienting Fashion* suggest one way to do this: focus on the conditions surrounding contemporary Asian dress, from a resurgence of interest in traditional or indigenous dress, to the simultaneous adoption and adaptation of Western dress by Asians, to the embracing and reworking of Asian fashion elements by Western designers and consumers. While the precise implications of the individual instances documented in this volume vary, these chapters all seek to consider the ramifications of and conditions for using dress to make meaning in a variety of settings. The authors question the self-evident interpretations of particular moves by exploring them in context, as strategies of internal and self-Orientalizing that are part of social, cultural, economic, and political landscapes rife with specific and often contradictory stakes. They do so through an ethnographic focus on performance practices by those individuals and nations who have been marginalized by Orientalism and globalization, yet who nonetheless possess some ability to shape the conditions of their self-representations.

It is here that a focus on mid-level actors in Asian fashion becomes instructive. This volume looks at those who fall squarely in the middle between the supposedly powerful and powerless: the Asian designers, merchants, and consumers who make decisions about what clothing to make, to sell, and to wear. Often invisible in studies of globalization and fashion that focus on the macro and the powerful or in anthropological works which tend to explore the lives of the clearly dispossessed, mid-level actors need to be examined as economically, politically, and culturally of crucial importance. They are producers, but not the disempowered working classes assumed in the literature on women and development. They are consumers, but not the type of powerful "global dictators" heralded by theorists of consumption such as Daniel Miller (1995a). By critically engaging with Orientalisms in all their forms, and reorienting attention to the intermediate players in global exchanges, the chapters expose the struggles, political limits, and possibilities mid-level actors face. Instead of voiceless victims or powerful agents, these are people who are betwixt and between, whose dress decisions involve complicated moves of internal and self-Orientalizing and are as likely to yield material benefit or cultural status as they are to reproduce economic, social, cultural, or symbolic marginality. That's what makes them so interesting.

Four of our authors (Niessen, Leshkowich, Ruhlen, and Bhachu) take as their point of departure the rediscovery of Asian women's so-called traditional dress, either by Asian women themselves or by interested external parties. One way to interpret this trend is to understand these fashions as continuations of ancient traditions. In attending in fine detail to each of these instances, the authors find that cases of apparent tradition are in fact strategic rediscoveries and remakings of tradition. In this way, wearing traditional dress can be seen as trendy, modern, or fashionable precisely because it is a self-Orientalizing move that often involves a distanced gaze or nostalgia for a precapitalist past. Indeed, the chapters by Niessen, Leshkowich, Ruhlen, and Bhachu challenge typical stereotypes of Asian women as easy symbols of either modernity or tradition. Rather, many of the women they describe are strikingly aware of the stakes involved in their choices. At the same time, transnational and domestic interactions involving divisions of class, gender, and ethnicity often shape how and when women choose to perform self-Orientalizing moves and whether these moves enhance or diminish the performer's status.

Sandra Niessen explores three scenarios from the history of Batak clothing to show how the design changes effected by this North Sumatran group's supposedly traditional weavers have been profoundly entangled in global fashion dynamics. Niessen begins by tracing how tumultuous social change during the Dutch colonial era and ongoing trade with Malays led Karo Batak weavers to discard their customary blue indigo dye in favor of the rarer and higher-status red – a color that is now seen as typically Karo Batak. Today, that same dynamism and incorporation of outside influences are apparent in the creation of what Niessen refers to as "modern traditional" outfits. These are clothes, such as the "Toba Batak sarong," that are recent innovations, combining traditional Batak patterns or weaving techniques with external design influences and materials to create ethnic-chic outfits. Niessen's account of Batak clothing highlights the dynamism of this fashion system in ways that challenge conventional notions of a dichotomy between unchanging traditional dress and ever-changing Western fashion. Such accounts should prompt us to reconsider how scholars define fashion and understand its workings, an argument which Niessen explores further in the Afterword to this volume.

It is important to see Bataks as having a fashion system, but Niessen's chapter also highlights the disadvantages of participating in larger circuits of clothing design and marketing. What for Bataks is a combination of income-earning and the reproduction of ethnic identity is also the reproduction of class and ethnic inequality in the larger Indonesian and global context. From colonial times to the present era of globalization and ethnic chic, Batak weavers clearly have exercised agency in responding to outside forces and making "strategic design decisions." But their survival has entailed a loss of control. They have become laborers whose designs are commissioned by outsiders or quasi-outsiders, such as the cosmopolitan "Ibu M.," a Batak woman living in Jakarta whose access to high-end fashion boutiques has given her a self-Orientalizing perspective. She knows how to translate Batak designs into fashions that will sell in urban Indonesia and abroad. As the styles gain currency through the design work of Ibu M., the weavers' agency gets erased. Lacking the privilege necessary for self-Orientalizing to be interpreted as a mark of status, they are instead assigned the label of traditional, the internal and eternal Others within the Indonesian nation who are left to drift into "anonymous obscurity."

Ann Marie Leshkowich's account of the Vietnamese ao dai offers a parallel case of how the circumstances of globalization have prompted a self-Orientalizing reinvention and rediscovery of so-called traditional dress. Here, however, the outcome seems more positive, because both the Vietnamese nation and the urban middle-class women in Ho Chi Minh City who tailor, sell, buy, and wear the garments benefit from the reconfiguration of an imagined tradition in the ao dai. By tracing the garment's circulation historically and during the 1990s' "ao dai craze," Leshkowich shows how this supposedly indigenous garment has in fact emerged through the incorporation of external stylistic elements: from China, France, and the United States in the past, and from international fashion trends and diasporic kin today. These influences have made the garment a hybrid product, one that seems familiar and yet fashionable to its contemporary wearers in Vietnam and in the Vietnamese diaspora. The garment is also familiarly exotic to outsiders, and their appreciation for it only enhances its status within Vietnam. While Vietnamese tend to celebrate the garment as reflecting a charming traditional femininity, Leshkowich suggests that this tradition has become valuable precisely because of its emergence as a modern, popular trend consistent with the global turn toward homogenized heterogeneity. As she writes, "The decision to wear an ao dai is just as influenced by global fashion trends as is the decision to buy Levi's" (000). The women who make or buy ao dai are thus engaging in self-Orientalizing to position themselves as conversant with cultured modernity by claiming knowledge of their ethnic heritage and a globally informed understanding of why that heritage is valuable and fashionable. The enduring appeal of finding national unity and difference on the bodies of Vietnamese women is clear, but so is the fact that being part of such a trend can afford middle-class women personal pleasure, social status, and material benefit.

In a different context, the Korean feminists whom Rebecca N. Ruhlen studies chose to wear the hanbok at national and international women's events and for fund-raising purposes, but not because they necessarily embraced some essentialist version of Korean traditional femininity. Quite the contrary, for as feminists they explicitly advocated challenging elements of women's traditional roles. Instead, they saw the moment of the Asian Economic Crisis and foreign financial intervention through the IMF as a politically charged context in which to reestablish Korean national identity to both foreign NGO observers and to themselves. They found an available and readily understandable avenue for doing this through an appeal to the past and through a sense of frugality, messages they felt they could convey through a hanbok that was nonetheless reconfigured as modern fashion and dubbed a "lifestyle hanbok." At the same time, this symbol of femininity seemed attractive precisely because it softened the potentially hard edges of feminism and insulated the wearers from accusations that feminism is a form of Western neo-imperialism that produces "Yankee whores" (page 130). The women may have claimed that wearing hanbok is just something that Koreans do, but there seemed a self-awareness to their decision to self-Orientalize. We have already described how Ruhlen's discussion vibrantly captures the stakes involved in such a move. Here, let us simply reiterate that the success of the hanbok as a feminist strategy depends in part on the concealment of it as a conscious, political move, at least on the terrain of gender. To the extent that wearing the hanbok seems natural, however, essentialized notions of Korean femininity go unchallenged and risk becoming reinscribed.

With Parminder Bhachu's study of the British South Asian women who design and market salwaar-kameez, we see women who are astutely aware of what is at stake in the contest over their appearances. The British Asian clothing merchants whom Bhachu studied have been able to exploit and profit from a trend toward salwaar-kameez in the United Kingdom, as well as other Western European settings, precisely because of their savvy awareness and creation of trends. Interestingly, this awareness has come from what might otherwise seem to be women tailors' and designers' positions of marginality, as intergenerational cycles of multiple migration have constructed them as outsiders in various new locales, and yet made them expert in understanding the contours of those differences and how to navigate them. Bhachu demonstrates that British South Asian women have successfully recoded the salwaar-kameez as both an expression of national and personal pride and a trendy fashion garment appealing to an increasingly diverse clientele, including Princess Diana. As a result, the designers have experienced commercial success. Yet, given the fact that the period of Bhachu's research coincided with the spread of violent racial conflict on British streets, we wonder to what degree celebrations of Asian styles, in particular a romanticized, feminized representation centered on women's dress, provide a kind of superficial multiculturalism that ultimately still refuses to address the racialized differences of British social life. Of all the chapters in this volume, the benefits of self-Orientalizing seem greatest for the women described by Bhachu, and they welcome the affirmation provided by the salwaar-kameez's entry into high fashion. It may be that these fashion developments provide a point of entry for substantive cross-cultural engagement and dialogue. There is nonetheless still a danger that the agency and creativity of South Asian designers will be interpreted by others as the essentialized and unreflexive expression of their femininity and South Asianness.

The chapters in this volume seek to destabilize the link between woman and nation by revealing how the connections are always historically specific, politically oriented, and the result of cultural work. In their exploration of representations of ethnic minority women in Vietnamese government propaganda posters, Hjorleifur R. Jonsson and Nora A. Taylor find that the foundations for a national need to identify and control ethnic difference lie significantly in a postcolonial condition. Jonsson and Taylor argue that the versions of ethnic difference through which the Vietnamese state has promoted national unity, both in the mid-twentieth century and in the 1990s, relied on a self-Orientalizing link between traditional women's dress and national identity. They trace this discursive strategy to French efforts to entrench colonial rule through ordering and classifying the different races dwelling in their domain. A newly independent Vietnamese government, faced with the task of defining itself and the people in whose name it rules, turned to the preexisting Orientalist classificatory apparatus of the French colonial state, imbuing it with Marxist rhetoric about nation, modernity, and progress. Even as the state today propagates a multiethnic vision of the modern Vietnamese nation, it deploys highly stylized and partial icons of that difference in order to feminize it and hence render it controllable, manipulatable, and ordered. The propaganda poster is the contemporary heir of the French divide-and-rule policy, a vehicle for expressing the magnanimity of the ethnic Vietnamese majority state toward its internal, and eternally backward, minority Others. As Jonsson and Taylor found, the response of these Others can often be to reject these markers by embracing non-signified dress. Women's dress thus becomes a pliable symbol for signifying backwardness at certain moments, and national superiority at others. That the minority people being signified do not respond by embracing and recoding their supposedly ethnic costumes as trendy fashions, as in the cases described by Bhachu and Leshkowich, testifies to their alienation from material and discursive centers of power. They simply do not have the privilege of self-Orientalizing.

Just as the chapters in this volume belie the impression of ethnic dress as easy continuations of timeless tradition, they also complicate what seem to be instances of simple adoptions of "Western" style. Carla Jones describes how Indonesian women who chose to adopt dress styles in ways that might be interpreted as a wholesale embrace or unconscious, but failed, imitation of the modern. These women's interest in global trends might also seem like an example of the sort of unreflexive, superficial pursuit of status or face that is a common stereotype of Asian women consumers. But Jones's account of Indonesian women who enrolled in courses on appropriate and professional appearance emphasizes the importance of class position when analyzing questions of dress and personal identity. In these courses, middle-class and aspiring middle-class women in the Javanese city of Yogyakarta sought expertise from wealthier and higher-status women who had greater access to global trends. Jones shows how these students treated research and choices about dress as a way of participating in the struggle over national culture in Indonesia. State development programs for women during the New Order regime of President Suharto engaged in self-Orientalizing claims that linked an invented version of traditional dress to conservative forms of femininity, domesticity, and housewifery. Official rhetoric suggested that women's dress choices be read as indexes of moral rather than class difference, even as this period saw the creation of increasingly deep class divisions under the regime's embrace of industrial capitalism. As a result, what might appear to an outside observer as a direct copy of a Western suit, in fact communicated the wearer's attempt to claim some control over her own appearance and propriety. At the same time, the wearer's use of that suit as a tool for attempting upward class mobility complicated official narratives that had decoupled dress from class. Jones shows that through Indonesian public concern over the appropriate form of the model woman citizen, the connections between nation and woman have to be continually remade, in part through the fashioning of the Indonesian woman's body.

In a similar way, but on the other end of the design spectrum, Lise Skov's analysis in Chapter 7 reveals the double bind Hong Kong fashion designers feel. Skov describes Hong Kong fashion designers who see no contradiction between being proudly Hong Kongers and their desire to create "Western" fashions, yet foreign buyers who exercise control over orders and commercial success reinscribe fundamental Orientalist differences they see between East and West. Such designers experience frustrating limitations on their creativity, professional and financial success, and personal identities, yet do not understand their desire to "make it" in the world of "Western" fashions as being inconsistent with pride in their Chinese heritage. Skov's piece reveals how Hong Kong designers find the global trend for "Chinese" fashions to be ultimately disempowering. While Shanghai Tang chic provided enormous cachet and wealth to Hong Kong entrepreneur David Tang and a select few elites, many aspiring and less powerful Hong Kong designers found the trend suffocating, preventing them from viable economic success unless they designed "Chinese" styles. If they took this route, however, they risked being seen as "ethnic" designers doing what supposedly comes naturally to them as a legacy of their heritage, and hence not as independent agents pushing the boundaries of fashion. Not having made it in the fashion business means that experimenting with self-Orientalizing design strategies poses the same risk of a loss of agency for cosmopolitan Hong Kong designers that Niessen described for rural Batak weavers.

Against a backdrop of Orientalism that has defined and continues to shape the meaning of Asian dress styles and practices, even in this era of globalization, the seven chapters of this volume demonstrate that self-Orientalizing and internal Orientalizing have become widespread and viable techniques for attempting to acquire material and discursive power. These moves, however, inevitably involve trade-offs, as certain kinds of difference get challenged and reworked to advantage, while others get reinscribed. Dress may be key to a performative construction of identity, but the effects of that performance seem largely to lie beyond the performer, with an audience that may or may not be amenable to having its assumptions exposed and its discursive constructions questioned.

In her Afterword, Sandra Niessen points to another way in which this volume exposes assumptions and questions discursive constructions: namely, what she describes as the Orientalist discourse that assumes "fashion" as stylistic innovations over time to be exclusively a Western phenomenon. Niessen provocatively suggests that this conception of fashion, one that remains largely unchallenged by fashion theorists, rests on an oppositional West/Rest construction. Empirically speaking, this opposition no longer holds, for the chapters in this volume amply demonstrate how thoroughly Asian dress has become enmeshed in global fashion practices. Discursively, however, the opposition remains strong, and has even gathered momentum, as people around the world evaluate their own dress practices through the lens of a dichotomy between the modern West and the traditional Rest. Accepting this dichotomy thus amounts to confirming the discursive terms on which the international fashion industry bases its power. Playing on this volume's title, Niessen calls for a "re-orientation" of fashion theory to take account of the production of fashion/anti-fashion oppositions as integral to the discursive and material power of global fashion.

Conclusion

Taken together, the studies in this volume highlight the ways in which the globalization of Asian dress, both in terms of the spread of Asian style throughout the world and in terms of the growing prevalence of other forms of dress in Asia, has been accomplished through Orientalist ways of knowing, particularly the construction of an opposition between a modern, masculine West and a traditional, feminine Orient. Interest in Asian style during the 1990s may have stemmed from a genuine desire for cultural appreciation or a recognition of the growing global power of Asian economies, but it tended to reduce heritage and difference to a feminized, essentialized, and unthreatening accent or an exotic flair.

These processes are particularly interesting in their effects on people who get caught in the middle because of their class, race, and gender identity or their economic, social, and cultural practices. In this introduction, we have argued that, as a whole, the case studies in this volume suggest a productive methodology for tracking these effects: an attention to performance practices that combines insights from both practice theory and performance theory. By looking at the practice of Asian dress performances, we can explore the decisions Asians, within and outside of Asia, make in ways that highlight the agency in their creation of self, while at the same time exploring the constraints on those choices – constraints typically posed by preexisting discourses and positions. We can also look at the ramifications of those choices, particularly the circumstances under which the highly fraught strategies of self-Orientalizing and internal Orientalizing succeed or fail in garnering material and symbolic power for those who deploy them.

The volume's title *Re-Orienting Fashion* reflects our goal of revealing how the globalization of Asian dress has been accompanied by a contradictory traffic in representations of Asian men and women through the surfaces and appearances of their bodies. The chapters in this volume analyze Asian dress practices within constrained terrains as often simultaneously empowering (and hence re-orienting of global power structures) and disempowering (and therefore re-Orientalizing of Asia and Asians). By attending to the material and

discursive stakes of fashion as a site for performing racial and gendered difference, we suggest that the authors in this volume position fashion and gender
as fundamental, yet under-studied, elements of the global circulation of wealth
and images. What people choose to make, sell, or wear is a vibrant site for the
generation of wealth under global capitalism that relies on circulations of value
that are not only economic but also psychic, personal, and national. These
chapters reveal contradictions between images of Asian women as passive
preserves of national cultures or as evidence of corruption and Western masculine
domination. One goal of this volume is to offer a correction to these images
through ethnographies of those women and men who stand to lose or gain by
making fashion choices. By charting their choices, the limitations they face,
and the meanings they make, the authors expand our understanding of how
both globalization and Orientalism continue to be refashioned in everyday life.
As a result, each chapter carefully disabuses us of any simple confirmation that
power, both material and discursive, is written onto women's bodies. Rather,
this volume challenges us to recognize the players and the stakes involved in
shaping what we all wear, and why what we wear matters.

Notes

1. This introduction is the result of three years of conversation and collaboration.
During that time, we have benefited from the kind assistance and keen insights of
several readers. Sandra Niessen and Bruce Knauft have offered insightful critique of
numerous versions of this text and have been constant and patient sources of support,
for which we are most grateful. We would also like to thank Carla Freeman, Joanne
Eicher, and one anonymous reviewer for reading and commenting on drafts of this
chapter. The Vernacular Modernities Program, funded by Emory University and the
Ford Foundation, and a Research and Publications Grant from College of the Holy
Cross provided us with the funds to develop and reflect on the ideas in this chapter.
We would also like to thank our families, particularly Meredith Leshkowich, whose
care and good humor allowed us to concentrate on this project.

2. In using the term "Asian" to describe the globalization of Asian dress, we do not
mean to suggest that such a singular or homogeneous place called "Asia" exists. To
the contrary, this volume seeks to highlight the problematic use of a label to capture
or describe a diverse and vibrant region that has come to be labeled Asia. Yet precisely
because the appeal of the category has been so successful in Western rhetoric about
an Asian Other, we use the term in this introduction to refer to the discursive category
that is popularly known as Asia.

3. To North American audiences, *National Geographic* is perhaps the most familiar
example of mass-media images of a primitive and authentic Other. As Catherine Lutz
and Jane Collins argue about the narratives of difference and progress promoted in
that magazine, exotic dress has been a particularly salient way for editors and readers

to interpret difference through an evolutionary framework as variously primitive, authentic, or just "bad taste" (1993: 93).

4. These discourses were by no means limited to Asia or the Middle East. As Jean Comaroff argues, colonial discourses of difference and superiority were made in the context of imperial conquest in Africa as well. She states that the joint endeavor of the civilizing missions of Protestant missionaries, colonial conquest, and industrial capitalism in South Africa made clothes "at once commodities and accoutrements of a civilized self. They were to prove a privileged means for constructing new forms of value, personhood, and history on the colonial frontier" (1996: 19).

5. Tarlo's discussion of colonial dress focuses largely on the politically charged and limited choices men made in the colonial period. Tarlo does not address the issue of women's dress, rather suggesting that women seemed to maintain "traditional" forms of dress. As discussed below, Partha Chatterjee's research argues that women's dress in India had as much to do with a strategically nationalist invented tradition as it did with an apparently natural and continued tradition.

6. During this time, Dutch colonists were likewise affected by this unequal traffic in ideas, enacting in the Indies new forms of gender relations that offered both new freedoms and limitations to European women. Taylor links these to European women's early embrace of the sarong in the eighteenth century, and to their ultimate abandonment of it in the late nineteenth and early twentieth centuries in favor of European fashions that enforced racial and gender boundaries. However, the colonial state particularly deployed the masculine symbolism of the uniquely colonial suit, one that included Javanese batik and embroidery. In so doing, the colonial suit not only imitated the dress of the European middle-class gentleman, but also acquired "a significance as the costume of the ruler rather than of the citizen" (Taylor 1997: 97).

7. In a similar vein, Lata Mani's research on the debate of the practice of *sati* in colonial India reveals how wresting political and military control from the native man was founded on the fantasy of European liberation of the native woman (1998).

8. Vicente Rafael argues that this trope of the native "penchant for mimicry" was central to the American discourse of "benevolent" colonialism in the Philippines. Because Filipinos were perceived to have no capability for original thought, they required instruction on how to be civilized, thereby justifying the American presence as teachers and rationalizing Filipinos into subjects for subjugation (2000: 34).

9. Chakrabarty analyzed bourgeois domesticity in colonial Bengal through domestic science textbooks and magazines for women. He found that these texts focused on crafting cultural distinctions between "European" and "Indian" through the domestic sphere. As such, there was agreement on the need to adopt apparently culturally neutral practices like hygiene, discipline, and order in the home, but more negotiation about what companionate marriage meant. The notion that a Bengali wife should also be her husband's friend was, Chakrabarty argues, threatening to the very order of authority in the home, for it suggested that a wife should be "a modern individual" (1992: 13). Similarly, Stoler and Cooper (1997) argue that indigenous bourgeoisies were highly influenced by the colonial rhetoric in which these classes were formed. Domestic arrangements, notions of family intimacy, and dress were all linked to attempts to form morally comparable complements to colonial superiority.

10. India is not the only example of how European styles were seen as inappropriate for new national femininities. Tai (1992) argues that the image of the "New Woman" was problematic for 1920s Vietnamese anticolonial revolutionaries. They wished to link a new, modern Vietnamese femininity to an emerging sense of the nation, but rejected European forms of femininity, as exemplified by wearing Western fashions and cosmetics such as lipstick. Similar imagery is common in the revolutionary era-writings of the Dutch East Indies. See, e.g., Achdiat Kartamihardja's *Atheis* (1981 [1952]), or Adboel Moeis's *Salah Asoehan* (1982 [1928]), in which female characters who wear European-style clothes, lipstick, and perfume fail to find happiness or meet tragic fates.

11. Because globalization involves the flow of things, ideas, and people across national borders, the current era is also often described as one of transnationalism. The difference between the terms lies mostly in the scope of the activities they describe. Globalization often refers to abstract processes not located in any particular place, while transnationalism describes the more concrete movement of people and things across nation-states (Kearney 1995; Basch et al. 1994; see also Appadurai 1996; Cvetkovich and Kellner 1997; Giddens 1990; Hannerz 1996; Robertson 1992; Wilson and Dissanayake 1996).

12. For overviews of the homogenization perspective, see Miller (1995a, 1995b) and Howes (1996). Arjun Appadurai notes that left-leaning scholars in media studies were particularly influential in making such arguments and cites Hamelink (1983), Mattelart (1983), and Schiller (1976) as examples (Appadurai 1996: 32). Ethnographic studies of local resistance to commodity capitalism (see, e.g., Taussig 1980 and Lan 1985) bolstered this view.

13. Within anthropology, consumption has gone from being criticized as inauthentic, superficial, and uncreative to being seen as a meaningful, personal, and innovative way to construct and express identity or as a potentially subversive site of resistance. See, for example, Abu-Lughod (1990, 1995b), Bourdieu (1984), Breckenridge (1995), Burke (1996), Carsten (1989), Comaroff (1990), Douglas and Isherwood (1978), Freeman (2000), Hannerz (1996), Howes (1996), McCracken (1988), Mackay (1997), Rutz and Orlove (1989), Toren (1989), and Weismantel (1989).

14. This observation has become so prevalent that at least four different terms have been coined to describe it: "hybridization" (García Canclini 1992), "creolization" (Hannerz 1996), "domestication" (Tobin 1992), and "localization" (Appadurai 1996). The difference between these terms seems to stem from the extent of local agency, the amount of creativity involved, and the degree to which the particular product in question becomes transformed (see, e.g., Howes 1996).

15. Examples include those focusing on "ethnic" art, clothing, dance, and tourism, such as Abu-Lughod (1990), Breckenridge (1995), Cvetkovich and Kellner (1997), Errington (1989), Freeman (2000 and 2001), Hendrickson (1996), Howes (1996), Kondo (1997), Price (1989), Savigliano (1995), Schein (2000), Steiner (1994), Tarlo (1996), and Tobin (1992).

16. Similar points have also been made about the creation of visions of culture for internal, domestic consumption. For example, Richard Wilk claims that the idea of something called Belizean culture emerged in the late 1980s, through the operation

of a global system promoting *"structures of common difference*, which celebrate particular kinds of diversity while submerging, deflating, or suppressing others" (Wilk 1995: 118, italics in original).

17. Arjun Appadurai identifies a similar category of elites: the transnational migrants who move across various global "scapes" (1996).

18. This distinction between cosmopolitans and locals mirrors other social scientists' understanding of the global/local dichotomy (see, e.g., Ong 1999; Wilson and Dissanayake 1996).

19. The article appears originally to have been published by the *Washington Post* (Harden 1985). All references in this introduction are to that version.

20. Economically speaking, the smuggling routes might be a primary way that such items enter Nigeria. The original article's discussion of the scope of illegal trade – $5 billion in 1983 alone, or approximately half of the country's total income from exports – provides support for this assessment (Harden 1985).

21. For example, Ong notes that transnationality among Chinese subjects, whether it be through flexible citizenship, migration, or multiple residences, is conditioned by "family regimes that generally valorize mobile masculinity and localized femininity" (1999: 20).

22. For more detail and analysis on the rhetoric of that moment, see Nonini and Ong (1997).

23. This gender bias has an interesting history. Davidoff and Hall (1987) trace it to the late eighteenth- to early nineteenth-century origins of a British middle class that viewed the world as separated into two domains, the public and the private, the former being male and powerful, and the latter being female and of lesser significance. Mica Nava (1997) argues that by the Victorian era this link between women and domesticity had so deeply entrenched fears of women's entry into the public sphere that social commentators and subsequent scholars rhetorically lambasted shopping as a wanton, lustful display of unrestrained feminine desire. Women's shopping was thus glossed as private, sexual, and dangerous, rather than as public, economic, necessary, and positive. According to Susan Bordo (2000), this conflation of consumption with dangerous feminine appetites continues today and can be seen in ads that simultaneously urge women to give in to their desires, while also suggesting that those desires are illicit. In contrast, as Campbell (1997) and Gladwell (2000) demonstrate, ads targeting men show none of this complexity or ambivalence and instead espouse clear utilitarian messages about how the items illustrated would unproblematically fulfill men's basic needs.

24. The distinction between the "fake" world of style and the "real" world of work was one shared by Second Wave feminists in the United States, who critiqued consumption in general and fashion in particular for trapping women in unfulfilling domestic roles and objectifying them as sexual objects to be displayed through dress and makeup. Women were urged to reject consumption by entering the productive world of work and embracing a more utilitarian or natural appearance (cf. Friedan 1963; Brownmiller 1984).

25. This view is, of course, complicated by a factor that Maria Mies (1986) points out: women exist on both sides of this divide, in both the First and Third Worlds. In

the First World, they act primarily as consumers; in the Third, they serve as producers. Mies's analysis equates the international division of labor and consumption with a patriarchy in which First World women consumers are singly oppressed, while Third World female producers are doubly so. While we see ample cause to complicate Mies's consumer/producer dichotomy, her claims support the idea of an unquestionably masculine global industrial regime.

26. Descriptions of Japanese luxury goods shoppers by both Japanese and foreign observers are striking in their implication that these individuals, most of them women aged 25–35, lack restraint, maturity, and agency. An article on the Japan Economic Foundation website describes "carefree young women with deep pockets" whose "brand fever" and "buying binge" are unchecked by economic recession (Japan Economic Foundation 2001). In a special *Time Magazine Asia* issue on how the world sees Japan, Natalie Warady describes the "factory-like" scene in the Paris Louis Vuitton store, as Japanese tourists wishing "to buy anything with a logo" wait for hours and are then briskly processed by curt salespeople (2001). In the same article, Naoki Takizawa, a designer for Issey Miyake, is quoted as worrying that "some of them [Japanese women] feel much more security when they wear the same thing as everyone else." Mari Kawasjee, the communications director at Louis Vuitton Japan "loves her job," but worries that "'brand-name articles are like drugs'" (Kobayashi 2002). Fumiteru Nitta's research (1992) challenges such dismissive characterizations. Nitta found that Japanese tourists in Hawai'i often purchase luxury items as gifts for families and friends back home and invest considerable research, time, and thought in doing so.

27. This view is consistent with recent challenges in scholarship on gender and development to Maria Mies's (1986) earlier characterization of First World women as consumers and Third World women as producers. See for example Freeman (2000), Mills (1999), and Mohanty (1997).

28. Butler's now well-known interpretation of the personal dress styles of lesbian women makes this point nicely. She argues against the suggestion that the choice to wear either "butch" styles, which mimic masculine dress, or "femme" styles, which mimic feminine dress, simply reinforces the dominant heterosexual narrative. Rather, to Butler, such choices are politically subversive precisely through their mimicry.

29. Scholars working in anthropological, sociological, and cultural studies have found performance theory especially useful in interpreting embodiment, gender, and resistance. See, for example, Bettie (2000), Boddy (1989), Combs-Schilling (1989), Garber (1992), Herdt (1993 [1984]), and Herzfeld (1985).

30. This moment seems to confirm what Chandra Mohanty has identified as a central limitation of transnational feminism, namely the continued reinscription of nation and woman as mutually codetermining, with "third world woman" as a timeless victim (1997).

31. Kondo develops this concept from Marta Savigliano's analysis of the Argentine rediscovery of tango (1995). Scholars working in other world regions have found similar counter-Orientalist strategies at work (see, e.g., Conklin 1997). A particularly striking example is the phenomenon of veiling among elite and middle-class women

in a variety of countries, such as Egypt, Indonesia, and Malaysia. These movements have strategically relied on rhetoric that can be called counter-Orientalist, but which scholars have argued also brings unique and unintended consequences for the women in and excluded from these movements (see, e.g., Abu-Lughod 1995a, Brenner 1996, Ong 1990). Edward Said, in the afterword to a later edition of *Orientalism*, also comments on the limits of using Orientalist logic in political critique. He argues that attempts to prove an essential positional superiority usually re-inscribe problematic stereotypes (1994 [1978]).

References

Abu-Lughod, Lila (1990), "The Romance of Resistance: Tracing Transformations of Power Through Bedouin Women," *American Ethnologist* 17(1): 41–55.

—— (1995a), "Movie Stars and Islamic Moralism in Egypt," in *Social Text* 42: 53–68.

—— (1995b), "The Objects of Soap Opera: Egyptian Television and the Cultural Politics of Modernity," in Daniel Miller (ed.), *Worlds Apart*, London and New York: Routledge.

Alarcón, Norma, Kaplan, Caren, and Moallem, Minoo (1999), "Introduction: Between Woman and Nation," in Caren Kaplan, Norma Alarcón, and Minoo Moallem (eds), *Between Woman and Nation: Nationalisms, Transnational Feminisms and the State*, Durham: Duke University Press.

Appadurai, Arjun (1990), "Disjuncture and Difference in the Global Cultural Economy," *Public Culture* 2(3): 1–24.

—— (1996), *Modernity at Large*, Minneapolis: Minnesota University Press.

Basch, Linda, Schiller, Nina Glick, and Blanc, Cristina Szanton (eds) (1994), *Nations Unbound*, Langhorne, PA: Gordon and Breach.

Bettie, Julie (2000), "Women Without Class: *Chicas*, *Cholas*, Trash, and the Presence/Absence of Class Identity," *Signs* 26(1): 1–35.

Bhabha, Homi (1997), "Of Mimicry and Man: The Ambivalence of Colonial Discourse," in Frederick Cooper and Ann Stoler (eds), *Tensions of Empire: Colonial Cultures in a Bourgeois World*, Berkeley: University of California Press.

Boddy, Janice (1989), *Wombs and Alien Spirits: Women, Men, and the Zar Cult in Northern Sudan*, Madison: University of Wisconsin Press.

Bordo, Susan (2000), "Hunger as Ideology," in Juliet B. Schor and Douglas B. Holt (eds), *The Consumer Society Reader*, New York: The New Press.

Bourdieu, Pierre (1977 [1972]), *Outline of a Theory of Practice* (trans. by Richard Nice), Cambridge: Cambridge University Press.

—— (1984), *Distinction*, Cambridge, MA: Harvard University Press.

Breckenridge, Carol A. (ed.) (1995), *Consuming Modernity: Public Culture in a South Asian World*, Minneapolis and New York: University of Minnesota Press.

Brenner, Suzanne (1996), "Reconstructing Self and Society: Javanese Muslim Women and 'the Veil'," *American Ethnologist* 23(4): 673–97.

Brownmiller, Susan (1984), *Femininity*, New York: Linden Press/Simon and Schuster.

Burke, Timothy (1996), *Lifebuoy Men, Lux Women: Commodification, Consumption and Cleanliness in Modern Zimbabwe*, Durham, NC: Duke University Press.

Butler, Judith (1990), *Gender Trouble: Feminism and the Subversion of Identity*, New York: Routledge.

Campbell, Colin (1997), "Shopping, Pleasure, and the Sex War," in Pasi Falk and Colin Campbell (eds), *The Shopping Experience*, London: Sage.

Carsten, Janet (1989), "Cooking Money: Gender and the Symbolic Transformation of Means of Exchange in a Malay Fishing Community," in Jonathan P. Parry and Maurice Bloch (eds), *Money and the Morality of Exchange*, Cambridge: Cambridge University Press.

Chakrabarty, Dipesh (1992), "Postcoloniality and the Artifice of History: Who Speaks for 'Indian' Pasts?" *Representations* 37: 1–26.

Chatterjee, Partha (1993), *The Nation and Its Fragments: Colonial and Postcolonial Histories*, Princeton, NJ: Princeton University Press.

Collier, Jane Fishburne (1974), "Women in Politics," in Michelle Zimbalist Rosaldo and Louise Lamphere (eds), *Woman, Culture, and Society*, Stanford: Stanford University Press.

Comaroff, Jean (1990), "Goodly Beasts and Beastly Goods," *American Ethnologist* 17(2): 195–216.

—— (1996), "The Empire's Old Clothes: Fashioning the Colonial Subject," in David Howes (ed.), *Cross-Cultural Consumption: Global Markets, Local Realities*, London and New York: Routledge.

Combs-Schilling, M.E. (1989), *Sacred Performances: Islam, Sexuality, and Sacrifice*, New York: Columbia University Press.

Conklin, Beth (1997), "Body Paint, Feathers, and VCRs: Aesthetics and Authenticity in Amazonian Activism," *American Ethnologist* 24(4): 711–37.

Corliss, Richard (1993), "Pacific Overtures," *Time*, 13 September: 68–70.

Cvetkovich, Ann and Kellner, Douglas (eds) (1997), *Articulating the Global and the Local*, Boulder, CO: Westview.

Davidoff, Leonore and Hall, Catherine (1987), *Family Fortunes: Men and Women of the English Middle Class, 1780–1850*, Chicago: University of Chicago Press.

de Certeau, Michel (1984), *The Practice of Everyday Life* (trans. by Steven Randall), Berkeley: University of California Press.

Douglas, Mary and Isherwood, Baron (eds) (1978), *The World of Goods*, London: Allen Lane.

Errington, Shelly (1989), "Fragile Traditions and Contested Meanings," *Public Culture* 1(2): 49–59.

Fan, Hong (1997), *Footbinding, Feminism and Freedom: The Liberation of Women's Bodies in Modern China*, London and Portland, OR: Frank Cass.

Fanon, Frantz (1965), *A Dying Colonialism*, New York: Grove.

Freeman, Carla (2000), *High Tech and High Heels in the Global Economy: Women, Work and Pink-Collar Identities in the Caribbean*, Durham, NC: Duke University Press.

—— (2001), "Is Local : Global as Feminine : Masculine? Rethinking the Gender of Globalization," *Signs* 26(4): 1007–37.

Friedan, Betty (1963), *The Feminine Mystique*, New York: Norton.

Garber, Marjorie (1992), *Vested Interests: Cross Dressing and Cultural Anxiety*, New York: Routledge.

García Canclini, Nestor (1992), *Consumers and Citizens: Globalization and Multicultural Conflicts*, Minneapolis: University of Minnesota Press.

Giddens, Anthony (1990), *The Consequences of Modernity*, Stanford: Stanford University Press.

Gladwell, Malcolm (2000), "Listening to Khakis: What America's Most Popular Pants Tell Us about the Way Guys Think," in Jennifer Scanlon (ed.), *The Gender and Consumer Culture Reader*, New York: New York University Press.

Golden, Arthur (1997), *Memoirs of a Geisha*, New York: Alfred A. Knopf.

Hamelink, Cees J. (1983), *Cultural Autonomy in Global Communications*, New York: Longman.

Hannerz, Ulf (1996), *Transnational Connections*, London and New York: Routledge.

Harden, Blaine (1985), "Flying Smugglers Supply Nigerians," *Washington Post*, October 10: A29.

Harvey, David (1989), *The Condition of Postmodernity*, Cambridge: Blackwell.

Hebdige, Dick (1979), *Subculture: The Meaning of Style*, London and New York: Routledge.

Hendrickson, Carol (1996), "Negotiating Identities in Consumption: Global Markets, Local Realities," in David Howes (ed.), *Cross-Cultural Consumption*, London and New York: Routledge.

Heng, Geraldine and Devan, Janandas (1992), "State Fatherhood: The Politics of Nationalism, Sexuality, and Race in Singapore," in Andrew Parker, Mary Russo, Doris Sommer, and Patricia Yaeger (eds), *Nationalism and Sexualities*, New York: Routledge.

Herdt, Gilbert H. (ed.) (1993 [1984]), *Ritualized Homosexuality in Melanesia*, Berkeley: University of California Press.

Herzfeld, Michael (1985), *The Poetics of Manhood: Contest and Identity in a Cretan Mountain Village*, Princeton: Princeton University Press.

Honour, Hugh (1961), *Chinoiserie: The Vision of Cathay*, New York: Harper and Row.

Howes, David (ed.) (1996), *Cross-Cultural Consumption: Global Markets, Local Realities*, London and New York: Routledge.

Japan Economic Foundation (2001), "Brand Fever Bucks Recession," *Journal of Japanese Trade and Industry*, September/October, http://www.jef.or.jp/en/jti/200109_004.html, accessed 3 August 2002.

Kartamihardja, Achdiat (1981 [1952]), *Atheis*, Jakarta: Balai Pustaka.

Kearney, M. (1995), "The Local and the Global: The Anthropology of Globalization and Transnationalism," *Annual Review of Anthropology* 24: 547-65.

Kobayashi, Tsutomu (2002), "Publicist Finds Riding the Brand Name Wave Full of Thrills," Mainichi Daily News Interactive, 19 February, http://mdn.mainichi.co.jp/japano/0202/020219vuitton.html, accessed 3 August 2002.

Kondo, Dorinne (1997), *About Face: Performing Race in Fashion and Theater*, London and New York: Routledge.

Lan, David (1985), *Guns and Rain: Guerrillas and Spirit Mediums in Zimbabwe*, London: James Currey.

Levy, Howard (1966), *Chinese Footbinding: The History of a Curious Erotic Custom*, New York: W. Rawls.

Lutz, Catherine and Collins, Jane (1993), *Reading National Geographic*, Chicago: University of Chicago Press.

Mackay, Hugh (ed.) (1997), *Consumption and Everyday Life*, London: Sage.

Mani, Lata (1998), *Contentious Traditions: The Debate on Sati in Colonial India*, Berkeley: University of California Press.

Mattelart, Armand (1983), *Transnationals and the Third World: The Struggle for Culture*, South Hadley, MA: Bergin and Garvey.

McCracken, Grant (1988), *Culture and Consumption*, Bloomington: Indiana University Press.

McLaughlin, Patricia (1998), "Capricious," Internet document http://interactive.phillynews. com/sunmag/712/style.shtml, accessed 25 June 2002.

Mies, Maria (1986), *Patriarchy and Accumulation on the World Scale: Women in the International Division of Labor*, London: Zed.

Miller, Daniel (ed.) (1995a), *Acknowledging Consumption*, London: Routledge.

—— (1995b), "Consumption and Commodities," *Annual Review of Anthropology* 24: 141–61.

—— (1997), "Coca-Cola: A Black Sweet Drink from Trinidad," in Daniel Miller (ed.), *Material Cultures*, London: University College London Press.

Mills, Mary Beth (1999), *Thai Women in the Global Labor Force: Consuming Desires, Contested Selves*, New Brunswick, NJ: Rutgers University Press.

Moeis, Abdoel (1982 [1928]), *Salah Asoehan*, Weltevreden: Balai Poestaka.

Mohanty, Chandra Talpade (1997), "Women Workers and Capitalist Scripts," in M. Jacqui Alexander and Chandra Talpade Mohanty (eds), *Feminist Genealogies, Colonial Legacies, Democratic Futures*, London: Routledge.

Morris, Rosalind C. (1995), "All Made Up: Performance Theory and the New Anthropology of Sex and Gender," *Annual Review of Anthropology* 24: 567–92.

Nava, Mica (1997), "Women, the City and the Department Store," in Pasi Falk and Colin Campbell (eds), *The Shopping Experience*, London: Sage.

Nitta, Fumiteru (1992), "Shopping for Souvenirs in Hawai'i," in Joseph J. Tobin (ed.), *Re-made in Japan: Everyday Life and Consumer Taste in a Changing Society*, New Haven: Yale University Press.

Nonini, Donald and Ong, Aihwa (1997), "Chinese Transnationalism as an Alternative Modernity," in Aihwa Ong and Donald Nonini (eds), *Ungrounded Empires: The Cultural Politics of Modern Chinese Transnationalism*, New York and London: Routledge.

Ong, Aihwa (1987), *Spirits of Resistance and Capitalist Discipline*, Albany: State University of New York Press.

—— (1990), "State versus Islam: Malay Families, Women's Bodies, and the Body Politic in Malaysia," *American Ethnologist* 17(2): 258–76.

—— (1991), "The Gender and Labor Politics of Postmodernity," *Annual Review of Anthropology* 20: 279–309.

—— (1997), "Chinese Modernities: Narratives of Nation and Capitalism," in Aihwa Ong and Donald Nonini (eds), *Ungrounded Empires: The Cultural Politics of Modern Chinese Transnationalism*, New York and London: Routledge.

—— (1999), *Flexible Citizenship*, Durham, NC: Duke University Press.

Ortner, Sherry (1974), "Is Female to Male as Nature is to Culture?" in Michelle Zimbalist Rosaldo and Louise Lamphere (eds), *Woman, Culture, and Society*, Stanford: Stanford University Press.

Price, Sally (1989), *Primitive Art in Civilized Places*, Chicago: University of Chicago Press.

Rafael, Vicente (2000), *White Love and Other Events in Filipino History*, Durham: Duke University Press.

Robertson, Roland (1992), *Globalization: Social Theory and Global Culture*, London: Sage.

Rosaldo, Michelle Zimbalist (1974), "Woman, Culture, and Society: A Theoretical Overview," in Michelle Zimbalist Rosaldo and Louise Lamphere (eds), *Woman, Culture, and Society*, Stanford: Stanford University Press.

Rubin, Gayle (1975), "The Traffic in Women: Notes on the 'Political Economy' of Sex," in Rayna Reiter (ed.), *Toward an Anthropology of Women*, New York: Monthly Review Press.

Rutz, Henry J. and Orlove, Benjamin S. (eds) (1989), *The Social Economy of Consumption*, Lanham, MD: University Press of America.

Said, Edward (1994 [1978]), *Orientalism*, London and New York: Vintage.

Salaff, Janet W. (1995 [1981]), *Working Daughters of Hong Kong*, New York: Cambridge University Press.

Savigliano, Marta (1995), *Tango and the Political Economy of Passion*, Boulder, CO: Westview.

Schein, Louisa (2000), *Minority Rules: The Miao and the Feminine in China's Cultural Politics*, Durham, NC: Duke University Press.

Schiller, Herbert I. (1976), *Communication and Cultural Domination*, White Plains, NY: International Arts and Sciences Press.

Smith, Carol (1995), "Race-Class-Gender Ideology in Guatemala: Modern and Anti-Modern Forms," *Comparative Studies in Society and History* 37(4): 723–49.

Steele, Valerie and Major, John (1999), *China Chic: East Meets West*, New Haven and London: Yale University Press.

Steiner, Christopher B. (1994), *African Art in Transit*, Cambridge: Cambridge University Press.

Stoler, Ann Laura and Cooper, Frederick (1997), "Between Metropole and Colony: Rethinking a Research Agenda," in Frederick Cooper and Ann Laura Stoler (eds), *Tensions of Empire: Colonial Cultures in a Bourgeois World*, Berkeley: University of California Press.

Tai, Hue-Tam Ho (1992), *Radicalism and the Origins of the Vietnamese Revolution*, Cambridge: Harvard University Press.

Tarlo, Emma (1996), *Clothing Matters: Dress and Identity in India*, Chicago: University of Chicago Press.

Taussig, Michael T. (1980), *The Devil and Commodity Fetishism in South America*, Chapel Hill: University of North Carolina Press.

Taylor, Jean Gelman (1997), "Costume and Gender in Colonial Java, 1800–1940," in Henk Schulte Norholdt (ed.), *Outward Appearances: Dressing State and Society in Indonesia*, Leiden: KITLV Press.

Tobin, Joseph J. (1992), "Introduction: Domesticating the West," in Joseph J. Tobin (ed.), *Re-made in Japan: Everyday Life and Consumer Taste in a Changing Society*, New Haven: Yale University Press.

Toren, C. (1989), "Drinking Cash," in Jonathan P. Parry and Maurice Bloch (eds), *Money and the Morality of Exchange*, Cambridge: Cambridge University Press.

Visweswaran, Kamala (1994), *Fictions of Feminist Ethnography*, Minneapolis: University of Minnesota Press.

Wang, Ping (2000), *Aching for Beauty: Footbinding in China*, Minneapolis: University of Minnesota Press.

Warady, Natalie (2001), "The Customers," *Time Magazine Asia* 157(17), 30 April, http://www.time.com/time/asia/features/japan_view/fashion_sb1.html, accessed 3 August 2002.

Watson, James L. (ed.) (1997), *Golden Arches East*, Stanford: Stanford University Press.

Weismantel, Mary (1989), "The Children Cry for Bread," in Henry J. Rutz and Benjamin S. Orlove (eds), *The Social Economy of Consumption*, Lanham, MD: University Press of America.

Wilk, Richard (1995), "Learning to Be Local in Belize: Global Systems of Common Difference," in Daniel Miller (ed.), *Worlds Apart*, London and New York: Routledge.

Wilson, Elizabeth (1985), *Adorned in Dreams: Fashion and Modernity*, London: Virago.

Wilson, Rob and Dissanayake, Wimal (eds) (1996), *Global/Local*, Durham: Duke University Press.

Wolf, Diane (1992), *Factory Daughters*, Berkeley: University of California Press.

1

Three Scenarios from Batak Clothing History: Designing Participation in the Global Fashion Trajectory

Sandra Niessen

Toward the end of the twentieth century, individual designer-entrepreneurs from the Batak culture in North Sumatra, Indonesia (see Map 1a: Batak Regions of Sumatra), have tried to market their Western-style fashions constructed from indigenous handwoven cloth internationally. Such attempts to market indigenous fashion lines are neither unprecedented nor any longer unusual, and the smallness of scale of the Batak case renders it an insignificant arrival on the global fashion stage. However, the preparations leading up to the appearance of an item of indigenous clothing on the global stage are socially and historically deeply rooted. It is worth probing the composition of such an indigenous fashion event for explanatory insight.[1]

Accepted wisdom is that fashion is a Western phenomenon. The emergence of a non-Western item of dress on the international stage is therefore notable. What meanings may be attached to such a fashion event? Is the Western fashion phenomenon becoming a global phenomenon? An argument presented in this chapter is that the apparent globalization of fashion is really about Western fashion dominance – and responses to it – beginning in the industrial revolution and the colonial period.

Non-Western dress has been typified as unchanging, hence traditional. This characterization has been central to the classic claim that fashion occurs only in Western civilization (e.g., Simmel 1957 [1904]; Sapir 1937; Rouse 1989). While the evolutionary preoccupation with where fashion can and cannot occur has been displaced by a variety of other theoretical preoccupations, it is striking that statistically and, I would claim, vestigially the word "fashion" is rarely used in reference to non-Western clothing systems, even while it has been used variously, from its most restricted definition in reference to couture to its more inclusive form in reference to Western clothing systems in general. Items of non-Western dress on the international fashion stage should present a challenge to fashion theorists. That we confront the ways in which fashion has been defined and characterized is long due.

In an important contribution to fashion theory, Baizerman, Eicher, and Cerny (1993) have exposed a Western bias in the study of fashion. Since then, Craik (1994) has recommended dissolving and reconstituting what she calls the "European-dictator (ethnocentric or cultural superiority) model of fashion . . . European high (elite designer) fashion is one specific variant of fashion. Although it may dominate popular consciousness about fashion, other fashion systems co-exist, compete and interact with it" (Craik 1994: xi). As Craik has also noted, addressing the ramifications of a more inclusive and dynamic concept of fashion will be an enormous project. One goal of the present chapter is to contribute to the reconstitution of the concept of fashion by examining the dynamic principles of change in a non-Western system of dress of a society that Simmel would have characterized as tribal, and therefore least likely to exhibit features of fashion.[2] Many fashion theorists since and including Simmel are in agreement that the phenomenon of fashion can occur only in hierarchical, industrial societies where there is mass production and rapid change. This understanding abets the conclusion that the appearance of non-Western clothing traditions on the fashion stage is a sign of non-Western social progress.

Many earlier anthropological studies of indigenous dress explore correlations between dress forms and social position (e.g. Kuper 1973a and b; Langner 1959). These semiotic mappings create the impression that wearer choices are constant and clear, supporting thereby the stereotype of changelessness in non-Western dress. More recent approaches present new ways to understand clothing in terms of choices and innovations that do not just reflect, but constitute identity and social categories (e.g. Hendrickson 1996; Kondo 1997; Tarlo 1996). This chapter is built upon the assumption that principles of Batak clothing change may be discerned from the strategic decisions made by both wearers and producers of Batak clothing to resolve social dilemmas and express choice. The method offers the opportunity to explore clothing dynamics wherever they occur, that is to say, universally and in association with every kind of social organization.

The chapter traces some of the dynamics of the Batak clothing system by means of three dress scenarios that take place at the beginning and end of the twentieth century. During this tumultuous century, the Bataks were annexed by the colonial regime of the Netherlands East Indies. They changed from an isolated tribe into a differentiated and hierarchical society, strongly and eagerly participant in the nation, including its political and economic life. These changes presented profound challenges to the makers of indigenous Batak cloth. Weaving viable textiles was important not only to the financial security of the makers, but also to the identity and social presence of the wearers in every forum in which their activities took place. The brief clothing history presented below is a tribute to the skill and ingenuity of the weavers who were able to adapt their age-old arts from the production of tribal dress to the production of global fashions as fitting the changing social body. Locally, however, their success can only be recognized equivocally. In the process of putting together garments that would be hailed as fashion in external centers of power, weavers lost design control of their art to apparel designers. Furthermore, success on the global economic stage recapitulates, within Batak society, hierarchical distinctions that, at the advent of colonialism, placed traditional Batak society on the lowest rung and enforced an unprecedented gap between the genders. In the first scenario described below, a color change occurs in Karo Batak clothing. The transformation from the "blue Karo" to the "red Karo" is symptomatic of the concepts traditional (indigenous) and modern (modeled after the West) taking root locally, thereby setting the direction for subsequent Batak clothing change. The second scenario is about the adaptation of traditional textiles designed by Toba Batak weavers to recapture lost apparel markets and to construct a Batak clothing presence on the national stage. In the final scenario, which overlaps with the second, a women's business suit made from fabric designed and woven by Batak weavers is marketed internationally. In this context the weavers count only as labor, and the indigenous understanding of femininity that the weavers represent loses finally to the objectified femininity of global commodity capitalism.

Historical and Cultural Context

The Batak of Sumatra comprise six subgroups including the Karo, Toba, Simalungun, Pakpak/Dairi, Angkola, and Mandailing peoples. While their languages are mutually unintelligible, Batak languages, customs, and history are related, intermarriage was once politically strategic and continues to be common, and trade ties among them have existed since prehistoric times. Lake Toba is situated in the midst of the Toba, Karo, and Simalungun Batak homelands where it has facilitated relatively easy communication among them. Because of their perceived coarse manners, reputed cannibalism, and frequent internecine wars, they were feared by outsiders. As a result, the Batak cultures/subcultures were able to develop their distinctiveness through centuries of relative isolation. They are known for their houses on stilts, wet and dry rice agriculture, and backstrap loom weaving.

Nevertheless, the Batak had been engaged in trade on Sumatra's coasts since prehistoric times.[3] Western traders had been involved in that trade for the most recent 400 years, but were unable to penetrate the rugged interior of Sumatra all the way to Lake Toba until the middle of the nineteenth century. During the final two decades of the nineteenth century and the first decades of the twentieth century, social change was rapid and tumultuous. All the Batak territories were annexed by the colonial power. Having lost their autonomy, the Bataks began to function within externally imposed systems of values and customs.

The many daily-life changes that the Batak underwent are exemplified in their weaving arts. In the Toba Batak myth of origin, the earth is the creation of a weaver, and in the precolonial worldview, weaving was strongly associated with fertility. The "growth" of the textile in the loom as it was being woven was homologous with the life cycle of the human, the rice, and other crops, and even the cycle of time itself. The ideal bride was a weaver who could provide for the needs of her family. She could weave oblong cloths of various lengths, widths, and patterning. These were wrapped around the head, tied around the waist, or hung over the shoulder (different modes signaled regional and subcultural differences). These cloths announced identity, protected the body, and had tremendous protective spiritual significance.

During the twentieth century the Bataks learned to dress for the new social roles in which they found themselves upon colonial annexation. Western dress styles became increasingly popular throughout the twentieth century. (They had been traded into Sumatra's interior long before Westerners themselves had succeeded in penetrating the island.) After Indonesia won independence in 1949, a national dress style emerged that was strongly influenced by Javanese dress styles. Both external clothing traditions represented enormous challenges for Batak weavers. They eroded the market for indigenous cloth even as the growing need for cash was making the role of the market more central. Weaving for family needs became incidental, and the cash that weaving could bring in to supplement family income became very important, especially in poorer regions. Semiotically, the new clothing trends reinforced other demonstrations that the locus of power was located external to Batak society.

The scenarios presented below explore three responses of weavers and wearers of Batak clothing to the challenge of negotiating their identity, in apparel terms, vis-à-vis the foreign power. Analysis of the first (Karo Batak) is based on archival research,[4] while field research undertaken by the author in 1979/80, 1986, 1990, and 1995 has provided the data for the latter two (Toba Batak) scenarios.[5]

Dress Scenario #1: The Red Rage in Karo Batak Dress

When he visited Sumatra's East Coast in 1823, the Englishman John Anderson was not specifically interested in the Karo people who were tribal rice agriculturists from the interior, and just one of many ethnic groups he encountered during his trade mission. However, he was meticulous in his observations of the cloth that was traded along the coast, the local tastes and preferences, and the kinds of trade inroads that had been, and could be, made with English cloth. Like other European visitors who were to succeed him (e.g. Hagen 1883: 47; Joustra 1910: 126; von Brenner 1890: 272–3), he remarked that the Karo people (he met members of the "Karau Karau" clan) "were dressed entirely in blue cloth" (Anderson 1971 [1826]: 52). Blue was not just the color produced by the indigo plant that grew wild on Karo hillsides, it was a signifier of Karo identity. By the middle of the twentieth century, however, the same people were wearing red textiles.

It appears that the desire for cloth was a great enticement for the Karo to come down from the highlands to the coast to perform wage labor for the Malay. They purchased lengths of white cloth that they carried back to their villages located farther inland. There, the cloth was first worn white and later (if not immediately) dyed with indigo.[6] The same was true of the wide lengths of cloth (*abit*) that women wrapped around their lower body if they were married, or from breasts to ankles if they were not yet married. (In Figure 1.1 the women have their breasts covered probably as a concession to Western propriety.) The imported material was used as a substitute for the indigenous cloth that Karo women could weave on their backstrap looms. By dyeing and draping even their foreign cloth imports in the manner of indigenous textiles, the Karo expressed a conservative tendency in their system of dress.

The description of the Karo people as wearing "simple blue cloth of indigenous manufacture," accurately depicts a folk without a high degree of social stratification,[7] and possessing relatively little wealth in comparison to the coastal Malays. Such a description corresponds well with the Western understanding that fashion does not occur among tribal peoples whose dress is characteristically stable and unchanging. While certain status divisions were evident from Karo dress, the Karo use of their dye pots supports the classic claim that "primitive fashions" emphasize ethnic rather than internal social divisions (Simmel 1957 [1904]: 545).

However, it is also true that, using their limited means, the Karo participated eagerly in the fashion ferment of the nineteenth century on the island of Sumatra. They demonstrated curiosity, delight in novelty, and an experimental attitude toward clothing. Occasionally they used their own handwoven cloth

Figure 1.1 A Karo Batak Chief and his family. The photograph was taken by Tassilo Adam ca. 1914-1921. Tropenmuseum, Amsterdam 572.9 (992.263), no.77.

to cut and tailor the waist-length jacket-like blouses (*baju*) that were inspired by Chinese and Malay traditions.[8] The coastal trade activities offered them at least visual access to a broad array of fabrics and clothing types. The Karo worked all of their trade ties, not just those to the coast, to acquire desirable cloth and clothing. They obtained expensive and sumptuous silks from Aceh to the north,[9] shared ikat designs with the Simalungun Batak to the south, and relied on Toba Batak weavers to the west to supply certain designs of hand-woven cloth. John Guy has observed that, "The diverse peoples of Sumatra had a seemingly insatiable appetite for new textiles and modes of dress. In exchange for the wealth of the interior, they avidly acquired cloths from across the archipelago and beyond" (Guy 1998: 68). This was the dynamic tendency that infused the indigenous Karo Batak clothing system.

Europeans were latecomers to the clothing and textile ferment found in the East Indies, and scrambled to gain a toehold in the colorful and lucrative trade (van Leur 1983 [1955]), first by trading Indian cloth so indispensable to success in that trade and then by imitating its production.[10] The European presence in Southeast Asia engendered increasingly hegemonic trade – supporting the subsequent globalization of *Western* fashion.[11] It was with these Western fashions, and the powerful political and economic forces that brought them to Sumatra's shores, that not just the Karo, but all of the Bataks were to enter into close dialogue.

The Economics and Politics of the Color Transformation in Karo Clothing

The East Coast Malays controlled the trade on Sumatra's shores, which included mediating between the inland inhabitants who had access to the local resources and the foreign visiting traders. Initially it was to their advantage to maintain good relations with the Karo and intermarriage was a useful strategy. While the ethnic difference between Karo and coastal Malay was bridged by a genetic continuum, the economic gulf between them widened as the plantation economy grew on the coast.[12] The Malays were able to use their control over trade to considerably expand their wealth, and gain European favor, thus also considerably expanding their power. They used their wealth to produce displays of hierarchy, such as monumental palaces for their sultans and sumptuous (especially red-dyed) silk clothing incorporating gold and silver yarn.

The relatively peaceful symbiosis that had prevailed between the Karo and the Malay crumbled into discontent during the colonial era when the Malay assumed ownership of Karo lands, however unjustified, and brokered them for plantation use. European military might, applied to the degree that the Karo rebelled (the strongest rebellion was put down in 1872), supported the Malay practices. The Karo were pushed back to the interior mountains and plateaus. Their distrust and resentment of the Malays and Europeans grew. When the Dutch forcefully annexed the Karo highlands in 1904, the capacity of Karo resistance was largely broken. Resistance and resentment did not end suddenly, however. It is remarkable that as late as 1910, Joustra described highland Karo clothing as still "fairly pure" (126–7). I deduce that the conservative blueness of their apparel, despite the close trade, labor, and marriage ties with the coast that altered the fabric of their clothing, was a visually striking symbolic form of resistance against the encroaching powers.[13] Eventually, the Karo nation had no choice except to function within the new political environment of the Netherlands East Indies. This was when the blueness of their attire began to redden.

The indigenous political organization had been relatively egalitarian.[14] The indigenous economy was subsistence-based and wage labor was unknown, ensuring that wealth differentials within the society were never large. The villages were administered by ward chief(s) invested with an authority sanctioned by the villagers. Dutch colonial rule infused Karo society with unprecedented hierarchical features by placing ultimate authority in the hands of the colonial power. The village unions were co-opted for administrative purposes, thereby ending their sovereignty. Five indigenous chiefs responsible to the European administration were appointed to administer the five highland territories carved out by the Dutch (Middendorp 1929: 54–5; Joustra 1915: 13). (Figure 1.1 depicts one of these chiefs and his family.) Similarly, the judicial system came under the control of the colonial establishment. Taxation and fines were levied, contributing to demand for cash through the selling of labor. A new educational system, developed by and for the colonial order, came into being. The Christian mission in Karo supported colonial structures intentionally and unintentionally (Kipp 1990: 226). Each of these systems offered new positions, opportunities, and status more or less exclusively to men, and Karo men quickly recognized that if they were to achieve a high social status, it would be within the framework offered by the new political regime.

Karo Men's Dress   To explain the dynamic of Western fashion, the early sociologist of fashion, Georg Simmel, articulated principles of clothing change that are also applicable to the Karo: imitation and differentiation, union and segregation (1957 [1904]). To dress for their wage positions created under the colonial regime, Karo men integrated more or less obvious elements of European dress into their attire. These were external displays of their aspirations, commitment, and collaboration with the new order. The process of integration was gradual, as new dress conventions were established slowly. European jackets were easily adopted, early forms (*baju*) having been popular before the arrival of the colonial power. Expensive and flashy novelties, such as watches on chains, umbrellas, and shoes, were carried or worn with pride. Despite an initial reluctance to wear European-style trousers (Joustra 1910: 127), Neumann (1916: 143) noted that a bridegroom in 1916 wore white ones covered by an indigenous hipcloth. Even this uncomfortable European clothing item was eventually accepted as a status marker. In the new political environment, elements of indigenous attire were forfeited. The upper-body shawl was no longer worn, and the long knife, symbol of an independent, self-reliant spirit and an indispensable part of dress prior to colonial takeover, disappeared. Indigenous jewelry was left off because it was seen as old-fashioned. These changes represented imitation of the European clothing systems and differentiation from the Karo system of the past.

The "traditional look" did not entirely give way to the "modern look," however. Experimentation with colonial attire became more fine-tuned. Decisions had to be made about the occasions on which a Batak male would wear an indigenous head covering, and when a European cap; when trousers would be worn, when covered over with an indigenous handwoven cloth, and when with an imported sarong. New combinations had to be tried on, new meanings established. Social distinctions, which had not been found in the subsistence community, could be expressed using the range of newly available apparel choices to indicate the holders of government or Church office. In Figure 1.1 the men are still wearing their indigenous hipcloths and shouldercloths, but the prevalence of blue indigenous cloth declined as it came to be seen as appropriate only for indigenous ritual occasions.

The establishment of new clothing signifiers was complicated further by relations with the coastal Malays. Many lowland Karo, who were under the administration of the coastal sultanates, converted to Islam, as did many highland Karo, despite the presence of the Christian mission (Kipp 1990). The Moslem Malays were situated socially between the Europeans and the Karo. Figure 1.2, a photo taken circa 1890 of the Sultan of Deli with his entourage (Agthe 1979: 124), is a revealing exposition of ethnicity and power. It depicts a group of men wearing blends of European and Malay clothing. The Sultan himself is wearing the same style of trousers as the European beside him, although his jacket is sumptuously embroidered unlike the sober version of his European counterpart. Other lower-status, indigenous (presumably Malay) gentlemen in the photograph are also wearing European jackets. One of them has a short sarong (quite likely red silk with gold inlay patterning, although the color is impossible to determine from the black-and-white photograph)

Figure 1.2 The Sultan of Deli with his attendants. The photograph was taken by Bernard Hagen in Medan, ca. 1890. Photoarchives Museum der Weltkulturen, Frankfurt.

wrapped around his white, Western-style trousers. All are wearing shoes. The Malay dress blended with European elements acknowledges the power held by the Europeans; only the dress of the European is not a blend – and it didn't need to be.

Just as the Malay look was changing in a way that expressed solidarity with the European power, so Karo Batak traditional dress was incorporating Malay elements. Malay textiles were fine, often made of silk, on looms that permitted a different kind of weave.[15] High Malay social status was associated with this same finery and color choices. Their demonstrated preference for red textiles with gold or silver supplementary patterning locates the origin of the Karo preference for the same.

During fieldwork in the 1970s, 1980s, and 1990s, I observed that Karo men still used indigenous attire on ritual occasions to express traditional values, and Western dress to express modernity, or their association with Western systems/values. Importantly, neither dress form had been constant or unchanging. The two had coexisted and intersected in an unresolved duality of union and segregation. The indigenous clothing system incorporates both European and Malay features in such a way that today's traditional appearance is yesterday's modern dress. Western, Malay, and indigenous dress are used to explore and continually relocate the boundaries of the traditional and the modern within changing Karo social space.

Karo Women's Dress   Geographic proximity to the great economic changes occurring on the East Coast obliged migrant Karo (male) laborers to explore the relations between them and the outside world. Karo women's social roles, on the other hand, changed little. They remained at home, looking after the children, performing household duties, and working in the fields. Roadway communications from Medan to Kaban Jahe were improved in 1909.[16] At first oxcarts were used. Motorized traffic beginning in 1914 (Joustra 1915) dramatically expanded transportation capacities. While women's labor in the fields intensified to meet the growing demand for cash crops grown in their cooler climate and fertile soil, the variety of social roles available to women remained restricted. Their dress changed little compared to men's dress (Figure 1.1). Consequently, gendered styles of Karo dress diverged more than previously in their history. It may be argued that the divergence signaled a colonization of gender relations in Karo society.[17]

Furthermore, weaving and dyeing were the exclusive purview of Karo women, and numbered among their household chores. When the women's time was more profitably invested in farming the land, Karo handweaving and indigo dyeing declined precipitously (Joustra 1910: 289), another significant factor in the loss of the Karo blue look. Their demand for clothing, including much of their ritual clothing, had to be met by expanding their already familiar reliance on textile imports.

On a daily basis, in place of the white/blue hipcloth or torso covering, women began to wear imported sarongs that they could purchase on the market relatively inexpensively compared to the homemade variety. Covering the upper body became the norm, as dictated by European morality. The massive silver earrings worn in many Karo areas were eventually left off, although wearing headgear remained the norm in public. Handwoven shouldercloths also remained a stable part of daily dress in the public arena, such as the market. Finer sarongs (handwoven Karo or imported varieties), finer blouses (all imports), and finer and more elaborate headcloths and shouldercloths (mostly imported handwovens) were reserved for ritual use.

Women had little access to what has been referred to above as the modern or Western-influenced sector into which men were thrust. It was not until the latter decades of the twentieth century, and then only among urban, professional Batak women, that the full Western dress complement of the male suit, i.e., skirt, blouse, and pumps, became common. Again, the limitations of the terms modern and traditional are evident with respect to Karo women's fashions. Their traditional clothing began to incorporate Malay elements with the result that here, too, the more modern, or recent appearance of the traditional became different from the traditional of previous years. Furthermore, because the blue-to-red color transition took place in handwoven textiles, the color revolution was found more generally in the range of women's clothing. Karo women still wear handwovens on a daily basis, while for men handwovens are restricted to ritual attire.

The Technology and Trade of the Karo Color Transformation

As Karo women gave up their weaving and dyeing for more lucrative pastimes, they expanded their reliance on foreign textile production, especially from their Malay and Toba neighbors who became the primary suppliers of their ritual clothing.

Toba weavers on Samosir Island and along the northwest coast of Lake Toba had been weaving for the Karo for centuries and trade between them was both regular and common.[18] The Toba did not have a road built into this territory and they did not experience the economic benefits that the Karo experienced from their road. The territories remained difficult to access and poor. Weaving in these economically deprived regions represented, and continues to represent, one of the few cash-earning options for women. The opportunity to cater to Karo consumer demand was welcome and textile production became prolific and competitive as Toba weavers avidly experimented to meet Karo taste. The fruits of the Toba Batak backstrap looms in this region include appropriated and modified silk Acehnese and Malay textile types rendered in cotton. In addition, the Toba adapted a range of Karo blue textile types by weaving them in red yarn. These are generically called *uwis gara*, "red cloths."

This kind of weaver adaptation did not constitute a new theme in Batak textile history, however. Robyn Maxwell (1990) has parsed the designs of Southeast Asian textiles demonstrating that they are layered compositions. Indonesian weavers throughout the archipelago and throughout the ages have selected from succeeding waves of foreign cultural influence and transformed it into cloth of their own distinctive traditions.[19] The dynamic factor in Batak clothing is also found at the technical level, in the strategic choices made by weavers. Each adaptation implies its own unique set of technical challenges. During the course of the twentieth century, the weavers had to contend with different weights and qualities of cotton and synthetic yarn; adjust loom size; experiment with pattern heddle rods to make new supplementary weft patterns; and continually select materials and designs to keep their wares viable on the marketplace.

The earliest Karo textiles in museum collections reveal that red had always been a precious color for the Karo, even if blue was predominant. It was used for embellishment in the form of fine stripes, decorative twining, or appliqué. Red silk was the textile of choice for men's headgear. Red, however, was difficult to procure. It had to be purchased from the Toba Bataks south of Lake Toba (Jasper and Pirngadie 1912: 69) who used the dye plant *Morinda citrifolia*. After an intensive and lengthy process, this plant produced a sober, auburn color. Bright red was more desirable.[20] Meint Joustra observed that when the Weaving School was set up south of Lake Toba early in the twentieth century (Joustra 1914), the Toba Batak weavers were delighted with the broad and bright synthetic color palette made available to them by the Christian missionaries. Like weavers around the globe, they responded rapidly to the mid-nineteenth-century invention of synthetic red.[21] It was considerably easier and faster to use than the vegetable indigo. Consumers, too, could only have been delighted by their ability to more easily and inexpensively express, in clothing, their longing for a status closer to that enjoyed by the Malay. Use of the synthetic red dye probably rendered the Toba textiles more viable on the Karo market, and facilitated the blue-to-red transition.

Summary

Upon closer examination, the visually striking blue-to-red transformation in Karo Batak clothing that took place immediately after colonial annexation was symptomatic of a complex set of changes – not all of which were as immediately evident to the eye of an outsider. While the blue-to-red color transformation was a specifically Karo response to tumultuous social change during the colonial era, the dress principles referred to in the course of the above analysis have been found more generally in the dress systems of the different Batak subgroups, all of which were forced to give up their sovereignty and to accommodate dominant, external social forces. In my previous research (Niessen 1993, Niessen in press) I have found conservative and dynamic tendencies in all of the Batak clothing systems, although manifested variously by the different subgroups. Everywhere the contrast of the West and the East that took hold during the colonial era engendered a deeply rooted notion of the modern relative to the traditional. Everywhere, the Bataks moved back and forth between the two, from resistance/rebellion (in which color often played an important visual role) to innovative accommodation and adaptation. Everywhere men were first to have access to modern social positions while women remained guardians of tradition. Rather than the traditional apparel choices remaining constant and timeless in contrast to the indomitable forces of modern change, however, the contrast between West and East, modern and traditional, appears to have given the Batak an outlet for continually renegotiating their identity in different social environments.

In this brief history of Batak fashion, we now shift our focus from the Karo and Toba Batak at the north end of Lake Toba, to the Toba Batak south of Lake Toba in the final decades of the twentieth century.

Dress Scenario #2: The Setelan: A Toba Batak "Modern Traditional" Outfit of Postcolonial Elaboration

While I was conducting fieldwork in the Silindung Valley in the 1980s, weavers told me with great pride about a visit by Ibu Tien, wife of former President Suharto. Apparently she purchased and wore a Toba Batak outfit, called a "setelan," made by weavers in the Valley. Modernized outfits inspired by traditional textile designs had been controversial, often eschewed by some older Toba Bataks. Ibu Tien's endorsement of this fashion trend gave it validity. Her purchase consisted of a sarong (cylindrical lower-body wrap) and slendang (draped shouldercloth). This outfit was national, yet Batak; it had the general appearance of being acceptable attire for a woman, suitable even for the wife of the nation's president, yet it was embellished with recognizable, traditional Toba Batak patterning.

"Modern Traditional" in the Silindung Valley

The Silindung Valley is nestled in the Barisan mountain range south of Lake Toba. In the center of the Valley is the town of Tarutung where the weavers bring their finished textiles to market. Their villages are clustered around the town. Everywhere in the Valley the visitor can hear the clatter of looms as weavers beat in their wefts, and see the weavers hard at work on the front porches of their colonial homes. The Valley is fertile, but it has too little arable land to meet the subsistence needs of the dense and still growing population. The women rely heavily on their looms to be able to make ends meet. The textile culture of the Valley is vibrant, and the modern textiles from the Valley are distinctive.

This distinctiveness relates to the social history of the Valley that was selected to be a local seat of the colonial government, as well as the Christian mission. The inhabitants experienced a long and intense association with colonialism. They learned to pride themselves on the impacts in their society that were symptomatic of their involvement with churches, schools, and other cultural manifestations of their external power-holders. They saw themselves as more refined and modern than Toba Batak people in other regions. After Indonesia gained political independence (1949), the definition of modern came to be heavily influenced by national trends, with Jakarta now functioning as the center of new fashion impulses. The Silindung Valley inhabitants then began to avidly follow these new trends. If parents had the means, they enabled their children to pursue an education and subsequently obtain good salaried employment in urban centers. Many migrated to Medan and Jakarta where they could practise their modern lifestyles. Only those females who were left behind and who had severely limited means would become the weavers of cloth.

Silindung Valley Bataks, just like their Karo neighbors, wore both traditional and modern clothing forms. In addition to their traditional repertoire, the weavers enthusiastically updated old styles and invented new styles (Niessen 1999). In the indigenous ritual sphere, the core of traditional Batak thought and expression, dress codes for indigenous ritual events were kept strict, such that the innovative textiles dyed with bright colors and simpler patterns were appropriate to wear only outside the ritual spheres, for example to church (which deplored Batak ancestor worship and textiles used in that connection) or modern political meetings. A division of weaving labor in the Silindung Valley grew up around the dichotomy of traditional/modern with some weavers specializing in the traditional cloth types and others in the modern varieties, mostly shouldercloths.

In the Karo region at the beginning of the century, the men were the first to modernize their traditional apparel as they jockeyed for positions within the new social order. In the Silindung Valley, half a century later, the trend was to flourish in women's apparel. While women's non-Western dress emphasized their traditional social role within the household, those who married well began to require items of apparel that announced their urban identity of high social standing, wealth and sophistication – as well as their role as guardians of hearth and home. They adopted the national women's dress form: sarong wrapped around the lower body with matching *slendang* (shouldercloth) worn over a blouse-like *kebaya* (see Jones in Chapter 6 of this volume for further discussion of Indonesian national dress/*pakaian nasional*). They selected from Malay and Javanese sarongs to wrap around the lower body,[22] but felt that the colorful, modernized, locally handwoven Silindung Valley textiles were appropriate to complete the outfit. As the century wore on, hierarchy became increasingly entrenched and prominent in Toba Batak social life. Despite initial resistance from those who wished to preserve customary law, the increasing importance of monetary wealth gradually facilitated the penetration of these innovative textile displays of wealth and status in the ritual context. This penetration marked a shift in the boundary between modern and traditional. These innovative shoulderclothes are the kind of attire that I refer to here as "modern traditional." The corresponding men's apparel to this handwoven, indigenous women's outfit is ethnically "odorless," (see Skov in Chapter 7 of this volume for a discussion of the use of this term) consisting of some kind of uniform, tailored for business, the civil service, army, or church.

Clothing for men and that for women always form a complementary set and must always be analyzed as relative to each other. Of importance to the present study of Batak indigenous apparel is the recapitulation in this colonial territory of the gender/clothing complementarity exhibited by the European colonialists, and found generally in Western society after the industrial revolution: men in functional uniforms symbolic of their participation in the modern state,[23] and women as objects of display, their clothing symbolizing their exclusion from the men's world (Wilson 1985: 14). It is specifically the addition of the indigenous component in the women's outfits that situates women, not just outside modernity, but firmly in traditional spheres, "in opposition to the cultural colonization of imperialism" (ibid.).[24]

In the 1980s, the Silindung Valley was abuzz with the newly invented "Batak sarong." The coarse, heavy, sober-colored, wraparound Batak hipcloths worn prior to colonialism had long been replaced by imported sarongs. From discussions with Toba Batak women in the Silindung Valley, I learned that they had become only a vague memory. Most had been sold on the antique markets, or had accompanied the dead to the grave. The Batak version of the sarong was an unprecedented dress form in that culture, consisting of two woven panels joined along their selvedge edges, and then stitched together at the ends to form a cylinder. Rather than the coarse versions worn in the past, these sarongs were made of fine yarn, and rather than the sober colors that characterized the traditional Batak clothing repertoire, weavers made use of the full range of their synthetic color palette. The designs were still typically Toba Batak, but they tended to emphasize supplementary weft patterning, just as

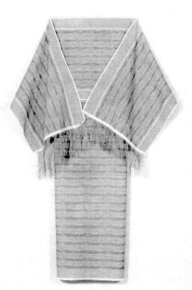

Figure 1.3 *Setelan,* comprising a hipcloth and shouldercloth, woven by Nai Ganda of Hutagalung in the Silindung Valley. In this invention, she has made use of synthetic dyes, and derived the ikat hook motif from an older motif that is no longer made. Photographer: Linda Turner.

Malay textiles do. Such a sarong, with a matching shouldercloth (Figure 1.3), is what Ibu Tien Suharto purchased and wore to great effect. The set signified the ability to participate in sophisticated national settings without entirely forfeiting an indigenous identity, indeed wearing it with pride. This was a significant accomplishment in a nation whose definition of sophistication is built upon Javanese court culture, and where the Batak culture is commonly perceived stereotypically as typifying quite the opposite.

The Production and Trade of "Modern Traditional"

Like other Batak weavers, the Silindung Valley weavers are poorly remunerated for their work. While there are still weavers of sober, conservative, traditional textiles in the Valley, the need for cash has provided a powerful stimulus to find/develop more lucrative market niches. The process of incorporating external design influences, described above as the dynamic tendency in the Karo Batak clothing system, has a technical component. It is the weavers who literally materialize this tendency using their technical knowledge. Their ability to translate social categories and trends into cloth is key to the viability of the textiles and thus the economic survival of the weavers.

Weaving in the Silindung Valley is a high-pressure occupation. On the Saturday market, the weaver buys her yarns from the profit of her most recent textile sale. She weaves the yarn into a new cloth by week's end so that she may keep her meager profits flowing. The speed required, and the accuracy and precision in executing the expanding array of fine, modern textiles that may be sold on the most lucrative urban markets have engendered an unprecedented division of weaving labor. There are specialists who make the ikat patterns, specialists who wind the warp, and others who do nothing but weave. Control over the resulting cloth is increasingly in the hands of the person who commissions the cloth and farms out the labor. Most often this is a person who owns/manages a textile stall in the marketplace. This person is most familiar with the style trends, and consumer demands, and has the most available cash with which to experiment and take risks. Elsewhere in Toba, where the weavers live at a greater distance from the market, there are mediators who specialize in taking the goods to market for sale, take stock of trends, and translate their observations and orders into weaver commissions.

The hum and buzz around the local Batak markets involves close contact among makers, sellers, and wearers of Batak indigenous clothing. Buyers hunt for their cherished designs; sellers watch what sells and what does not; middlemen and weavers buy yarn and dyes, receive and hand out commissions; creative designers and weavers survey textile imports for inspiration. The marketplace is the crucible where fashions are adopted, adapted, and discarded. The fashion scene is on display and accessible to all who would like to participate in it. Here, the fashion system is constructed collaboratively by the whole society. (See Leshkowich in Chapter 2 of this volume for a parallel discussion of the importance of the market negotiations for the production and dissemination of new styles in Vietnam.) Traders come to the Silindung Valley market from Karo, Simalungun, Pakpak, and other regions of Toba, where they get a sense of market trends, and buy up cloth for resale in their home markets. In this way, the Silindung Valley weavers are able to influence the newest textile trends in the entire northern Batak region.

Dress Scenario #3: A Batak Business Suit in Europe

In the final phase of this brief Batak fashion history, the focus shifts to Jakarta, capital city of Indonesia. This final period is still the closing decades of the twentieth century, and overlaps temporally with Dress Scenario #2.

Ibu M. is a wealthy Toba Batak designer and entrepreneur who lives in Jakarta. She grew up in North Sumatra, and understands the weaving culture there as well as the upscale market for exotic clothing in Jakarta. She converted part of her house into a design studio where her employees work on her projects. When I visited her, there was a heap of handwoven cloth imported from North Sumatra in a corner of the room. The cloths were decorated with a prominent motif characteristic of the textile locally named "Ragidup." The Ragidup, *according to* adat *or indigenous customary law, is the most important Toba Batak ritual textile worn only by those of high social standing, as this is defined in very specific ways by* adat. *However, Ibu M. creatively combines the hand-woven pattern section with commercial cloth to construct women's business suits of distinctive appearance. She received me as a visitor after her return from a marketing trip to Europe. She was subdued about her trip and gave the impression that she understood the daunting task ahead of her if she was to successfully corner a profitable international market for her products.*

In the 1970s, indigenous weavers/entrepreneurs throughout the world were exploring how to make their woven goods more viable on the tourist market (e.g. see Lambert 1976; Morris 1991; Salvador 1976). In the Batak region, and especially in the Silindung Valley, lengths of cloth with indigenous patterning were woven by or commissioned from weavers to make blouses, jackets, dresses, skirts, pants, ties, belts, handbags, scarves, shoes, et cetera (Figure 1.4). This kind of initiative was usually undertaken by entrepreneurs who had more wealth than the weavers, and a social position that granted them understanding of, and access to, modern markets. They commissioned the cloth from the weavers, and transformed it into Western-style items in studios/workshops, under their direction. Their outlets included hotel shops catering to tourists, modern boutiques along shopping streets, and separate, more exclusive markets in the major centers, with an urban clientele. It was a small step for ambitious, wealthy, and talented entrepreneurs to try to market the Western-styled indigenous items on international markets, which, despite the bustle of the local tourist markets, are the more lucrative markets to penetrate (Pye 1988: 25). This is the modest appearance that Batak fashions have been able to make on the international stage.

Ibu M. makes clothes of Western design for women. (The male counterparts of her buyers are still safely and unadventurously dressed in business suits.)[25] She targets what is popularly known as the fashion world, precisely that world that, by definition, excludes tribal dress. By adding ethnic flavor to her conservative, Western-style designs, she hopes to find/create a viable market niche. Her clothes are Western but Batak, modern but indigenous. Her work is an attempt to carve out/express a recognizable Batak identity in the current urban context. Hers is an initial foray into the kinds of markets that Skov and Bhachu

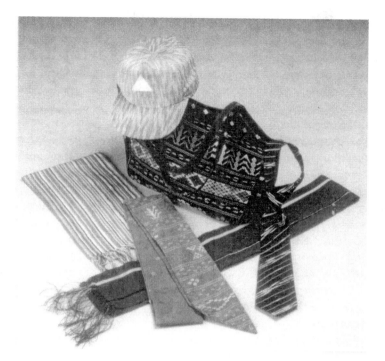

Figure 1.4 A variety of modern apparel items are made from handwoven indigenous cloth. In this image, there is a hat, handbag, tie, sash, scarf, and shawl. Photograph by Lotus Studio.

(respectively Chapters 7 and 4 of this volume) describe for the challenges that they present to the Eastern designer. Ibu M. represents a new class of Batak designer. Her market is both the local moneyed class and, as is her hope, international. She is a mediator between the local and the global just as the centuries of Batak weavers before her have been – but she does it now, according to current circumstances, as a fashion designer and not as a weaver. She operates within a new social class that has developed in response to external influences since the colonial era.

Production

The weavers are far removed, both socially and geographically, from Ibu M.'s markets, and also from her design studio. They are laborers who rarely even have the opportunity to see the finished product. Some comparable Jakarta fashion designers who like to use indigenous fabrics in their creations have moved weavers (from other ethnic groups) to the capital city so that they can

weave under the supervision of the design studio, although they do not participate in the decision-making process. Other designer-entrepreneurs have
found that their need for fabrics of a consistently high standard cannot be met
by backstrap weavers who tend to work seasonally, make cloth of varying
quality, and can only rarely fill sudden, large orders. A designer in Medan, for
example, won a presidential award in the 1980s because her studio generated
work and income for impoverished Batak weavers. When I spoke to her
afterwards she pointed out that to compete successfully she would need faster,
standardized, mechanically produced cloth. She recognized that her planned
factory production would further undermine the economic position of the
backstrap weavers to whom she had initially given employment.

In this scenario, the cloth producers figure as paid labor. The success of the
weavers in keeping their craft viable in changing social and economic circumstances during the twentieth century in the end has entailed that they forfeit
design and marketing decisions to members of the society of a higher class with
more extensive means, and who are conversant with the exclusive modern
markets. This places the weavers in a yet more vulnerable, dependent position,
unable to realize the larger profits that might result from the entrepreneur's
use of their work.

The bifurcation into traditional and modern that has become so basic to the
Batak clothing system, in other words, also pertains to markets, with weavers'
strategies informing the direction only of the traditional market. When possible,
weavers enhance their security by working for more than one market. They
may accept commissions when they are available, and send their goods to the
local market when that is the best option. The latter may offer greater latitude
for individual creativity, while the former may also introduce new designs and
technical ideas. It is also the case that, in addition to their obligation to meet
external expectations, the high-fashion designers look to the creations of the
weavers for inspiration. The bifurcation of modern and traditional in production appears to be as fundamental, but no more clear and discrete, than the
clothing forms denoted by those terms.

A Global Fashion Trajectory

The central argument presented in this chapter is that the modest emergence
of Batak clothing design in an international context has historical roots beginning in the colonial era – or centuries earlier if one factors in the tendency and
learned ability of weavers to incorporate external influences in their cloths.
Three dress scenarios from twentieth-century Batak clothing history were
selected to illustrate principles of change that have guided the direction of that

history. At the outset I pointed to the challenge presented to fashion theory by the inclusion of indigenous non-Western clothing designs on what has been defined as an exclusively Western stage, and that this chapter is intended to contribute to the project advocated by Jennifer Craik (1994: 18) of reconstituting the "outmoded, conventional notion of fashion."

Contending with the dominance of an external social force with its own distinctive clothing system immediately presented the Bataks with two sets of clothing choices, the foreign one "modern" and their own "traditional." Their selections and their innovative combinations simultaneously united them with one and differentiated them from the other. In the early phase of colonial encroachment, blue Karo clothing expressed resistance, an extreme form of differentiation from the dominant political power. Since that time, the dynamics of Batak dress – and identity – have been a series of strategies to negotiate a satisfying balance between their traditional identity and their participation in the modern world. Simmel (1957 [1904]) proposed that expressions of union and differentiation are both a product of, and propulsion for, Western fashion change. Simmel may have described a universal principle common to all dress systems and not, therefore, exclusively characteristic of Western fashion. The principle has been key to the present understanding of change in Batak dress.

According to Blumer, the flow of Western fashion is given direction by the way the past is left behind:

> By presenting new models and subjecting them to the process of competition and collective selection, the fashion process offers a continuous means of adjusting to a changing and shifting world. The fashion mechanism detaches social forms from the grip of the past, as suggested by the derogatory connotation of such expressions as 'old-fashioned' and 'out of date'; yet, in growing out of the preceding mode fashion maintains continuity of development (Blumer 1968: 344).

This classic, conventionally held understanding of fashion differs from what is found in the Batak system of dress. A characteristic of the latter appears to be *not* to leave behind what is traditional, but to continually reincorporate it in the process of constructing an identity between two competing worlds. Above I have referred to the continual splitting of the Batak dress system into its modern and traditional aspects as the principle of bifurcation. It appears to be a constant feature of postcolonial Batak clothing. The traditional is continually updated with reference to modern fashion trends – hence the term "modern traditional" to describe the clothing inventions in the second dress scenario. The modern, too, when crafted by Batak designers, is differentiated by the introduction of something distinctively Batak, as described in the third dress scenario above. Moreover, the kinds of balance that have been struck between traditional and modern have highlighted the changing relations between the genders and their changing social roles since the colonial era.

According to fashion theory, clothing that is characterized as traditional is unchanging and timeless. Batak traditional clothing is *conceptually* unchanging and timeless, despite the inventions of "modern traditional" dress forms. I use the term "modern traditional" in this chapter to designate a dynamic *trend* in traditional dress rather than a particular *form* of dress, recognizing that the forms of "modern traditional" are also constantly being updated. In this way, traditional Batak clothing change exhibits a characterizing feature of fashion, defined by Eicher and Sumberg as "a process involving change, from the introduction of a variation of a cultural form to its acceptance, discarding, and replacement by another cultural form" (1995: 299). It is important to note that fashion theorists Polhemus and Proctor also have made the distinction between measurable and conceptual change in the wake of their recognition that traditional Western apparel items such as the coronation gown of Queen Elizabeth II, while different from the gowns of her predecessors, is *conceptually* unaltered and traditional to those who see it (1978: 13-14). While Polhemus and Proctor do not apply their distinction to the non-fashion arena of "traditional societies," their observations may nevertheless represent an implicit acknowledgement that the apparently unchanging styles found in "traditional societies" could similarly be changing while remaining conceptually unaltered. As this volume demonstrates, this sleight of mind is found not just among the Batak people, but also in Vietnam and Korea (see Leshkowich and Ruhlen, Chapters 2 and 3 of this volume). Significantly, the Batak conceptualization of their "unchanging" traditional garb is consistent with the European Orientalist notion of unchanging traditional society, and may represent one of the cognitive shifts brought about by colonial domination such that self-identification of the ruled became consistent with the Orientalist perception of the Other held by the power holder. If this is a form of self-Orientalizing, it did not preclude pride, ingenuity, and agency in the invention of modern traditional Batak textiles.

That the Bataks modify their traditional dress relative to external, dominant fashion forms is a fundamental feature of their dress system that differentiates it from Western fashion. Eicher and Sumberg have made the points that "World, ethnic, and national dress are inter-related in today's global community" (1995: 304) and that "Western dress represents a style with origins in the tailored garments of Euro-Americans, but now, as a way of dress shared by millions of people, it no longer merits that name" (Eicher 1995: 4). The postcolonial Batak clothing system provides a good illustration of both points. However, the impression of unity and sameness that accompanies "world dress" masks a power differential. Clothing hides as well as reveals. By wearing "world dress," the Batak are not only opting for apparel forms suitable to a particular occasion, they are negotiating their relationship to the cultural centers of origin of that dress form.

The power differential strongly informs the kinds of strategy adopted by Batak producers and wearers of clothing. The strategy of using indigenous, handwoven cloth to make exogenous forms (Western and national) of apparel, for example, is notably a dramatic inversion of what was happening almost two centuries earlier and prior to colonial domination, when Karo men traded on the East Coast for cloth that Karo women fashioned into indigenous clothing styles. Given the current emergence of a range of other indigenous clothing forms on the international fashion stage, the question that must be asked is whether the direction of clothing change experienced by the Bataks is indicative of what I call a global fashion trajectory, *a direction of clothing transformation that ensues when indigenous clothing systems interact with the dominant Western clothing system*. The direction is set by the power differential, and the trajectory is as singular as the global hegemonic power. The Western fashion system sets the terms on which indigenous fashions compete to make their appearance on the global stage. Because people dress to fit the social roles to which they aspire, dressing is ineluctably a political act and cannot but reveal differential relations of power.

The principles of change guiding Batak clothing history weaken the West/ Rest dichotomy implied by the conventional definition of fashion, while sharpening awareness of the specific similarities and differences that characterize relations between the two. Most notably the power differential that has shaped the kinds and direction of change undergone by Batak dress is obfuscated by the conventional dichotomization of world dress systems. The emergence of items of non-Western dress on the international fashion stage offers the appearance of fashion globalization, particularly when the society whence it originates has hierarchical and industrial features. Batak dress history suggests, however, that such appearances are the result of deeply rooted historical processes characterized by the negotiation, in the apparel forum, of this power differential. If fashion were to be understood, like dress, as a global phenomenon with a Western variant, rather than a Western phenomenon gone global, I propose that among indigenous dress systems are the fashion systems that "coexist, compete, and interact with the western fashion system," the study of which may provide theoretical renewal in fashion theory and Craik's recommended reconstitution of the "outmoded, conventional notion of fashion" (1994: 18).

The brief Batak clothing history presented above traces the creative agency of weavers. Cloth and clothing are easily seen just for their plastic features while the skillful hands that put it together go unrecognized. Batak textile designs are weavers' interpretations of the world. Recent textile studies emphasize what Janet Catherine Berlo has called women's aesthetic strategies,[26] "the diverse ways by which women invest meaning in textile arts" (1991: 438). "Textiles are eloquent texts, encoding history, change, appropriation, oppression and endurance, as well as personal and cultural creative visions" (439). These are equally the texts of Batak handwoven dress. The history of Batak dress is a display of an aspect of Batak women's history, a history that cannot be found in the verbal domain, but is encoded in the plastic features of Batak cloth.

During the twentieth century, the viability of the cloth on the marketplace became a central measure of the weaver's skill in translating the social order into cloth. The irony of the weavers' success becomes apparent in the third dress scenario when the designer torch is passed on to specialists of a higher social class who have the ability to connect with external markets. Then the Batak weavers are phased out of their designer role and disappear into the same anonymous obscurity as the cutters and stitchers of Western fashion (Nielsen 1990). The women's business suit in the third scenario signals the modern image of the Batak woman of high social status, a very different image from the woman in the Toba Batak myth whose ability to provide for her family was understood to be her procreative power and was the foundation of her social status. At that time, the weaver's work was like the origin of life itself. A class system as well as ideological conversion are signaled by the changing responsibility in design production. The definition of female success in the modern sector has less to do with procreation than with the means and habits of fashionable consumption. This chapter has revealed that Batak femininity has been constructed both by wearing and by producing clothes, and that these processes, too, are deeply bifurcated as traditional and modern. Moreover, the "success" of the indigenous weaver is clouded by the inevitable obsolescence of her role as a designer, while the success of the designer in the modern sector meets images of femininity that are externally constructed, engendering unresolved problems of identity that Jones and Ruhlen explore more fully in Chapters 6 and 3 of this volume.

Notes

1. An earlier version of this article, entitled "How Batak Weavers Use Thread to Realize the Challenge of Designing a Future," was presented to the Association of Asia Studies 1999 Annual Meeting for the Panel: Designing Women: The Use of Fashion to Construct International Modernity, National Tradition, and Gender in Indonesia, Vietnam, and within the South Asian Diaspora. The paper was dedicated to Professor P.E. de Josselin de Jong at the State University of Leiden, The Netherlands, my doctoral thesis advisor, who passed away during the last minutes of 1998. Another version was

presented to the Department of Human Ecology at the University of Alberta. I thank Anne Lambert, Tim Babcock, and my co-editors, Carla Jones and Ann Marie Leshkowich, for important comments on different drafts of this chapter, and to the Series Editor, Joanne Eicher, and the external reader for their comments.

2. Craik has concerned herself with Western fashion only.

3. It was primarily the exotic tree products that the Bataks harvested, as well as their need for salt, and their desire for exotic commodities such as iron and cloth, that pulled the Batak into trader activities along the coasts.

4. Among these archival records, I include Karo Batak textiles and photographs, as well as written (published and unpublished) colonial and precolonial records. In the absence of being able to conduct interviews and having only the occasional chance reference to clothing/textiles in the extant written records, the researcher of Batak apparel history must rely heavily on visually decoding textiles and photographs. My insights for Dress Scenario #1 have been derived from an examination of what people wore in the context of the social, economic, and political circumstances of the time. I have correlated changes in dress with social changes in much the way that a present-day analyst of brand-new fashions that appear on the street or the runway will do. My deductive hypotheses about the meanings of apparel forms are informed by my understanding of principles of clothing dynamics.

5. The present chapter has developed from long-term research into the indigenous classification of textiles in the northern Batak regions. The research has been supported by the Dutch ZWO/WOTRO, and by the Canadian SSHRC, as well as through various funds at the University of Alberta, most notably Killam Postdoctoral funding. In North Sumatra, support was provided by Universitas HKBP Nommensen.

6. From Neumann's 1916 account of a ritual ceremony, this was still the case in the early twentieth century: "Most were wearing a clean upper body covering [likely what Anderson had referred to as a "bajoo"], white or blue depending on what they owned, because the white torso coverings are often first worn until they are dirty, and only then dyed with indigo" (1971 [1826]: 48; my translation from the Dutch).

7. Middendorp (1929: 46–7) noted that "the Karos were not the inhabitants of a kingdom with a stable government. The Karo lands . . . consisted of hundreds of village 'kingdoms', independent of each other and always at war with one another and with the Karos of the lowlands. There were 250 states . . ."

8. Examples are found in museum collections (e.g., Museum der Weltkulturen, Frankfurt, depicted in Niessen 1993, fig. 11).

9. The Batak did not cultivate silkworms or weave silk, and such cloth was particularly desired as an indicator of means to those of higher social position. Village leaders used it as headcloths and their wives used it as shouldercloths. The few handwoven museum textiles that incorporate appliquéd pieces of Acehnese silk attest to the preciousness of even small pieces of this fabric.

10. "Unable to establish trade with China, the [East India] Company was equally unsuccessful in its attempt to dispose of English woollen cloth upon the spice-islanders. It was soon discovered that the only commodity acceptable there was Indian textiles" (Irwin and Schwartz 1966: 9).

11. In the eighteenth century, Marsden's records indicate that "the overwhelming bulk of cloth imports [to Sumatra] were Indian cottons" (Guy 1998: 68). While arguably the onset of globalization may be traced to the colonial era, with respect to clothing and textiles, the roots of globalization are much deeper. Long prior to the European presence in Southeast Asia, India had clothed the world (Gittinger 1982). If a concept of globalization had been present in the Karo indigenous worldview, it would have been most applicable to the time of active trade of diverse cloth by participants of many nationalities before European domination. By the middle of the nineteenth century, "the [Indian] handicraft industry was largely destroyed by the English imports into India of machine-made cloth and yarn . . ." (Wolf 1982: 287). Indian cotton production survived only a little longer.

12. The first European planter to cultivate tobacco arrived on Sumatra's East Coast in 1863. Tobacco plantations rapidly expanded. The East Coast also became centrally important to the colonial regime for the production of rubber and oil.

13. Emma Tarlo notes how this strategy was employed in India. "The simplest and least controversial way to resolve the difficulty of how to modernise one's dress without appearing to desert one's 'traditional' identity was to adopt European fabrics but retain Indian styles" (Tarlo 1996: 45). The Batak case does not appear to revolve around the desire to modernize, but rather the problem of incorporating available and necessary fabric without appearing to collaborate with the oppressive force that supplied it.

14. Indigenous social organization was based on five exogamous patrilineal clan divisions (Karo Karo, Tarigen, Ginting, Peranginangin, and Simbiring) connected by marriage alliances. Hierarchy characterized relations between wife-givers and wife-takers, but this was both negotiable and relative because alliances were continually being crafted and every clan was obliged to function in both capacities – although not at the same time.

15. The Batak backstrap loom produces a warp-faced textile, while the Malay frame loom produces a more balanced weave in which the weft has more prominence.

16. "In 1909 the road between Kaban Djahe and Medan (81 K.M.) was completed. It was this road that made such a tremendous and rapid change in the Karo community.

For instance: Previous to 1909 a man who wished to export potatoes would have had to walk for three days with a sack containing 25 K.G. of potatoes on his back, partly over steep mountain paths, to sell them in Medan. That was not worth the trouble. Since 1909 the same man can transport about 400 K.G. of potatoes by ox-cart, with no difficulty, to Medan and return with salt, oil etc. This improved system of transportation opened up possibilities for the cultivation of vegetables and influenced changes in clothing, morals and health conditions" (Middendorp 1929: 63).

17. Jean Gelman Taylor (1983: 143) points out that "European women still wore a modified form of Indonesian costume at home before the second world war" consisting of sarong and *kebaya*. This is in striking contrast to the unmodified styles of European dress worn by European men. The complexity of postcolonial gender construction is a theme addressed by all of the chapters in this volume.

18. When collectors for the World Exhibition in Amsterdam in 1883 visited Samosir Island and the west bank of Lake Toba, they found weavers who claimed to have

specialized in catering to Karo tastes for as far back as memory served. Samosir Island still today specializes in the very wide, blue textiles used by the Karo for ritual purposes. The red headcloths worn by Karo women are made on the west coast of the lake, and the northwest shore of Samosir Island specializes in weaving the fine shouldercloths with flashy supplementary weft patterning.

19. In an earlier publication (Niessen 1993), I have traced some of the historical threads that have been woven into Batak textile design.

20. A brighter red dye was rumored to have been in use in by Bataks on the edge of Karo territory on the shore of Lake Toba, but given the lack of more information, it is likely that, if it existed, it was rare (Niessen, in press).

21. In Guatemala, for example, some communities of weavers stopped using indigo blue and moved to a wholesale adoption of red (Carlsen and Wenger 1991: 370).

22. By adapting Malay features in their clothing in the beginning of the century, the Karo (as described above) were participating in a more generalized, modern indigenous clothing trend found among all the Batak groups. Textiles with metallic (or metal-colored) supplementary weft in Malay patterning are currently the most esteemed among Christian and Moslem buyers alike. Especially where there are such sharp political divisions between adherents of the two religions as in Indonesia, this shift in taste suggests that the textile design is perceived as being more closely aligned with high social status than with Islam. Even brides in the strongly Christian Silindung Valley elect to wear sumptuous silk, Malay-style sarongs on their wedding day.

23. "Uniforms were another manifestation of this bureaucratic attempt to offset the anonymity of the metropolis. They symbolized the advance of the modern state into the life of the individual . . ." (Wilson 1985: 35).

24. In her history of fashion, Wilson supports the claim that "the most fundamental distinction in dress is not, as we might suppose today, that between male and female, but the distinction between the draped and the sewn" (1985: 17). At this stage in Batak clothing history, the gender distinction parallels the distinction between draped and sewn garments, women wearing the draped versions, and men the sewn versions.

25. A notable exception is the popular use of the Javanese batik shirt as acceptable men's business attire in Indonesia.

26. While not everywhere weavers are women, in Indonesia weaving is women's work. The connection that Berlo makes between weaving and women's work applies in the Batak case.

References

Agthe, Johanna (1979), *Arm durch Reichtum. Sumatra: Eine Insel am Äquator*, Frankfurt am Main: Museum für Völkerkunde.

Anderson, John (1971 [1826]), *Mission to the East Coast of Sumatra in 1823*, Kuala Lumpur: Oxford University Press.

Baizerman, Suzanne, Cerny, Catherine, and Eicher, Joanne B. (1993), "Eurocentrism in the Study of Ethnic Dress," *Dress* 20: 19–32.

Berlo, Janet Catherine (1991), "Beyond Bricolage: Women and Aesthetic Strategies in Latin American Textiles," in Margot Blum Schevill, Janet Catherine Berlo and Edward B. Dwyer (eds), *Textile Traditions of Mesoamerica and the Andes: An Anthology*, New York: Garland.

Blumer, Herbert (1968), "Fashion," in David Sills (ed.), *International Encyclopedia of the Social Sciences* 5: 341–5.

Brenner-Felsach, Joachim von (1890), "Reise durch die unabhängigen Battak-Lande und auf der Insel Nias," Mitteilungen der Kaiserlichen und Königlichen Geographischen Gesellschaft in Wien 33(5&6): 276–305.

Carlsen, Robert S. and Wenger, David A. (1991), "The Dyes used in Guatemalan Textiles: A Diachronic Approach," in Margot Blum Schevill, Janet Catherine Berlo and Edward B. Dwyer (eds), *Textile Traditions of Mesoamerica and the Andes: An Anthology*, New York: Garland.

Craik, Jennifer (1994), *The Face of Fashion: Cultural Studies in Fashion*, London and New York: Routledge.

Eicher, Joanne B. (1995), "Introduction" in Joanne B. Eicher (ed.), *Dress and Ethnicity*, Oxford: Berg.

—— and Sumberg, Barbara (1995), "World Fashion and Ethnic and National Dress," in Joanne B. Eicher (ed.), *Dress and Ethnicity*, Oxford: Berg.

Gittinger, Mattiebelle (1982), *Master Dyers to the World*, Washington: The Textile Museum.

Guy, John (1998), *Woven Cargoes: Indian Textiles in the East*, New York: Thames & Hudson.

Hagen, Bernard (1883), "Eine Reise nach dem Tobah-See in Zentralsumatra," in Dr. A. Petermann, *Mittheilungen aus Justus Pethes' Geogr. Anstalt*, 29: 42–53, 142–9, 167–77.

Hendrickson, Hildi (ed.) (1996), *Clothing and Difference: Embodied Identities in Colonial and Post-Colonial Africa*, Durham, NC and London: Duke University Press.

Irwin, John and Schwartz, P.R. (1966), *Indo-European Textile History*, Ahmedabad: Calico Museum of Textiles.

Jasper, J.E. and Pirngadie, Mas (1912), *De Weefkunst, De Inlandsche Kunstnijverheid in Nederlands Indie*, Vol 2, 's-Gravenhage: Mouton.

Joustra, Meint (1910), *Batakspiegel*, Uitgaven van het Bataksch Instituut 3, Leiden: S. C. van Doesburgh.

—— (1914), "De Weefschool te Lagoeboti," *Eigen Haard* 40: 66–7.

—— (1915), *Van Medan Naar Padang en Terug* [*Reisindrukken en- Ervaringen*], Uitgaven van het Bataksch Instituut 11, Leiden: S.C. van Doesburgh.

Kipp, Rita S. (1990), *The Early Years of a Dutch Colonial Mission*, Ann Arbor: University of Michigan Press.

Kondo, Dorinne (1997), *About Face: Performing Race in Fashion and Theater*, London and New York: Routledge.

Kuper, Hilda (1973a), "Costume and Identity," *Comparative Studies in Society and History* 15 (3): 348–67.

—— (1973b), "Costume and Cosmology: The Animal Symbolism of the Ncwala," *Man* 8(4): 613–30.

Lambert, Anne (1976), "Textile Transposals: Guatemala in Interchange with Outside Markets," *Ethnographic Textiles of the Western Hemisphere*, Proceedings, Irene Emery Roundtable on Museum Textiles, Washington: The Textile Museum.

Langner, Lawrence (1959), *The Importance of Wearing Clothes*, New York: Hastings House.

Leur, Jacob C. van (1983 [1955]), *Indonesian Trade and Society: Essays in Asian Social and Economic History*, KITLV Reprints on Indonesia, Dordrecht: Foris Publications.

Maxwell, Robyn J. (1990), *Textiles of Southeast Asia: Tradition, Trade, and Transformation*, Melbourne: Australian National Gallery and Oxford University Press.

Middendorp, W. (1929), "The Administration of the Outer Provinces of the Netherlands Indies," in B. Schrieke (ed.), *The Effect of Western Influence on Native Civilisations in the Malay Archipelago*, Batavia: Royal Batavia Society of Arts and Sciences, G. Kolff & Co.

Morris Jr, Walter F. (1991), "Marketing Maya Textiles in Highland Chiapas, Mexico," in Margot Blum Schevill, Janet Catherine Berlo and Edward. B. Dwyer (eds), *Textile Traditions of Mesoamerica and the Andes: An Anthology*, New York: Garland.

Neumann, J.H. (1916), *Een jaar Onder de Karo-Bataks*, Typ. Varekamp & Co.

Nielsen, Elizabeth (1990), "Handmaidens of the Glamour Culture: Costumers in the Hollywood Studio System," in Jane Gaines and Charlotte Herzog (eds), *Fabrications: Costume and the Female Body*, New York: Routledge.

Niessen, Sandra A. (1993), *Batak Cloth and Clothing: A Dynamic Indonesian Tradition*, Kuala Lumpur: Oxford University Press.

—— (1999), "Threads of Tradition, Threads of Invention: Unraveling Toba Batak Women's Expressions of Social Change," in Ruth B. Phillips and Christopher B. Steiner (eds), *Unpacking Culture: Art and Commodity in Colonial and Postcolonial Worlds*, Berkeley: University of California Press.

—— (in press), *The Batak Textile Repertory: Design, Technique, Nomenclature*, Zutphen: Walburg Pers.

Polhemus, Ted and Proctor, Lynne (eds) (1978), *Fashion and Anti-Fashion*, London: Thames & Hudson.

Pye, Elwood (1988), *Artisans in Economic Development: Evidence from Asia*, Ottawa: International Development Research Centre.

Rouse, Elizabeth (1989), *Understanding Fashion*, Oxford: BSP Professional Books.

Salvador, Mary Lynne (1976), "The Clothing Arts of the Cuna of San Blas, Panama," in Nelson Graburn (ed.), *Ethnic and Tourist Arts: Cultural Expressions from the Fourth World*, Berkeley and Los Angeles: University of California Press.

Sapir, Edward (1937), "Fashion," *Encyclopedia of the Social Sciences*, The McMillan Co.

Schevill, Margot Blum, Berlo, Janet C. and Dwyer, Edward B. (eds) (1991), *Textile Traditions of Mesoamerica and the Andes: An Anthology*, New York: Garland.

Simmel, Georg (1957 [1904]), "Fashion," *The Journal of American Sociology* LXII (6): 541–58.

Tarlo, Emma (1996), *Clothing Matters: Dress and Identity in India*, Chicago: University of Chicago Press.

Taylor, Jean Gelman (1983), *The Social World of Batavia: European and Eurasian in Dutch Asia*, Madison, WI: The University of Wisconsin Press.

Wilson, Elizabeth (1985), *Adorned in Dreams: Fashion and Modernity*, London: Virago.

Wolf, Eric R. (1982), *Europe and the People Without History*, Berkeley: University of California Press.

2

The Ao Dai Goes Global: How International Influences and Female Entrepreneurs Have Shaped Vietnam's "National Costume"

Ann Marie Leshkowich[1]

On 10 September 1995, the Miss International Pageant in Tokyo awarded the prize for "Best National Costume" to Miss Vietnam, Truong Quynh Mai. The Vietnam Airlines flight attendant wore a blue and white silk brocade *ao dai* (pronounced "ow-zai") consisting of three elements: (1) a long, close-fitting tunic with mandarin collar and high slits up the side seams, (2) loose pants, and (3) a donut-shaped coiled hat. The outfit is often referred to as Vietnam's traditional or national costume. Today, a formal ao dai like Miss Vietnam's is typically worn by brides, performers, and models, and on special occasions (Figure 2.1). Worn without the hat and fashioned from less sumptuous fabric, the ao dai is a common uniform for civil servants, tour guides, hotel and restaurant workers, and high school students.

Within Vietnam, Miss Vietnam's victory was heralded as more than simply a prize for a beautiful outfit. An article in Vietnam's fashion press described the ao dai as symbolizing Vietnam's "national soul" that had "once again been honored in front of thousands of international spectators" in Tokyo (*Thoi Trang Tre* October 1995: 43).[2] By affirming the ao dai as the embodiment of Vietnam's traditions and signifying the country's incorporation into the modern global community, Truong Quynh Mai's award represented a victory for her entire homeland.

Figure 2.1 A fashion show featuring a style of brocade ao dai similar to that worn by Miss Vietnam, Truong Quynh Mai. Photo by Ann Marie Leshkowich.

International recognition boosted the ao dai's domestic appeal. While Miss Vietnam was accepting her award in Tokyo, I was living in Ho Chi Minh City in order to study female traders in the cloth and clothing industry (Leshkowich 2000). Within days of Miss Vietnam's victory, many of the market stalls and tailor shops where I conducted my research had posted pictures and signs promising customers custom-made ao dai "just like Miss Vietnam's." While these signs testify to many entrepreneurs' speed in capitalizing on a potentially lucrative news event, the Miss Vietnam advertisements and increased interest in ao dai are in fact part of a larger effort by Vietnamese designers and sellers to market the garment as a domestic product that has earned the approval of foreign fashion experts, thus making it both traditional and stylish, or what Vietnamese tellingly call "*mo-den,*" a term taken from the English word "modern."

This chapter focuses on three issues that are crucial to understanding the origins and significance of the "ao dai craze" during the mid- to late 1990s. First, I explore recent anthropological studies of consumption and globalization to highlight how so-called traditional costumes have emerged as powerful and fashionable, yet essentialized, markers of national and gender differences. The women who choose to wear such outfits often do so precisely because of global fashion discourses. The choice to don even a modern version of a "traditional costume" does, however, carry the very real danger of self-exoticizing. At the same time, women's positions as consumers of this fashion trend challenge other stereotypes that depict Third World women as participating in globalization only as oppressed laborers.

While global circumstances have prompted nations around the world to develop and promote a "traditional costume," understanding Vietnam's ao dai craze requires attention to a second question: why has this particular garment been selected to portray Vietnam on the international stage? The answer lies in the garment's history. Although the ao dai has become synonymous with traditional Vietnamese culture and feminine virtues, the garment in fact has a relatively brief history marked throughout by significant foreign influence – first Chinese, then French and American. I suggest that the ao dai can best be viewed as possessing a hybrid character. In today's environment of globalization that demands and structures standardized displays of cultural distinctiveness into a kind of homogenized heterogeneity, the ao dai's hybridity makes it particularly well suited to convey comprehensible and compelling messages about Vietnam's national character to both domestic and foreign audiences. In this capacity, it also serves as a vehicle for debating the positive and negative effects of globalization on Vietnamese cultural identities.

As important as the ao dai's history has been in shaping its role as the quintessential symbol of Vietnamese-ness, the garment is also a material object designed, produced, and marketed by individuals. The third part of this chapter focuses on the roles of these individuals, most of them small-scale female shop owners and market stallholders, in producing and circulating ao dai. As the ao dai is created in homes and tiny tailor workshops across the country, each step in its production involves minute decisions about cut, pattern, fabric, and decoration.

Even on this mundane level, however, the supposedly "global" and "local" are intertwined. Conscious of their customers' desire to keep abreast of international fashion trends, the female entrepreneurs I studied regularly turn to their personal contacts overseas, primarily relatives, for information about the latest styles. Fashion catalogs, Vietnamese-language calendars produced in the United States, pattern books, and fashion magazines both inspire local producers to develop stylistic innovations and provide concrete evidence to convince wary consumers that the resulting items are truly "*mo-den.*"

In charting the ao dai's "cultural biography" (Kopytoff 1986) as both a potent national symbol and a concrete object produced under specific material and cultural conditions, I seek to make three broader points about the cultural and economic effects of globalization. First, as a methodological tactic, I wish to draw attention to sites and processes of circulation as not just middle points bridging production and consumption, but as arenas for the mediation and transformation of style through specific marketplace encounters. The crafting and marketing of ao dai is a creative process involving communication and negotiation by multiple agents whose interaction shapes both productive processes and consumer desires. In contrast to more abstract discussions of global cultural flows (Hannerz 1996; Appadurai 1990, 1996), attention to marketplace encounters allows us to see how tastes are formulated, by whom, with what possibilities, and under what constraints.

Second, through an examination of the ao dai's distant and recent history, I suggest that contemporary global processes have placed a premium on identifying and ordering cultural diversity into a system of homogenized heterogeneity. As a result, the authentic, traditional, and local need to be viewed not as timeless, discrete properties characterizing people, things, or experiences, but as hybrid and discursive productions. While these dynamics are clearly compelling both foreign and domestic interest in Asian fashion today, the ao dai's history suggests that it has always been such a hybrid product. It may be that a garment's hybridity, far from violating its cultural distinctiveness, is exactly what makes it such a useful and comprehensible marker of ethnic or national identity in the contemporary global commodification of diversity.

Third, the creative energy of the female entrepreneurs I studied belies any attempt to depict Third World producers as simply the passive victims of forces of global capital. While scholars of gender and economic development have rightly drawn attention to the ways in which global capital can marginalize certain groups, my research on the ao dai suggests globalization can create opportunities for certain types of small-scale female entrepreneurs to serve as active agents in the circulation of styles and information. By performing their traditional role as maintainers of kin relations within the relatively new circumstances of a global Vietnamese diaspora, the female entrepreneurs I met have privileged access to information about global consumer trends. Cosmopolitan in their orientation (Hannerz 1990, 1996), these savvy businesswomen serve as cultural brokers who use the knowledge they acquire through diasporic kin networks in order to craft and promote a garment whose appeal lies precisely in its synthesis of perceived national tradition and international modernity.

The Circulation of Fashion and Gender in Globalizing Marketplaces

My focus on the concrete circumstances shaping the ao dai craze in Vietnam during the mid- to late 1990s coincides with a broader shift in the anthropology of economic life away from a traditional concern with relations of production and exchange and toward a new focus on consumption.[3] This change in focus has led to several significant realizations. First, consumption is profoundly implicated in the self-conscious creation of gender, class, national, racial, and ethnic identities, not just in the developed "First World," but in the "Third World" as well. Second, groups and individuals tend creatively to reinterpret the items they consume, so that even the use of mass-produced products need not be a form of false consciousness perpetrated on unsuspecting consumers by hegemonic, neo-imperialist capitalist structures.[4] Third, anthropologists have come to recognize that gender biases led scholars in the past to valorize the "male" realm of production as the locus for creating individual and social worth, and also to denigrate the "female" realm of consumption as frivolous, superficial, or inauthentic.[5] A more fruitful approach would be to view consumption as a significant form of economic and cultural work (see, e.g., Jones, Chapter 6 of this volume).

Taken together, work in anthropology, postcolonial studies, and gender studies documents an important shift in the ideology of consumption. No longer viewed as the "radical leveler" (Marx 1977 [1867]) inexorably obliterating cultural distinctiveness or seducing women into accepting second-class status as keepers of the domestic realm, the commodity is now seen as a value-neutral tabula rasa, ready to be inscribed with meanings by its purchasers and users and then deployed by them to display those meanings.

As with any adoption of new areas of concern, however, the rush to consider consumption has created gaps and biases of a new kind. The tendency to celebrate consumption's potential to express and fulfill individual desires has led some to underemphasize the constraints – be they economic, religious, gendered, familial, racial, ethnic, or otherwise – that limit the exercise of consumer choice or that enable others to reinterpret the meaning of such choices in service of broader discourses. Focus on the act of consumption as an encounter between individuals and the goods that they select, acquire, and use also risks making goods seem the natural and functional concretization of consumer desires. But how does a particular array of goods come to be available for consumers to select? What persons and processes enable goods to be delivered to and desired by particular consumers?

On a philosophical level, while I agree that objects in theory do not possess intrinsic significance and instead acquire their meaning from people and the uses they make of those objects, the reality is that in a global flow of people, ideas, and objects, the vast majority of the things that we encounter in daily life are already saturated with meaning. As such, they carry rich semantic loads that have been assigned to them over the course of their history as objects. Meaning is not recreated anew each time a consumer confronts a commodity. Rather, meaning comes from somewhere, and each new interpretation exists in dialogue with its antecedents.

In short, explorations of consumption risk truncating the political, historical, social, cultural, and symbolic trajectories that both people and goods must follow so that they may come together. How can we address these gaps? One fruitful approach is to focus on circulation. Through documenting the concrete details of retail encounters, we can explore how one's position in systems of production and access to sites of exchange serve to shape consumption preferences. We can also consider how the expression of these preferences then drives the production and exchange of goods, tastes, and identities.

An endless range of goods can be examined to shed light on these issues,[6] but I find clothing to be a particularly useful means for exploring the interconnection between meaning, taste, and agency in the context of globalization. As items that envelop wearers' bodies, clothing is the individually consumed commodity most available for public display. As a result, it is increasingly through fashion that cultural and other differences are being displayed, assessed, standardized, commodified, valorized, contested, and appropriated. These processes play a key role in propelling not just Vietnam's ao dai craze, but global fascination with Asian style and national costumes more generally. An exploration of the circulation of the ao dai thus draws our attention to two distinct, yet interdependent, contexts: the international circulation of information about national costumes and identity, and the Vietnamese locations in which ao dai and information about them move between producers and consumers.

National Costumes and the Global Circulation of Difference

One of the most striking features of globalization is the frequency, speed, and ease with which people and things from different parts of the world come into contact with each other. Given that this contact has largely been prompted by capitalist forces originating from Europe and North America, most early observers of globalization found cause to be concerned that the encounter between different things and people would be a homogenizing one in which non-Western cultures would be transformed in the West's image. Something about this contact, however, led not to the erasure of difference, but to its validation. In today's global economy of mass-produced goods, the new and the unique have come to be prized as such, and possessing such items or knowledge about them marks one's status as a facile navigator of global cultural "scapes" (Appadurai 1990, 1996).

This development is a double-edged sword. On the one hand, an appreciative global audience for such things as African art, Chinese acupuncture, and Indonesian textiles leads to the continued use and production of those items or practices. On the other hand, what may seem a practical feature of globalization – the ability to encounter and appreciate difference – has in fact become an ideological technique for maintaining power. As with colonialism and Orientalism in past centuries, globalization has been a vehicle for serving up elements of the world so that these features can be assessed and appreciated by cognoscenti. The effect is what Jones and I (in our Introduction to this volume) refer to as "homogenized heterogeneity" or what Richard Wilk (1995) has called "structures of common difference": certain types of diversity are picked up and placed into categories so that they can be understood and controlled. We might think of this as a kind of patchwork quilt of cultural diversity. The color and pattern of each square may be individually or locally produced, but the way they are stitched together, the overall structure of the quilt, the commissioning and placement of each square, and even the very idea that a quilt should be constructed at all – these decisions are all controlled by globalization's powerful centers, typically located in North America and Western Europe.[7]

Homogenized heterogeneity is perhaps most evident in the idea of a "national costume." It has become standard practice at international events such as the Olympics, beauty contests, world's fairs, visits by foreign dignitaries, and even international policy meetings (see Ruhlen in Chapter 4 of this volume) for different groups to display their identities through the donning of traditional dress, usually by women.[8] Participation in the global community in fact seems to require as a price of admission that each member develop and be prepared to display a costume that visually signals its history and distinctiveness so that it can be remembered and understood as it circulates through staged displays of global culture. Although the national costume's status as an unspoken requirement might seem oppressive, peoples distant from global power centers more often seem to interpret it as a chance to capture the attention and respect of a global audience, however stereotypically or fleetingly. To have one's cultural identity validated, even when one does not control and may be ambivalent about the process of display, can nonetheless be a desirable achievement.

While the presentation of a national costume on a global stage is an interesting site for exploring the commodification and circulation of cultural diversity, I am even more fascinated by the impact of such displays on the home audience. What happens when the traditional costume, now bearing the stamp of global approval, returns to its purportedly original context? How do the supposed owners of the traditional costume respond to it? Addressing these questions requires attention to another site for the circulation of difference: a domestic context in which national identity, images of traditional femininity, the lure of international power, and the simultaneous desire for "local" authenticity and modern cosmopolitanism mingle to shape perceptions of the so-called national costume. For the ao dai, these conditions have combined to make the national costume a trendy fashion, as processes of "self-exoticizing" (Kondo 1997, Tarlo 1996, Savigliano 1995) lead young, urban Vietnamese women and the media to see and newly appreciate the ao dai as outsiders might. It is in this way that people, particularly women, become globalized consumers of externally produced versions of the traditions that appear to be uniquely theirs.

Attention to the international and domestic circulation of national costumes thus challenges the image of tradition as localized, timeless, authentic, or uniquely the product of the group with which it is associated. We come to see that people wear or appreciate these outfits, not because they are performing some kind of essentialized identity, but because they have acquired global cultural criteria for discerning the value of specific visions of their own traditions. In addition, by showing women in places such as Vietnam participating in the globalized consumption of fashion, such a project challenges another cherished notion: that Third World women are involved in globalization exclusively as oppressed, localized producers.

Using Circulation to Challenge Producer/Consumer Binaries

One of the most popular ideologies of globalization is that it has fostered an increasingly stark dichotomy between First World citizens as consumers and Third World citizens as producers of the items consumed in the First World.

According to this account, the rise of consumption in the European and North American societies of the so-called First World (or what Wallerstein (1974) calls the "center") has been accomplished through the expansion of global systems of capitalist production that exploit workers in the Third World ("the periphery"). As feminist scholars have pointed out, this gap between First World consumer and Third World producer is often gendered, so that a contrast emerges between the housewife as the prototypical First World consumer and the Third World factory worker as a young woman with "nimble fingers, slow wit" (Ong 1987: 151) whose disempowered status as a woman makes her particularly vulnerable to exploitation in the workplace.[9]

With respect to clothing, this logic of globalization has become so prevalent that just about any consumer of clothing in the United States expects items bearing a "Made in X" (i.e., not "the USA") label to have been created by oppressed Third World women working under harsh conditions. It is for this reason that students of mine are often surprised by my pictures of a Ho Chi Minh City marketplace that show female vendors proudly displaying their stock of Levi's jeans, both genuine and fake. The conventional wisdom about the global circulation of Levi's does not include the possibility that Third World persons can be active agents of consumption, let alone a part of global culture partaking of and reinterpreting fashion knowledge generated in the First World.

The image of those same young Vietnamese women wearing ao dai sits more comfortably. Wearing ao dai "fits" Vietnamese women, for they are consuming the clothing that has rightfully been bequeathed to them through history. Such a conclusion is deceptive, for the ao dai's history and contemporary examples of its manufacture and use, as I describe below, demonstrate that the decision to wear an ao dai is just as influenced by global fashion trends as is the decision to buy Levi's.

Whether Third World women wear ao dai or Levi's, recognizing that they are not just producers of fashion but globally aware consumers whose choices fuel fashion trends does not necessarily simplify our interpretation of their actions. When they are doing so with respect to a supposedly traditional item of clothing, understanding their intentions and the effects of their actions becomes even more complicated. Consider a young female Vietnamese garment worker who uses part of her earnings to buy an ao dai to wear to a special event. Is she expressing her identity as a traditional Vietnamese woman, an identity that has remained largely unchanged, despite the transformations wrought by colonialism, war, socialism, and globalization? Or, is she responding to the international recognition of the ao dai as a beautiful Vietnamese national costume that has made "ethnic chic" trendy? Is the ao dai an expression of her personal taste? Or, is she buying one because she's been told (by elders, by peers, by the media) that she must have one because it is appropriate for a certain occasion?

Faced with such an act of consumption, I find myself asking why we should be forced to choose between these divergent interpretations. The consumption of fashion is not simply a system ordained by some invisible panel of experts, nor is it an unconstrained process of individual selection or identity construction. Answering these questions requires looking beyond the act of consumption to try to understand the forces and processes that enable that consumption. What is needed is attention to contexts in which production and consumption, global symbolic meanings, and local interpretations appear simultaneously and are mediated through the agency of individuals.

Circulation is one such arena. Through the circulation of clothing items in marketplaces, shopping malls, and curbside venues, consumers confront products, form and realize consumption preferences, and provide retailers with valuable cues about fashion trends. By documenting how small-scale traders and tailors in Ho Chi Minh City design and market Vietnam's national costume to their customers, I wish to demonstrate the utility of a focus on the circulation of fashion. Located between various sets of extremes – the local and the global, the traditional and the modern, production and consumption – the traders I studied serve as cross-cultural translators and fashion mediators. These processes of mediation depend in large part upon and are facilitated by exchanges of information, money, and fashion materials among traders, tailors, and their overseas kin. A major theme emerges from this account: contrary to images of petty traders as mere drones in the retail network,[10] the successful Ho Chi Minh City stallholders and boutique owners I met participate in global networks of circulation and have capitalized on them in order to fashion themselves as what Ulf Hannerz (1990) has described as savvy cosmopolitans: skillful cross-cultural translators of style positioned at the heart of the formation of consumer tastes. What is perhaps most surprising about this example is not just that female stallholders and their middle-class customers in Vietnam are embracing cosmopolitan orientations toward fashion, but that they are doing so with respect to a garment supposed to be the quintessential emblem of Vietnam's enduring cultural distinctiveness. While this is obviously a feature of contemporary globalization, the history of the ao dai reveals that the garment has long played this same role of helping Vietnamese both fit into and distinguish themselves from powerful foreign cultures.

Hybrid Origins: How the Ao Dai Came to Represent Vietnam on the International Stage

Historian David Marr has described Vietnamese identity as forged in contrast to others, a sameness constructed to oppose difference. After years of research, he found that he was "repeatedly struck by the degree to which the Vietnamese have tended to define themselves in terms of their neighbors" (Marr 1971: 7). This practice has fueled struggles for independence and territorial expansion, but it has also led to a striking willingness to borrow from the cultures of both conquerors and conquered. The history of the ao dai places Vietnam's "national costume" squarely within this tradition of simultaneous adaptation and differentiation. What is today touted as the embodiment of a rich national culture and ancient ethnic traditions is in fact a bricolage constructed in response to powerful foreign influences. As such, charting the ao dai's distant and more recent history provides an instructive example of how global processes construct supposedly local cultures.

Chinese Confucianism and the Emergence of the Ao Dai

While the lines of the ao dai's long tunic and wide-legged pants seem so integral to Vietnamese dress, the outfit was unknown for most of Vietnam's history. In the centuries following the end of Chinese colonial rule in AD 939, most Vietnamese women wore an outfit consisting of a skirt (*vay*) and a halter top (*yem*).[11] Similar garments can be found among other ethnic groups in Vietnam, as well as in other Southeast Asian countries. Vietnamese scholar Doan Thi Tinh describes how women laboring in muddy rice paddies would raise the *vay* and tie the front and back hems together (1987: 65). The *yem* consisted of a diamond-shaped piece of fabric with two sets of ties securing it around the neck and back. By covering the chest, the stomach, and part of the back, the *yem* preserved some modesty but enabled women to bare their arms as they worked.

While the *yem* was suitable for working in the fields or at home, most women considered it too revealing for more public occasions. At such times, they would cover the *yem* with a long shirt known as the *ao tu than*, or four-paneled tunic. The *ao tu than* was worn open, with the flaps either falling loose in front or tied together about the waist. The neck of the tunic was either collarless or had a thin stand-up, mandarin-style collar. Women might also wear shorter versions of the *ao tu than* belted with fabrics in contrasting colors.

The purported immodesty of the *vay* and *yem* made them the target of numerous sartorial campaigns. During the fifteenth century, troops from China's Ming Dynasty occupied Vietnam for twenty years and pursued a brutal policy of assimilation. Condemning the *vay* as immoral and immodest, the Ming forced women to adopt Chinese-style pants and prohibited them from showing their feet (Nguyen Van Ky 1995: 237; Doan Thi Tinh 1987: 39). After recovering the country's independence in 1427, the victorious Le Dynasty embarked on its own program of Confucianization, which included promoting more modest garments, but most women continued to wear the *vay* and *yem* (Nguyen Van Ky 1995: 237).

Four centuries later, the newly ascendant Nguyen Dynasty likewise pursued a series of orthodox Confucian reforms.[12] In 1826, Emperor Minh Mang banned the *vay*, which was derided as unseemly "'bottomless pants'" (Nguyen Van Ky 1995: 238). Compliance with these laws varied by class. Pants became most popular among women from the ruling mandarin classes, who donned the garment as a sign of their high status. Peasants, particularly in the North, continued to find the *vay* the more convenient garment for working in the fields and engaging in petty trade. By the time of French conquest later that century, most women in the North had resumed wearing the *vay* (Nguyen Van Ky 1995: 238).

During this period, a precursor to the modern ao dai became popular for daily wear in northern cities and for holidays and festivals in the countryside. The outfit consisted of a loose-fitting shirt with a stand-up collar and a diagonal closure that ran along the side from neck to armpit and down the ribs. Although resembling the *ao tu than*, this ao dai had prominent features, such as its closure and collar, that were directly inspired by Chinese garments, themselves adapted from Manchu fashions. These associations, plus the garment's inconvenience for manual labor, may explain its greater popularity among the upper classes. Most women wore the ao dai over a brightly colored *yem*, but for festivals during the colder winter months they would often layer three or more ao dai of different colors. The upper buttons would be left unfastened, thus revealing the different layers (Doan Thi Tinh 1987: 70).

French and American Influences

In the 1860s, French forces began an assault on Vietnam. They quickly established a colony in the south and by the 1880s had extended their control to the central and northern regions. The ensuing seventy years of colonial rule heightened preexisting cultural differences between the city and the countryside and led to the emergence of an urban, Westernized middle class.

Catering to the developing tastes of this new bourgeoisie, a series of French-educated designers remodeled the loose-fitting ao dai into a garment closely resembling the one worn today. The most famous of these designers was Hanoian Nguyen Cat Tuong, who was more commonly known as Le Mur, the French translation of his given name. In 1935, Le Mur released a new, "trendy" ao dai. Directly inspired by the cut of European shirts and skirts, this ao dai featured puffy sleeves, lacy collars, buttoned cuffs, and scalloped hems. The outfit appeared in bright or pastel colors, which younger women would pair with white pants, instead of the traditional black. Even more notable than the decorative elements of this ao dai was the way Le Mur changed its fit. While the tunic still flowed open over the lower part of the body, the top fit much more closely to the figure, with darts at the chest and a nipped-in waist. This prompted many women to start wearing brassieres or corsets in place of the traditional *yem* (Doan Thi Tinh 1987: 77). Le Mur also tailored the pants in accordance with French fashion. Instead of being loose and belted, they were cut to fit more snugly through the waist and hips, gradually flaring down to the ankles. Le Mur publicized his design as well suited to "'show off the personal beauty of each person'" (Nguyen Van Ky 1995: 249). While peasants clung to the *yem*, *vay*, and *ao tu than*, and older urban women continued to prefer the looser ao dai, young women embraced these new ao dai and the European-inspired notions of the feminine form that inspired them. Just as the earlier loose-fitting ao dai had been associated with the Confucianized upper classes, the new ao dai served as a marker for an urban, educated elite which included comparatively liberated "new women" who came into frequent contact with Europeans.[13]

In 1954, the Geneva Accords ended French colonialism by dividing Vietnam into a communist North led by Ho Chi Minh and a democratic South under the presidency of Catholic Ngo Dinh Diem. The ao dai quickly fell into disfavor in the North, both because of its associations with the bourgeoisie and colonialism, and because the new leaders viewed it as impractical for workers constructing a socialist nation. Northern women did continue to wear the garment on special occasions and for important political functions, but in its looser, pre-Le Mur form.

Meanwhile, in the South, experimentation with the ao dai continued. Fueled by massive inputs of American aid, a consumer boom swept the capital city of Saigon. New body-conscious ao dai styles proliferated. Waists became even more cinched and sleeves tighter. Collars became higher, which emphasized the neck and restricted the wearer's movement, thus marking her as a member of the non-laboring classes. More radical experiments followed. The wife of Ngo Dinh Nhu, brother of the South Vietnamese president, popularized a type of ao dai with an elongated open neckline, but many reviled this design as immodest and aesthetically unappealing. Nevertheless, other ao dai styles with open necks, square necks, and shorter sleeves did become popular. Many women favored the "ao dai maxi," which featured a mandarin collar and was buttoned down the center, usually with Chinese-style fabric "frog" closures (Vai net 1995: 17). In the late 1960s, some Saigonese women began wearing miniskirts. Ao dai designers followed with their own "ao dai mini," a shorter version of the garment in which the tunic fell to the top of the knee. The slits in this ao dai were high enough to reveal skin from the waist to the ribs (Doan Thi Tinh 1987: 99). Around the same time, two Saigon tailors developed the final innovation that distinguishes today's ao dai: raglan sleeves. Cut diagonally from the neck to the armpit, these sleeves eliminate wrinkling around the shoulder or underarm, enabling an even closer fit, which emphasizes the upper body.

Socialism and the Creation of a National Symbol

On 30 April 1975, Northern tanks and troops streamed into Saigon and captured the Republic of Viet Nam's capital, which they promptly renamed Ho Chi Minh City.[14] The victorious communist government decried most aspects of Southern urban culture as decadent, bourgeois, and un-Vietnamese. This included the newer ao dai styles. Everyday clothes became simple and utilitarian. Ao dai were worn only on special occasions, such as weddings, and the preferred form of the garment was the more modest, pre-French and pre-American one. Doan Thi Tinh's historical study of Vietnamese clothing, written in the late 1980s, clearly demonstrates the force of this condemnation of Southerners' sartorial decadence. When the author's discussion reaches 1975, what has heretofore been a straightforward and reliable description of stylistic changes suddenly becomes a polemical account of cultural purity and pollution. Only the classic form of the ao dai merits praise for surviving the cultural contamination perpetrated by the "American puppet" regime:

> We must recognize that in that tangled mass of bamboo shavings, in front of the sharp, ferocious tip of that massive, frenzied fashion invasion, the ao dai of Vietnam, although deformed in some ways, still survived as evidence of the protracted struggle, until April 30, 1975, the day the South was entirely liberated. (Doan Thi Tinh 1987: 102, my translation)

In addition to symbolizing the victorious regime's rejection of foreign decadence, a return to the traditional, supposedly unadulterated ao dai had the political advantage of emphasizing the cultural unity of the entire country. More than a century of separation by French colonialism and the Cold War had exacerbated preexisting differences in dress among the three regions of the country. In celebrating one particular style of ao dai as the common denominator uniting these regions, the government was also rhetorically asserting its own legitimacy as the ruler of the unified country. Doan Thi Tinh states this succinctly:

> The ao dai of Vietnamese women has become a symbol of Vietnam in the eyes of the world's people. Seeing a woman wearing an ao dai, foreign visitors know right away that this is a Vietnamese woman. The ao dai has contributed to demonstrating the unity of the three regions, North, Center, and South; it proves that there is only

one unified country of Vietnam, unshakable. The ao dai is an achievement of a unique creativity, of the enduring struggle in which the good must defeat the bad, and a pure people must prevail against that which is foreign and unseemly. (107–8)

Despite such praise for the ao dai as a constituent element of Vietnamese identity, the garment retained its elitist connotations. With its bright colors and restrictions on the wearer's movement, the ao dai seemed an extravagance in a time of food shortages and redistribution of resources. In the decade following reunification, the ao dai was replaced in newspaper and magazine fashion spreads by styles reflecting an aesthetic of socialist androgyny that prized simplicity, labor, and frugality.

Economic Reform and the Ao Dai Craze

The heyday of socialism did not last long. By the mid-1980s, Vietnam's economy was in crisis. Geopolitically, Vietnam was dangerously isolated. The Vietnamese Communist Party responded by announcing a series of market-oriented reforms, known as *doi moi,* or renovation, that were intended to promote economic growth, increase exports, and attract foreign capital for business investment.

Progress under *doi moi* has been dramatic, particularly in terms of the population's rising standard of living. With increased incomes, especially in urban areas, Vietnamese by the mid-1990s were demanding more consumer goods. This led to an explosion of interest in fashion. Coming primarily from the United States, Paris, and Tokyo, these clothing styles – mostly for women – were hailed as fashionably modern (*mo-den*). Newspaper articles directed Vietnamese consumers to stores where they might find these clothes and described the resulting "fashion craze" as evidence that Vietnam had, after years of colonialism, war, and isolation, finally entered global markets.[15]

The proliferation of foreign fashion produced a predictable reaction in Vietnam: the self-conscious display for domestic and foreign audiences of clothing that was represented as uniquely Vietnamese. Combined with economic prosperity, it is this age-old need to differentiate that which is Vietnamese from that which is foreign that has fueled a recent resurgence of the ao dai. Interest in the garment has led to an ao dai craze that can be observed on a variety of levels, from working classes to elites.

The ao dai's revival can be dated to the First Miss Ao Dai contest, which was organized by the Ho Chi Minh City *Women's Newspaper* in 1989. In speaking with me about this competition, most observers described it as a signal that the drab days of scarcity and austerity had given way to relative prosperity and a concern with the aesthetics of daily life. In the words of one designer, "In the past, we lived by the proverb, 'enough to eat, warm clothes to wear (*an no mac am*).' That was when the country was struggling, and having enough to survive was good enough. Today, we can live by the proverb, 'eat well, dress beautifully (*an ngon mac dep*).'" Tailors and stallholders echo this idea that increased material means alone can explain heightened interest in fashion in general and the ao dai in particular.

The Ao Dai on the World Stage

While growing wealth has certainly enabled Vietnamese consumers to increase their consumption of clothing and other consumer goods, the hyperbolic nationalistic rhetoric surrounding discussion of the ao dai suggests that this particular commodity carries a significant cultural load. The ao dai is a polyvalent symbol that both embodies Vietnamese identity and represents it to others. To the domestic Vietnamese audience, Miss Vietnam's award in Tokyo signaled that the ao dai has become part of the international language of fashion. This in turn has created two pressures, each of which presents drawbacks and opportunities.

The first pressure centers on the desire and injunction for cross-cultural communication. On the positive side, economic openness in the form of trade and foreign investment draws Vietnamese into systems of relationships that afford the opportunity to display Vietnamese culture to foreigners in a sort of free marketplace that places a premium on authenticity and distinctiveness. Miss Vietnam was one of forty-nine equal contestants – a metaphor for Vietnam being one of many countries whose traditions and history deserve outsiders' respect and appreciation.

The drawback is that something gets lost in the process of representation and translation. Communication of culture involves modification, and this can lead to static images in which the rich heritage being represented becomes flattened or caricaturish. The ao dai becomes a kind of free-floating symbol available to non-Vietnamese to be picked up and reinterpreted. This was already evident in the early 1990s, when the movie *Indochine* inspired an Asian-themed fashion trend known as Indo-chic. Taking the ao dai and the more common peasant outfit of brown or black pajamas as cues, design houses such as Chanel and Richard Tyler released their own variations. A *New York Times Magazine* fashion spread made the cycle complete by taking these clothes to Vietnam, where they were modeled by regular Vietnamese women. From the perspective of Vietnamese observers, the problem with such acts of translation and reinterpretation is that the clothing code associated with the garments' Vietnamese origins becomes garbled. A photograph taken in Ho Chi Minh City's colonial post office paired a lavish ao dai with a peasant conical hat – a combination that would be incongruous in daily Vietnamese life. The mandarin collar and frog closures originally celebrated as the height of modesty by a conservative Confucian dynasty were now described for Western eyes as "like erotic flash points" (Shenon 1993).

With cross-cultural communication, therefore, comes a loss of control over the meaning of the items being displayed and the risk that their integrity will be compromised or degraded. While the ao dai's history suggests that such integrity is in fact chimerical, for there has never been a single, pure form of the garment, the outfit's current availability as one style among many on the international market raises the stakes involved in the myth of authenticity, even as it makes that myth harder to maintain.

The second pressure comes from the opportunity that allowing foreign goods into Vietnam affords for borrowing and adapting ideas, developing exciting new clothes, and marketing items that the public will view as raising its quality of life. One man who has taken advantage of the opportunities offered by Vietnam's open markets is an artist named Si Hoang, who by the mid-1990s had become one of Saigon's top ao dai designers. Si Hoang's ao dai designs first appeared at the Miss Ao Dai competition in 1989. Credited as the first designer to paint, rather than embroider, the ao dai, he has liberally borrowed from non-Vietnamese artistic movements. From the West, he has adopted features of abstract art, such as in a recent collection of ao dai inspired by Picasso and Matisse (Figure 2.2). Closer to home, Si Hoang has turned to the ethnic minority groups living in Vietnam's highlands. In 1996 he released a collection of painted velvet ao dai that employed motifs from these groups' weavings. When I spoke to him at the time, he was working on a show that would feature ao dai inspired by each of Vietnam's fifty-four ethnic groups.

Just as foreign embracing of the ao dai sparks a fear that outsiders will misinterpret the garment's meaning, experiments with foreign influences by designers such as Si Hoang lead to the parallel fear that Vietnamese themselves might forget which version of the ao dai is "authentic" and thus lose this cherished form. Si Hoang himself seems acutely sensitive to such concerns. He repeatedly emphasized in our conversation that his designs consist exclusively of decorative innovations, such as painting or buttons. He has not tampered with what he refers to as the traditional design of the ao dai: "I think that the ao dai we have had up to now, its design has already reached perfection. If I changed the way of tailoring or designing it, then it wouldn't be an ao dai anymore, but something like the cheongsam of China or a dress worn by Westerners." To Si Hoang, then, the ao dai's form is what makes it quintessentially Vietnamese.

While Si Hoang asserts that the authenticity of the ao dai lies in its form, the history that I recounted above – one which is well-documented by Vietnamese and French historians – suggests that the ao dai's shape evolved in

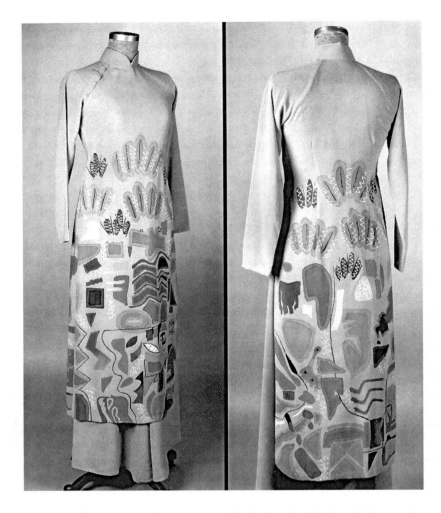

Figure 2.2 A Si Hoang ao dai showcases the designer's skills in adapting modern art styles. Photo by John L. Buckingham/College of the Holy Cross.

response to strong foreign influences. When I asked Si Hoang about this, he asserted that the ao dai is a uniquely Vietnamese and indigenous creation:

> In the past, Vietnamese women wore a type of ao dai which isn't like today's – the *ao tu than* – and after that it was improved slowly so it would be appropriate for an ever-developing lifestyle until it reached its present form. The Vietnamese ao dai isn't something which originated from China. No, it came from the *ao tu than*, the tunic with four panels which slowly became two.

The feature stories that followed Miss Vietnam's victory in Tokyo echo Si Hoang's adamant assertion that the ao dai is an indigenous garment that evolved in harmony with the material and cultural conditions of the Vietnamese people. One observer noted that when he looks at the S-shape of Vietnam on the map (see map 1b, p. xii), he "sees in it the graceful curve of the Vietnamese ao dai" (Thao Thi 1995: 11). One gets the image of the ao dai literally emerging of whole cloth from the soil of Vietnam.[16]

Others ascribe the Vietnamese-ness of the garment to its reflection of Vietnamese women's fundamental character. An article in a Saigon woman's newspaper recounts the history of the ao dai, noting that it has developed in response to significant outside influence. In the author's opinion, this evolution has allowed the garment to reach an ideal form that epitomizes the character of Vietnamese women:

> Something which must be noted about the ao dai of Vietnamese women is its "soul." It truly is appropriate only for those with the slight stature and slimness of Asian women. It demands that the wearer have a self-effacing bearing, cautious, moving deliberately, lightly. Because of that, it isn't without reason that there was a time when people forced female pupils from sixth to twelfth grade to wear the ao dai as a uniform. The goal was to train girls in a modest, cautious, and refined manner in their dress and their bearing, so that they can become young Vietnamese women of grace and politeness. (Vai net 1995: 17, my translation)

In this way, the ao dai is not just a vehicle for expressing Vietnamese femininity, but a pedagogical tool for inculcating it.[17] The article concludes with the following assertion of the ao dai's symbolic importance today:

> Many researchers in fashion and ethnic studies within and outside our country say that the ao dai of Vietnamese women today has achieved a standard dreamed of: merging both traditional features and contemporary features, both reflecting the unique essence of our people, and answering the increasing aesthetic needs of this age. (ibid.: 17)

While these accounts unabashedly celebrate the ao dai as an embodiment of the traditional and the modern, they also hint at an underlying ambivalence about what truly constitutes each of these qualities. Both get oversimplified: the traditional is held to be uniquely Vietnamese, pure, simple, and unsullied, while the modern finds expression in the drive for more sumptuous lifestyles in which aesthetic desires eclipse material necessities. At the core of this contrast lies the conflict that David Marr claims has haunted Vietnam throughout history: how can Vietnamese incorporate the new and the foreign without losing that which is old and unique? The ao dai, itself the result of significant foreign influence throughout its history, now becomes celebrated as the pinnacle of a Vietnamese tradition that must be carefully protected against undue outside influence, even as it simultaneously serves as a vehicle for encountering and mediating that influence by representing Vietnam in the global organization of cultural diversity.

In the rhetoric of contemporary cultural politics, the ao dai's protean identity as partly foreign and yet uniquely Vietnamese makes it a contingent and contested symbol susceptible to hyperbolic assertions of its "true" nature. Precisely because the meaning of the ao dai seems to originate from so many sources, it facilitates a discourse in which diverse people can participate. With its flowing lines and mandarin collar, it seems exotic to foreign fashion cognoscenti, but the French colonial influences on its cut and design mute this effect. Unlike other Vietnamese customs, such as teeth lacquering or betel-nut chewing, the ao dai is exotic enough to be enchanting, but not so Other as to be inaccessible or unpalatable.

The garment has a similar effect on domestic audiences. The ao dai is uniquely Vietnamese in that no other culture wears the costume on a regular basis, but part of its attraction lies in the fact that it is not an ordinary garment made banal by its prevalence in daily life. It occupies a middle ground between the foreign and the domestic that makes it well suited to represent Vietnamese resilience and the ingenuity required to incorporate outside ideas without losing one's identity. This hybrid character, rather than the ao dai's purported indigenousness, makes it the quintessential symbol of Vietnamese identity. That such a Vietnamese cultural icon is now celebrated by international audiences rather than demeaned as inferior, as was the case for other elements of Vietnamese society during the centuries of Chinese and French occupation, adds to its domestic appeal. The ao dai, like Vietnam, has arrived on the international stage.

The Making and Marketing of Ao Dai in Ho Chi Minh City

As a national symbol touted in cultural rhetoric, the ao dai provides a metaphor for debating the pros and cons of combining the local with the global and the traditional with the modern. The juxtaposition is not simply symbolic, but concrete, in that the ao dai's development to this point has entailed repeated borrowing and adapting of foreign design innovations and decorative details. The central players in this dramatic history have existed within the upper strata of society and culture: imperial courts, French colonial fashion houses, presidential palaces, contemporary design studios, and international beauty contests. Throughout the story, the ao dai as envisioned and worn by the upper, knowledge-producing classes seems to have an existence separate from that of the garment occasionally donned by a peasant to welcome the New Year. Today, this gap appears to be narrowing. As economic reforms lead to growing incomes throughout the country, Vietnam is experiencing a rise in mass consumerism, and the ao dai has become a garment of interest to a greater variety of classes. With the expansion of the media, more information becomes available, enabling more people to express diverse tastes. This means that ao dai innovation does not just emanate from the couture design studio of someone like Si Hoang, but occurs in the more mundane settings of the thousands of home workshops and tailor studios that produce the vast majority of the ao dai purchased in Vietnam. On this level, the growing cosmopolitan orientation of both producers and consumers drives ongoing efforts to incorporate global influences into the ao dai. One of the most important sources of information about these influences comes from ao dai tailors' and sellers' kin living overseas.

To Market, To Market: How Traders Market and Consumers Select Ao Dai

The average Vietnamese consumer purchases an ao dai in one of two ways: either she goes to a tailor, chooses a fabric from her inventory, and has her sew it, or she goes to a market, picks out the fabric herself, and then takes it to a tailor (Figure 2.3). The former offers convenience, while the latter offers greater selection and cheaper prices. As part of my dissertation research, I spent a year observing daily life in both these settings. My research focused on Ben Thanh market, a large and famous structure located in the center of Ho Chi Minh City. Offering just about everything the average Saigon consumer might need, Ben Thanh contains over 150 stalls selling fabric and 350 specializing in clothing. Women own and run approximately 85 per cent of these stalls. On the higher end of the retail spectrum are Saigon's downtown tailor shops. Also largely run by women, these shops cater to both foreign tourists and wealthier locals. In both settings, I spoke at length with merchants about how they selected and marketed their goods. I also observed hundreds of transactions with customers in order to get a sense of what features they sought and the strategies sellers employed to clinch the purchase.

As Saigon consumers become more fashion-conscious, the sellers of cloth and clothing in Ben Thanh market make a concerted effort to persuade a customer that a given item is the newest, most "*mo-den,*" and best suited for her particular coloring and figure. To do this, they often copy the designs of famous makers such as Si Hoang or use props such as catalogs and fashion magazines to convince the buyer of the popularity of a particular item. One day while I was speaking to a stall owner who specialized in ao dai fabrics, two customers, a mother and daughter, approached. They were looking for ao dai fabric for the daughter, a woman in her early thirties. The initial stages

Figure 2.3 A Ho Chi Minh City marketplace stall displays fabric panels, including ones used for making ao dai. Photo by Ann Marie Leshkowich.

of the transaction focused on what color and styles would be appropriate for the daughter's coloring, with green emerging as the consensus choice. The seller held up each of the panels being considered and wrapped them tightly around her chest in order to show the customers how the hand-painted design would look on the bosom and flowing toward the ground. She also showed the buyers "catalogs," which consisted of photo albums she had assembled herself from a variety of snapshots and Vietnamese fashion magazines. She mentioned that the panel in which the buyers seemed most interested was copied from a design by Si Hoang. Throughout the exchange, the potential customers maintained a rather cynical stance toward such claims, but they finally selected precisely the panel that the seller had identified as based on a *mo-den* Si Hoang design.

Like most other sellers in Ben Thanh market, this stallholder had carefully selected the panels displayed in her stall in accordance with her reading of local consumer tastes. She then marketed her designs as cheaper versions of these prestigious *mo-den* items. As the shopping encounter described above illustrates, however, the trader was not simply supplying items to meet pre-formulated consumer demands. Rather, she was an active shaper of ideas about what constitutes the *mo-den* and fashionable. Like most customers I met, the mother-daughter pair in this transaction came to the stall with vague preferences as to ao dai color and design. They actively solicited the trader's advice about how to concretize these desires, although they carefully cloaked their need for information in an air of indifference that would strengthen their bargaining position as the transaction moved toward a conclusion. Despite their skepticism, the consumers seemed swayed by the trader's performative display of fashion knowledge, particularly her familiarity with Si Hoang's designs and ability to produce evidence in the form of homemade catalogs to substantiate her claims. This marketplace encounter thus entailed a transformative process of negotiation and exchange in which a certain knowledge about the desirability of a Si Hoang design was produced. Two consumers who may previously have had only vague ideas about Si Hoang and his designs left the stall obviously pleased with their decision to partake of this fashion trend, while the trader subsequently decided to devote even more of her stall to knock-offs of designer creations.

In addition to copying famous local designers, many Ben Thanh market traders pay close attention to the tastes of overseas Vietnamese who comprise a significant portion of their customer base. In the year 2000, over 300,000 overseas Vietnamese visited Vietnam (*The Saigon Times Daily*, 10 January 2001). Most of these visitors stayed in the South, as this region had previously been their home and many of their relatives remain there today. As Saigon's most famous market, Ben Thanh is a popular stop for visitors, and most make sure to buy ao dai fabric for themselves, their relatives, and their friends abroad. At the end of December 1996, one fabric seller told me that the vast majority of her customers during the past few weeks had been returning Vietnamese. Climatic and cultural differences between Vietnam and the temperate regions where most overseas Vietnamese now live have prompted ao dai fabric sellers in Ben Thanh to stock a greater array of fabrics, particularly heavier ones such as velvet and thick brocade. They also offer more daring styles, such as flocked velvet, in which bits of pulverized material create a pattern against a sheer, see-through background. Designs have likewise become bolder, with velvet panels decorated with lavishly sequined dragons or phoenixes becoming increasingly popular. Finally, because many overseas Vietnamese prefer ao dai with the tunic and pants sewn from matching fabric rather than the customary white or black, many stalls now stock a wide array of undecorated ao dai fabric.

Overseas Vietnamese also have a direct influence on Saigon tailors' ao dai designs. During the late 1970s and early 1980s, when the ao dai had fallen out of favor in Vietnam, overseas Vietnamese in the United States continued to experiment with style innovations. A student of mine who grew up near Little Saigon in southern California recalls the 1980s as a time when Vietnamese-Americans wanted to make the ao dai look more "Western." Fashion shows featured puffy sleeves and sweetheart necklines, or even more daring variations, such as sleeveless and one-sleeved tunics. While most Vietnamese returning to have ao dai made in Vietnam request the more "authentic" traditional form, some do voice a preference for a different neckline, a certain cut, or a particular length. The resulting styles transform the ao dai into something closer to an evening gown, as befits the special occasions for which most overseas Vietnamese will wear the garment. The tailors with whom I spoke in downtown Ho Chi Minh City told me that while some of these designs might not be appropriate for domestic tastes, others could be adapted. Some described overseas Vietnamese ao dai as more luxurious (*sang trong*) – a fitting symbol of Vietnam's prosperity and the aspirations of many middle-class Vietnamese to the kind of lifestyles they imagine their kinfolk enjoying abroad.

Circulating Fashion Knowledge within the Diaspora

While overseas Vietnamese customers play a role in traders' and tailors' selection of ao dai merchandise, the overseas Vietnamese population with whom these businesswomen have the most frequent and prolonged contact are their relatives. By the late 1990s, remittance flows between the nearly three million Vietnamese émigrés and their kin in Vietnam were widely estimated to exceed one billion US dollars annually. More than 80 per cent of this money was sent directly to individuals, rather than being invested in official development projects. While much of this money is used to cover day-to-day living expenses or one-time expenditures, such as a new television or motorbike, many of the tailors and traders I know use remittances as investment capital for their businesses. Perhaps even more significantly, the packages relatives mail back to Vietnam contain more than money. In addition to letters, Vietnamese resettled abroad regularly send foreign videos, CDs, fashion catalogs, magazines, and snapshots of daily life or special occasions in their adopted countries. For small-scale fashion entrepreneurs, these materials provide a valuable source of information about international clothing styles and trends, and they waste no time in capitalizing on this knowledge. Tuyet, Mai, and Tien provide three typical examples of the ways in which capital and information from overseas Vietnamese can facilitate the development of small businesses.[18]

On one of my first shopping excursions when I arrived in Saigon in 1994, I visited nearly every store located on the main strip of tailor shops along Dong Khoi Street. After seeing about a dozen nearly identical displays of merchandise, I entered a large boutique featuring more colorful and innovative styles. Fashioned from the same materials – raw silk, brocade, and light silk – as the clothes in neighboring shops, the items in this store blended Western clothing forms and colors with Vietnamese accents. Thinking that this store featured the most chic and up-to-date styles, I asked the owner, Tuyet, about the origins of the designs; she replied that they were all her own creations. A woman in her late thirties, Tuyet had worked as a secretary for a state firm until about five years before. Noticing the rapid increase in tourists and explosion of domestic consumerism, she opened her tailoring and clothing store with capital pooled from immediate and extended family living both within and outside Vietnam. Tuyet's sister, who lives in Seattle, has encouraged her to expand her business and regularly sends her newspaper columns and magazine spreads about fashion trends. Tuyet prides herself on providing superior-quality silks and designing styles that appeal equally to Vietnamese and foreigners for wear in business and professional settings. While she also offers standard tourist articles, she sees her future success as lying in cross-cultural styles that transcend kitsch. Right before my return to the United States, she told me that her sister had offered to help her open a boutique in Seattle.

Mai and Tuan are a married couple in their forties who own a large clothing stall in Ben Thanh market that specializes in a variety of women's clothes, including dresses, suits, tops, and leggings. Mai designs all of the clothes herself. Her three younger sisters help with the sewing and patterns. Mai has been selling clothing for over twenty years. A college student when the North Vietnamese army captured Saigon in 1975, Mai was forced to leave school when her father, a colonel in the South Vietnamese army, was sent to a re-education camp and her mother was forcibly relocated to the Mekong Delta.[19] To support her siblings, she started selling clothing on the black market. At that time, most of Mai's goods were smuggled items sent into the country by Vietnamese who had escaped abroad. Mai slowly developed her business and acquired a stall in Ben Thanh market in the mid-1980s. After several unsuccessful attempts to flee Vietnam, Tuan eventually joined Mai full-time in running the stall. Their business has grown steadily since the advent of economic reforms in 1989.

Both Mai and Tuan pay close attention to new styles, particularly to catalogs that friends and relatives in the United States send them. Mai often adapts drawings from Vogue, Butterick, or Simplicity catalogs, which she then promotes to her customers as "sewn from a catalog just sent from America." With an average turnaround time of less than a week, Mai can quickly translate the newest foreign styles into items that she knows will appeal to her loyal customer base of small shop owners and other traders. Tuan's sister lives in North Carolina and occasionally sends them some money, but the amounts are small and typically intended to help support Tuan's elderly parents. Nevertheless, Mai and Tuan dream of expanding their business, and their overseas relatives and friends form a key part of the plan. Tuan explains:

I would like to open a factory, but I don't have the facility yet. In the future, I think that the piece of land Mai and I have bought could serve as the production plant. We'll buy machines and then have some other workers work from their homes. We could have about thirty people working for us, that would be good. Most of our customers would be domestic, but we also have so many friends and relatives [overseas] who can help us with the American market. They know fashion, they know what styles are popular there with the *Viet Kieu* [overseas Vietnamese], who like goods produced in their homeland.[20] They'd help us be able to sell and develop, and we would also make clothes cheaply following catalogs. The clothing would be popular and the price would be right, not too expensive.

Like Mai and Tuan, Tien, who owns a stall in one of Ho Chi Minh City's wholesale markets, sees his overseas relatives as a key resource helping him to expand the women's clothing and pajama business that he owns with his wife. Tien's mother-in-law has lived in the United States for ten years and recently sent the family a computer, complete with graphics programs to help Tien design clothing. She regularly mails Tien fashion catalogs such as McCall's, which he credits as the primary source of inspiration for his designs. Although a computer and occasional catalogs may seem like a relatively small contribution to Tien's business, Tien describes these kinds of exchanges as essential to maintaining his competitive edge: "In this way, *Viet Kieu* send back some of their gray matter [i.e., their knowledge and skills] to help us out in Vietnam."

While Tuyet, Mai, and Tien sell mostly Western-style clothing, information and goods received from overseas Vietnamese can also help traders reinvent supposedly traditional merchandise. The Ben Thanh ao dai trader described above freely admitted to copying a Si Hoang design; indeed the resemblance of her and other traders' items to Si Hoang creations makes them considerably more attractive to their customers and likely results in higher profits. I have also documented trends in ao dai styles and fabrics that I believe originated with overseas Vietnamese customers' preferences. Occasionally, I would hear a Ben Thanh trader tell a domestic customer that a type of fabric she seemed interested in was "very *mo-den*. The *Viet Kieu* who come back to visit home buy this type of fabric a lot." Downtown tailor shops stock many types of ao dai panels, and I have also heard boutique owners tell prospective customers that an overseas Vietnamese had just bought a large quantity of a certain style. The implication is that the style is somehow trendier or more fashionable because a Vietnamese living overseas, who presumably has more cosmopolitan tastes, selected it.

Unlike Mai's touting of her fashions as inspired by American catalogs, traders' statements about the ao dai's appeal to overseas Vietnamese stop short of suggesting that the ao dai designs themselves have anything but a local origin. One explanation may be that their statements are accurate; the ao dai is simply a homegrown product that is little affected by input from outside sources. My research, however, suggests a different interpretation. Given the variety and importance of traders' contacts with overseas Vietnamese in other aspects of their fashion businesses, it would be naive to assume that these relations have no bearing on their ao dai designs. Indeed, occasional offhand comments and my observations in the marketplace suggest that these interactions do have an impact on the ao dai. Unlike other articles of clothing, such as dresses, skirts, pants, and suits, however, the ao dai is a symbolically charged item whose appeal rests largely on its associations with Vietnam's national history and character. Just as Si Hoang downplays Chinese, French, or American fashion sensibilities in asserting that the ao dai evolved directly from the Vietnamese *ao tu than*, small-scale ao dai sellers are reluctant to admit that they have been influenced by overseas Vietnamese tastes or by ao dai-inspired styles from the foreign designers who have promoted Indo-chic. So much of the ao dai's cultural currency stems from its aura of supposed indigenous authenticity that too much discussion of the impact of foreign ideas, or even overseas Vietnamese tastes, might contaminate the article and threaten tailors' and stallholders' positions as its purveyors.

In representing an ao dai style as popular among overseas Vietnamese or in using information about the ao dai supplied by emigrated relatives to rework their own versions of the original item, traders must walk a fine line between concealing this interaction and reaping the benefits that such foreign prestige imparts to their products. When a panel of judges in Tokyo proclaims the ao dai to be the best national costume, they put an international seal of approval on the garment. This acclaim can be freely celebrated within Vietnam for it does not call into question the garment's sacred status as a marker of authentic Vietnamese identity. Similarly, Si Hoang can use cubist images or ethnic weaving motifs to decorate his ao dai, so long as he is careful to point out that he preserves and respects the garment's time-honored form. When, however, foreigners or quasi-foreign Vietnamese participate even marginally in transforming the ao dai sold to domestic consumers, they challenge perceptions of the garment's authenticity. The traders and tailors I know must balance the attraction of disclosing the sources of their stylistic innovation with this need to preserve the ao dai's sacred orthodoxy.

Conclusion: Cosmopolitan Women, Traditional Fashions

In this chapter, I have documented the historical emergence of the ao dai as an ambivalent but potent symbol of Vietnamese identity. Its hybridity makes it particularly appealing to contemporary domestic consumers, who see in the garment the opportunity both to assert national tradition and to embrace an international vision of cosmopolitan chic. They are supported in this project by ao dai producers and sellers, who use a combination of overt displays of local taste and covert acquisition of international knowledge from diasporic kin to fashion themselves and their goods as authoritative representatives of style.

By focusing on how small-scale traders and tailors design and market ao dai styles to their customers, I seek to address a gap in knowledge about the circulation of fashion. Located at a nexus between the global and the local, as well as between production and consumption, the traders I studied serve as cross-cultural mediators. As the above examples from my fieldwork suggest, traders' and tailors' abilities to act as mediators are significantly enhanced through ongoing relations with overseas kin and their gifts of money, information, and clothing. Advertising these channels of communication during marketplace encounters with consumers adds to the ao dai's appeal, even as traders try to conceal them out of a need to protect their own access to information and to preserve the aura of authenticity surrounding their product.

Their willingness to explore new style trends gives businesspeople such as Tien, Mai, and Tuyet what Ulf Hannerz (1990) has termed a cosmopolitan outlook. In a world marked by an "organization of diversity," Hannerz claims that cosmopolitans possess the following traits:

> a stance toward diversity itself, toward the co-existence of cultures in the individual experience . . . At the same time, however, cosmopolitanism can be a matter of competence, and competence of both a generalized and a more specialized kind. There is an aspect of a state of readiness, a personal ability to make one's way into other cultures through listening, looking, intuiting, and reflecting. And there is cultural competence in the stricter sense of the terms, a built-up skill in maneuvering more or less expertly with a particular system of meanings and meaningful forms. (1990: 239)

What is most useful about Hannerz's definition is that it combines an orientation, an interest in the novel and unique, with practicality, namely the ability to understand and interpret diversity.

It is precisely this cosmopolitan outlook that traders like the ones I studied are frequently assumed to lack because gender and the small scope of their enterprises are presumed to give them a local orientation.[21] At first glance, the traders and boutique owners I met seem to support such an expectation. Retail trade in general, and marketplace selling in particular, have long been gendered as feminine in Vietnam – a designation that both reflects and reproduces the lower status and presumed insignificance of traders and their activities

(Leshkowich 2000).[22] Employing no more than one or two dozen workers who produce garments at home, the "entrepreneurs" I studied work on a scale so tiny as to seem undeserving of this label. Producing new garments in batches of ten or twenty, they seem risk-averse and focused on day-to-day survival, rather than on long-term growth. Given the small size of their operations, they understandably rely on cheap and informal sources of information sent to them by kin, rather than more scientific marketing studies. As useful as such strategies may be, the specific economic and political circumstances of development in Vietnam suggest that they are tools of last resort used by those who lack more formal and more profitable means to expand their businesses. Even in an environment of economic reform, the state retains total political control and a firm grip on economic "liberalization." Complex foreign investment laws designed to protect unprofitable state-run firms, minimal steps toward privatization, incoherent and contradictory property laws, and ambiguous lines of authority over business regulation combine to create an uncertain economic environment. This setup favors those with formal or informal connections to the party: high-level bureaucrats, operators of state-run industries, their relatives, and private businesspeople with the connections or capital to pay hefty "fees" – a euphemism for bribes. Not surprisingly, the vast majority of these people are male.

Although such characterizations contain an element of truth, my account of traders' businesses and the items that circulate through their stalls demonstrates that their businesses are far more complicated and global in their scope. Mai, Tuyet, Tien, and others are sources of tremendous creativity and resourcefulness, and it is traders like them who continue to cater to the needs of most consumers in Vietnam. Their means of doing business are also relatively sophisticated, in that they rely on frequent information sent to them from abroad. Rather than leaving them behind, economic and cultural globalization has led to a democratization of knowledge and the opening up of opportunities for certain types of entrepreneurs – many of them female – to capitalize on this knowledge.[23]

While the term "democratization" suggests that access to international networks is no longer confined to Vietnam's elites, it would be misleading to assume that it has become universal. The mostly female entrepreneurs whom I studied tend to come from families like Mai's, which had been part of an urban middle class displaced by the communist victory in 1975. Tormented by or disenchanted with the new regime, many of these women's relatives fled the country. More than twenty years later, the displacement that led to their marginalization within a socialist society and scattered their families around the globe had been transformed into a valuable economic and cultural resource. The relatively new situation of a vast Vietnamese diaspora in which women serve as the primary conduits for ongoing communication presents substantial business opportunities. This interaction has clearly facilitated small-scale entrepreneurs' production and marketing of foreign-style commodities, but it has also had a profound effect on the revival of the ao dai. While other aspects of "traditional culture" are being resurrected or revived, no other Vietnamese outfit is experiencing the same exuberant resurgence as the ao dai.[24] It cannot merely be a coincidence that this item has also received significant international attention, a fact that traders learn about through newspapers, magazines, and their diasporic contacts.

In spite of impassioned cultural rhetoric touting the ao dai's indigenous authenticity, attention to the circulation of the ao dai domestically and globally in both the past and the present reveals that its enduring popularity stems from its multi-national, hybrid origins that make it a garment amenable to interpretation by both Vietnamese and non-Vietnamese in standardized displays of cultural distinctiveness, or homogenized heterogeneity. Whereas earlier versions of the ao dai were crafted by cross-cultural elites, such as a Confucianized emperor or a French-educated artist, today's ao dai is being shaped by thousands of independent tailors, mostly women, who draw on a varied cross-cultural array of resources. Through its history of incorporating foreign influences in uniquely Vietnamese ways, the ao dai is not just a fitting symbol of Vietnam's past, but of a globalized present in which innovative women engage in transnational, multi-faceted personal relations and transform them into productive, profitable resources.

Notes

1. I would like to thank the following people for their comments on this chapter and the 1999 Association for Asian Studies conference paper on which it is based: Carla Jones, Sandra Niessen, Mary Steedly, Hue-Tam Ho Tai, Jennifer Cole, Penny van Esterik, Stephen O'Harrow, Sara Friedman, Sandra Teresa Hyde, Christine Walley, Noah Berger, series editor Joanne Eicher, and one anonymous reviewer. John L. Buckingham, Kurt Hultgren, and Joel Villa of College of the Holy Cross graciously helped prepare the photos. My research in Vietnam was sponsored by the College of Social Sciences and Humanities of the National University of Ho Chi Minh City and benefited from the help and advice of Vo Van Sen, Ngo Van Le, Bui Khanh The, Tran Thi Kim Lien, and the stallholders of Ben Thanh market. Fieldwork was funded by the Joint Committee on Southeast Asia of the Social Science Research Council and the American Council of Learned Societies with funds provided by the Andrew W. Mellon Foundation, the Ford Foundation, and the Henry Luce Foundation; a Fulbright-Hays Doctoral Dissertation Research Abroad Fellowship from the United States Department of Education; a Merit Fellowship from Harvard University; and an International

Predissertation Fellowship from the Social Science Research Council and the American Council of Learned Societies with funds provided by the Ford Foundation.

2. My use of the term "fashion" requires explanation. As Sandra Niessen points out (in the Afterword to this volume), the term is hardly straightforward. Through its association with a systematized cycle of innovation over time, "fashion" has typically not been seen to include non-Western societies. As we look at clothing styles and uses around the world, however, it becomes increasingly apparent that exactly this kind of fashion does indeed exist outside the West. It is for this reason that I use the term fashion in this chapter. The Vietnamese language also suggests that Vietnamese clothing tastes and practices constitute fashion in this sense, for the word for fashion is *thoi trang*, a compound composed of *thoi*, or time, and *trang*, dress or decoration.

3. Mary Douglas (Douglas and Isherwood 1978) and Pierre Bourdieu (1984) were some of the earliest contemporary anthropologists to call for anthropological study of consumption. Other noteworthy studies include Abu-Lughod (1990), Breckenridge (1995), Burke (1996), Comaroff (1990), de Certeau (1984), de Certeau et al. (1998), Freeman (2000), Friedman (1994), Howes (1996), Mackay (1997), McCracken (1988), Miller (1987 and 1995a), Parry and Bloch (1989), Rutz and Orlove (1989), Tobin (1992), and Weismantel (1989).

4. The idea that regimes of commodity capitalism challenge indigenous and supposedly more authentic cultural and social systems has long roots in anthropology, dating from Malinowski (1961 [1922]) and Mauss's (1990 [1925]) use of anthropological evidence to attack the concept of *homo economicus*. While such oppositions certainly can exist (see, e.g., Taussig 1980), they cannot be assumed a priori. For a detailed history and critique of this good/bad opposition between authentic culture and inauthentic consumption, see Miller (1995b).

5. Several scholars have noted that this gender bias, as well as the male/female and production/consumption dichotomies upon which it rests, stems from the late eighteenth- to early twentieth-century emergence of manufacturing in Europe and North America. During that time, a rising middle class began to view the world as separated into the public sphere of male work and the private sphere of female housekeeping (see, e.g., Davidoff and Hall 1987 and Nava 1997). When women did enter the public sector to shop, their activities were critiqued as illicit and self-indulgent, a chastening rhetoric which Susan Bordo (2000) argues continues to this day.

6. Examples of commodities studied by anthropologists, mostly from the perspective of consumption rather than circulation, include Coca-Cola (Miller 1997), bread (Weismantel 1989), motor scooters (Hebdige 1988), soap (Burke 1996), soap operas (Abu-Lughod 1995, Das 1995, Miller 1992), home decoration (Gullestad 1992), personal stereos (du Gay et al. 1997), beauty contests (Wilk 1995), and sugar (Mintz 1985).

7. Richard Wilk likewise sees a link between displaying or understanding diversity and asserting power: "The *dimensions* across which they [different cultures] vary are becoming more limited, and therefore more mutually intelligible. In this way the societies competing for global economic and cultural dominance build their hegemony not through direct imposition, but by presenting universal categories and standards by which all cultural differences can be defined" (1995: 118). Wilk includes in these

categories things like feminine beauty, the focus of his study, but also economic indicators such as standards of living and GNP (131, n.8).

8. While the reasons for this mobilization of women to display national essences and traditions can vary according to context and historical circumstances, I suspect that a primary reason for the prevalence of the woman/nation association is colonialism and, in Asia, Orientalism. As Emma Tarlo describes for India (1996), Indian men tended to adopt variations on British suits as part of a mimicry strategy that, among other things, might help them access educational and employment opportunities. Women tended to continue to wear traditional forms of dress because to do otherwise would too clearly challenge notions of modesty and decorum. Women's dress thus came to be seen as a potent encapsulation of Indian identity, both for Indians seeking to ensure the preservation of national culture and for colonial authorities seeking to justify their rule as a mission to rescue Indian women from exploitation by traditional patriarchal culture.

9. This point is taken directly from Mies (1986). For discussions of the negative impact of globalization, economic development, and capitalism on women, see also Boserup (1970), Bonería and Sen (1981), Bonería and Feldman (1992), Bourque and Warren (1991), Guyer and Peters (1987), Lim (1983), Mohanty (1997), Nash and Fernandez-Kelly (1983), Ong (1987), Salaff (1995), and Wolf (1992).

10. The Vietnamese refer to small-scale market and street traders as *tieu thuong*. This term literally means small trader, with the word "*tieu*" having the same connotations as the English "petty": small, insignificant, or trivial.

11. According to Nguyen Van Ky, the skirt appeared in two variations: a closed garment made from a long piece of fabric sewn in a sheath stopping at the belt, and an open version that was shorter and not sewn (Nguyen Van Ky 1995: 237).

12. Woodside (1988) provides an excellent discussion of the Nguyen Dynasty's Confucian policies.

13. As Tai (1992) points out, these so-called new women were problematic figures, precisely because their Westernized manners and purported ease in public places and among foreigners, including men, challenged traditional notions of the modest and demure woman. Hence, when Le Mur's ao dai first appeared, it seemed quite shocking.

14. While Saigon today is officially known as Ho Chi Minh City, the older name is commonly used to refer to the central downtown area. I follow local convention in using the terms interchangeably.

15. While these accounts suggest an uncritical passion for things foreign, my discussions with young cosmopolitan women reveal greater ambivalence and selectivity in adopting "new" fashion. Undeniably enthusiastic about being able to exercise greater choice in clothing, every woman I interviewed nonetheless expressed concern about selecting "appropriate" styles. This term encompasses a host of criteria – lighter pastel colors, looser fit, more frills, and greater coverage of legs, midriffs, and arms – that, to Vietnamese women, serve to distinguish them from the more audacious foreign consumers who drive international fashion trends.

16. Looking at ao dai worn in Vietnamese beauty pageants in the United States, Nhi T. Lieu notes a similar tendency to claim, despite evidence to the contrary, that the ao dai is a pure and untainted Vietnamese product (2000: 128).

17. The pedagogical utility of the ao dai is reflected in the fact that it has once again become a common uniform for high school girls. By restricting their movement, the garment literally crafts them as gentle and modest females.

18. With the exception of the well-known designer Si Hoang, all names provided are pseudonyms, and identifying details have been changed to protect anonymity.

19. Mai's experiences parallel those of many other traders at the end of what Americans refer to as the Vietnam War and Vietnamese tend to call the American War. Like many middle-class Saigonese, Mai's parents supported the Republic of Viet Nam, the United States-backed regime of South Vietnam, as opposed to the communist government of the Democratic Republic of Viet Nam, based in the Northern capital of Hanoi and supported by guerrilla movements throughout South Vietnam. After the Northern victory, Southerners who had supported the Republic of Viet Nam or the United States were punished through imprisonment in reeducation camps or internal exile to remote rural provinces.

20. Although widely used by Vietnamese living inside and outside Vietnam, the term *Viet Kieu* can be pejorative, in that it can be used to mark Vietnamese as lesser citizens of their adopted countries and because *Viet Kieu* are often seen by other Vietnamese as having acquired certain negative personality traits and aggressive behaviors. While I retain this term when it appears in direct quotes, I prefer in my own discussions to use the neutral phrase "overseas Vietnamese."

21. Hannerz himself seems to make these assumptions, as evidenced by his unsubstantiated claim that Nigerian women smuggling goods between Lagos and London possess an unaltered "local" worldview (1996: 103).

22. So prevalent is this idea of trade as a female activity that male stallholders such as Tien must endure his female colleagues' continual teasing about his masculinity. Male traders often respond by assuming a stance of alienation from their work, typically by describing a hobby or alternative occupation as their true vocation (see Leshkowich 2000).

23. For similar discussions of how globalization and the spread of mass consumerism have created opportunities for diasporic female South Asian entrepreneurs, see Bhachu (Chapter 4 of this volume and 1997) and Khan (1992).

24. The revival of tradition has been most marked in the area of religious practices. See, for example, Malarney (1996), Kleinen (1999) and Luong (1992).

References

Abu-Lughod, Lila (1990), "The Romance of Resistance: Tracing Transformations of Power through Bedouin Women," *American Ethnologist* 17(1): 41–55.

—— (1995), "The Objects of Soap Opera: Egyptian Television and the Cultural Politics of Modernity," in Daniel Miller (ed.), *Worlds Apart*, London and New York: Routledge.

Appadurai, Arjun (1990), "Disjuncture and Difference in the Global Cultural Economy," *Public Culture* 2(3): 1–24.

—— (1996), *Modernity at Large*, Minneapolis: University of Minnesota Press.

Benería, Lourdes and Feldman, Shelley (eds) (1992), *Unequal Burden: Economic Crises, Persistent Poverty, and Women's Work*, Boulder, CO: Westview.

Benería, Lourdes and Sen, Gita (1981), "Accumulation, Reproduction, and Women's Role in Economic Development: Boserup Revisited," *Signs* 2: 279–98.

Bhachu, Parminder (1997), "Dangerous Design: Asian Women and the New Landscapes of Fashion," in Ann Oakley and Juliet Mitchell (eds), *Who's Afraid of Feminism?* London: Hamish Hamilton.

Bordo, Susan (2000), "Hunger as Ideology," in Juliet B. Schor and Douglas B. Holt (eds), *The Consumer Society Reader*, New York: The New Press.

Boserup, Ester (1970), *Woman's Role in Economic Development*, London: Allen and Unwin.

Bourdieu, Pierre (1984), *Distinction*, Cambridge, MA: Harvard University Press.

Bourque, Susan C. and Warren, Kay B. (1991), "Women, Technology, and International Development Ideologies: Analyzing Feminist Voices," in Micaela di Leonardo (ed.), *Gender at the Crossroads of Knowledge*, Berkeley: University of California Press.

Breckenridge, Carol A. (ed.) (1995), *Consuming Modernity: Public Culture in a South Asian World*, Minneapolis and New York: University of Minnesota Press.

Burke, Timothy (1996), *Lifebuoy Men, Lux Women: Commodification, Consumption, and Cleanliness in Modern Zimbabwe*, Durham, NC: Duke University Press.

Comaroff, Jean (1990), "Goodly Beasts and Beastly Goods," *American Ethnologist* 17(2): 195–216.

Das, Veena (1995), "On Soap Opera: What Kind of Anthropological Object Is It?" in Daniel Miller (ed.), *Worlds Apart*, London and New York: Routledge.

Davidoff, Leonore and Hall, Catherine (1987), *Family Fortunes: Men and Women of the English Middle Class, 1780–1850*, Chicago: University of Chicago Press.

de Certeau, Michel (1984), *The Practice of Everyday Life*, Berkeley: University of California Press.

——, et al. (1998), *The Practice of Everyday Life, Volume 2*, Minneapolis: University of Minnesota Press.

Doan Thi Tinh (1987), *Tim hieu Trang Phuc Viet Nam* (Investigating Vietnamese Costumes), Ha Noi: Nha Xuat Ban Van Hoa.

Douglas, Mary and Isherwood, Baron (eds) (1978), *The World of Goods*, London: Allen Lane.

du Gay, Paul, Hall, Stuart, Janes, Linda, Mackay, Hugh, and Negus, Keith (1997), *Doing Cultural Studies: The Story of the Sony Walkman*, London: Sage.

Freeman, Carla (2000), *High Tech and High Heels in the Global Economy: Women, Work and Pink-Collar Identities in the Caribbean*, Durham, NC: Duke University Press.

Friedman, Jonathan (1994), *Consumption and Identity*, Chur, Switzerland: Harwood Academic Publishers.

Gullestad, Marianne (1992), *The Art of Social Relations*, Oslo: Scandinavian University Press.

Guyer, Jane, and Peters, Pauline (eds) (1987), *Special Issue: Conceptualizing the Household, Development and Change* 2.

Hannerz, Ulf (1990), "Cosmopolitans and Locals in World Culture," *Theory, Culture, and Society* 7: 237–51.

—— (1996), *Transnational Connections*, London and New York: Routledge.

Hebdige, Dick (1988), *Hiding in the Light: On Images and Things*, London and New York: Routledge.

Howes, David (ed.) (1996), *Cross-Cultural Consumption*, London and New York: Routledge.

Khan, Naseem (1992), "Asian Women's Dress: From Burqah to Bloggs – Changing Clothes for Changing Times," in Juliet Ash and Elizabeth Wilson (eds), *Chic Thrills: A Fashion Reader*, Berkeley: University of California Press.

Kleinen, John (1999), *Facing the Future, Reviving the Past: A Study of Social Change in a Northern Vietnamese Village*, Singapore: Institute of Southeast Asian Studies.

Kondo, Dorinne (1997), *About Face: Performing Race in Fashion and Theater*, London and New York: Routledge.

Kopytoff, Igor (1986), "The Cultural Biography of Things: Commoditization as Process," in Arjun Appadurai (ed.), *The Social Life of Things*, Cambridge: Cambridge University Press.

Leshkowich, Ann Marie (2000), *Tightly Woven Threads: Gender, Kinship, and "Secret Agency" among Cloth and Clothing Traders in Ho Chi Minh City's Ben Thanh Market*, Doctoral dissertation, Harvard University.

Lim, Linda (1983), "Capitalism, Imperialism, and Patriarchy: The Dilemma of Third World Women Workers in Multinational Factories," in June Nash and Maria Patricia Fernandez-Kelly (eds), *Women, Men, and the International Division of Labor*, Albany: SUNY Press.

Luong, Hy V. (1992), "Economic Reforms and the Intensification of Rituals in Two North Vietnamese Villages," in Borje Ljunggren (ed.), *The Challenge of Reform in Indochina*, Cambridge, MA: Harvard Institute for International Development.

Mackay, Hugh (ed.) (1997), *Consumption and Everyday Life*, London: Sage.

Malarney, Shaun (1996), "The Limits of 'State Functionalism' and the Reconstruction of Funerary Ritual in Contemporary North Vietnam," in *American Ethnologist* 23(3): 540–60.

Malinowski, Bronislaw (1961 [1922]), *Argonauts of the Western Pacific*, New York: Dutton.

Marr, David G. (1971), *Vietnamese Anti-Colonialism: 1885–1925*, Berkeley: University of California.

Marx, Karl (1977 [1867]), *Capital: Volume I*, New York: Vintage.

Mauss, Marcel (1990 [1925]), *The Gift*, New York: W.W. Norton.

McCracken, Grant (1988), *Culture and Consumption*, Bloomington: Indiana University Press.

Mies, Maria (1986), *Patriarchy and Accumulation on the World Scale: Women in the International Division of Labor*, London: Zed.

Miller, Daniel (1987), *Material Culture and Mass Consumption*, Oxford and New York: Blackwell.

—— (1992), "The Young and the Restless in Trinidad: A Case of the Local and the Global in Mass Consumption," in Roger Silverstone and Eric Hirsch (eds), *Consuming Technologies: Media and Information in Domestic Spaces*, London and New York: Routledge.

—— (ed.) (1995a), *Acknowledging Consumption*, London: Routledge.

—— (1995b), "Consumption and Commodities," *Annual Review of Anthropology* 24: 141–61.

—— (1997), "Coca-Cola: A Black Sweet Drink from Trinidad," in Daniel Miller (ed.), *Material Cultures*, London: University College London Press.

Mintz, Sidney (1985), *Sweetness and Power*, New York: Viking Penguin.

Mohanty, Chandra Talpade (1997), "Women Workers and Capitalist Scripts," in M. Jacqui Alexander and Chandra Talpade Mohanty (eds), *Feminist Genealogies, Colonial Legacies, Democratic Futures*, London: Routledge.

Nash, June, and Fernandez-Kelly, Patricia (eds), (1983), *Women, Men, and the International Division of Labor*, Albany: State University of New York Press.

Nava, Mica (1997), "Women, the City and the Department Store," in Pasi Falk and Colin Campbell (eds), *The Shopping Experience*, London: Sage.

Nguyen Van Ky (1995), *Vietnamese Society Facing Modernity*, Paris: L'Harmattan.

Nhi T. Lieu (2000), "Remembering 'the Nation' through Pageantry: Femininity and the Politics of Vietnamese Womanhood in the *Hoa Hau* Ao dai Contest," *Frontiers* 21(1/2): 127–51.

Ong, Aihwa (1987), *Spirits of Resistance and Capitalist Discipline*, Albany: State University of New York Press.

Parry, J. and Bloch, M. (eds) (1989), *Money and the Morality of Exchange*, Cambridge: Cambridge University Press.

Rutz, Henry J. and Orlove, Benjamin S. (eds) (1989), *The Social Economy of Consumption*, Lanham, MD: University Press of America.

Salaff, Janet W. (1995 [1981]), *Working Daughters of Hong Kong*, New York: Cambridge University Press.

Savigliano, Marta (1995), *Tango and the Political Economy of Passion*, Boulder, CO: Westview.

Shenon, Philip (1993), "The Mist Off Perfume River," *New York Times*, 21 November.

Tai, Hue-Tam Ho (1992), *Radicalism and the Origins of the Vietnamese Revolution*, Cambridge, MA: Harvard University Press.

Tarlo, Emma (1996), *Clothing Matters: Dress and Identity in India*, Chicago: University of Chicago Press.

Taussig, Michael T. (1980), *The Devil and Commodity Fetishism in South America*, Chapel Hill: University of North Carolina Press.

Thao Thi (1995), "It dong tan man ve ao dai va khan co Tam (Some scattered lines about the ao dai and the Miss Tam turban)," *Phu Nu*, 20 October: 11.

Thoi Trang Tre [New Fashion] (1994–1997), various issues.

Tobin, Joseph J. (1992), "Introduction: Domesticating the West," in Joseph J. Tobin (ed.), *Re-made in Japan*, New Haven: Yale University Press.

"Vai net ve lich su chiec ao dai Viet Nam (A Few Characteristics about the History of the Vietnamese Ao dai)," (1995), *Phu Nu*, 1 November: 15–17.

Wallerstein, Immanuel (1974), *The Modern World System*, New York: Academic Press.

Weismantel, Mary (1989), "The Children Cry for Bread," in Henry J. Rutz and Benjamin S. Orlove (eds), *The Social Economy of Consumption*, Lanham, MD: University Press of America.

Wilk, Richard (1995), "Learning to Be Local in Belize: Global Systems of Common Difference," in Daniel Miller (ed.), *Worlds Apart*, London and New York: Routledge.

Wolf, Diane (1992), *Factory Daughters*, Berkeley: University of California Press.

Woodside, Alexander (1988), *Vietnam and the Chinese Model*, Cambridge, MA: Council on East Asian Studies, Harvard University.

3

Korean Alterations: Nationalism, Social Consciousness, and "Traditional" Clothing

Rebecca N. Ruhlen

One winter day during fieldwork I arrived half-frozen at the Korea Sexual Violence Relief Center.[1] A senior staff member, with her typical grace and hospitality, gave me a cup of sweet instant coffee and sat with me for a minute while I warmed my hands around the cup. A few years older than the other staff members and in a higher position, Hyekyung[2] was usually well-dressed, but almost always in Western clothing. That day she was wearing a lovely woolen Korean-style outfit in a rich shade of violet. It was one of the new styles of *hanbok*, with a calf-length dress under a waist-long embroidered jacket (Figure 3.1).

I remarked on how pretty she looked that day. She responded, smiling, "Oh, really? Thank you . . ." Then after a pause, she continued, "I have an appointment today with a potential donor – someone who might give us some money."

Sensing that she was explaining something rather than changing the subject, I prodded for a clarification: "Is that why you're wearing hanbok – Korean clothing – today?"

She replied, "Mm . . . that's right!" Then she was abruptly called back to her duties, leaving me to wonder what further meaning the pause, the smile, and the trailing tone of her voice had held. This chapter presents an educated guess at the answer to that question.

Through ethnographic examples and a study of news articles, I will argue that when feminist activists don new-style hanbok, they are responding to several threads in a cultural discourse about nationalist pride, activism, gender,

Figure 3.1 A senior activist wears "lifestyle" hanbok for her organization's year-end general meeting. She wore the same outfit earlier in the year to meet with a potential donor. Photo by Rebecca N. Ruhlen.

and consumption. Above all, they – and many others in Korea – deploy hanbok essentially as costumes in a public performance of political identity.

Hanbok Introduced

While I was conducting fieldwork on the Korean women's movement, I repeatedly encountered activists and other people wearing a style of Korean clothing that I had not observed on my previous visits in the early and mid-1990s. The previously singular style of hanbok around 1997 had suddenly been deemed "traditional" hanbok, and it competed for attention with a range of new terms and styles.

"Traditional" hanbok, of course, had its own history, development, and fashion trends. At some point, most likely during the colonial era (1905–1945) when both Japanese and Western culture was making deep inroads into Korean customs, the idea of a proper hanbok outfit became fairly definitive. A woman's costume, for example, consisted essentially of a long skirt (*ch'ima*) and short jacket (*cheogori*). The skirt was very full and so long that it reached from the upper chest all the way to the floor, while the length of the jacket was generally just enough to cover the top of the skirt, ending at about the level of the breasts. Certain undergarments were also worn, and an overcoat; ornamental ties or hairpins, and special shoes and stockings would accessorize the outfit nicely, but the basic structure was the skirt-jacket combination – in fact, another way of saying that a woman was dressed in hanbok was to say that she wore *ch'ima-cheogori*.

In addition, the proper context for wearing hanbok also became rigidly defined. By the 1970s, Western-style clothing predominated so thoroughly that hanbok became for most people a costume worn exclusively for special occasions, especially traditional holidays and ceremonies, and particularly by older women as opposed to young women, children, and men.[3] As a special-event formal wear, hanbok was thus thought most appropriately constructed of an expensive and delicate fabric, such as silk. Cheaper versions might use a synthetic fabric that approximated the shiny iridescence of real silk. Startlingly bright colors also became the rule, often with two contrasting colors for the woman's skirt and jacket.

On the other hand, with the new styles of hanbok that were becoming popular in the late 1990s, only the general shape of the garments was similar to that of traditional hanbok. Everything else was different. Instead of silk or a shiny synthetic fabric, the new garb was usually cotton or wool; instead of brilliant colors, it was usually in dark or muted earth tones. The women's skirts were shorter and not so full, and (I was told) the men's garments fastened with modern devices like zippers. Even more striking was that some women who dressed in this new style wore the garments traditionally restricted to men: hip-length jackets, vests, and baggy trousers.

The first term I heard to describe this new style of traditional clothing was *kaeryang hanbok*: "reformed Korean clothing." But as I pursued the topic, other names emerged as well, each with its own set of contested meanings. I began to perceive the deployment of this clothing as a statement of political and national identity. The range of garments and styles seemed to function as a system of encoded nationalist ideologies, building upon ideas about class, gender, and nature. In the end, I concluded that the new hanbok styles were part of a repertoire for the performance and consumption of nationalist identity, available to all Koreans but used especially by activists.

The New Hanbok in Mainstream Feminism and Activist Nationalism

The first place I remember seeing new-style hanbok was at a celebration of International Women's Day in early March of 1998. It was an annual gathering of some twenty-five progressive women's organizations to mark the occasion and celebrate the movement. It took place in a sleek new performance center at Yonsei University.

Outside the doors a lively atmosphere prevailed; one group was raising funds by offering a chance to be photographed peering through a large signboard. The signboard portrayed a black-robed, cigarette-smoking, blue-haired witch on a broomstick – adorned with the international symbol for woman. Female students in jeans lined up to be photographed there. Just inside the doors, a tight security checkpoint was staffed by security men in sober suits, for the wife of the newly elected Korean president was speaking at the event. The lobby was filled with booths arranged by the participating organizations, each distributing literature, collecting signatures on petitions, recruiting new members, or hawking various goods for fund-raising.

The Korea Women's Hotline booth consisted of two tables displaying its various publications for sale. At one end stood a rack of new-style hanbok that they were selling to raise funds. One of their full-time staff members wore a similar outfit. The only other person dressed likewise whom I observed at this event was later onstage as a mistress of ceremonies. Everyone else – hundreds of women from all walks of life – wore various styles of Western clothing, like nearly everyone in Seoul. Clearly, the new hanbok was hardly a dominant theme in progressive Korean feminism, at least on International Women's Day; yet one of my fieldsite organizations was deliberately identifying itself with this clothing.

A few weeks later, the "new" hanbok caught my eye once again. I was at a meeting of a progressive feminist/culture group called "An Alternative Culture." They were holding a monthly discussion series on state violence against women, and the topic for the evening was the postliberation massacres on Cheju Island.[4] First on this otherwise solemn agenda, however, was a boisterous display of persimmon-dyed "new" hanbok and a chat with the New York-trained designer.

The clothing in question was displayed on a wire mesh screen and modeled by the designer as well as by the guest speaker who would later lead the discussion on the Cheju Island violence. Audience members rummaged through the stacks of garments for sale, trying on vests and hats to the amused delight of their friends. The clothing was described as completely natural in material and in color. A brochure distributed to that effect explained that persimmon juice was the traditional ingredient for dyeing clothing on Cheju Island. Its photographs showed various outfits jauntily accessorized and draped across a patch of cropped rice straw. The style of the garments ranged from a recognizably traditional short jacket to a thoroughly modern baseball cap, but all were dyed in various shades of the same brownish-orange persimmon. The all-women audience was quite surprised when the speaker removed her short jacket to reveal that the skirt, instead of a traditional *ch'ima* that ties around the chest, was in fact a sleeveless dress hanging on the shoulders. All agreed that this innovation was comfortable and convenient (*p'yeon hada*).

Several aspects of this event intrigued me and led me to think more seriously about the connections between "new" hanbok and broader social, cultural, and political issues. The most obvious in this case was the juxtaposition of supposedly Cheju Island-inspired clothing and the Cheju Island massacres in the late 1940s. These massacres took place as part of the brutal suppression of a grassroots rebellion on Cheju Island, after Korea's liberation from Japanese rule and the Cold War division of the peninsula. Over a period of several years, tens of thousands were killed by state forces under the control of the United States occupation, and memories of the events were officially suppressed for decades (Eckert et al. 1990: 339, 344; Kim Seong Nae 1989).

The rediscovery or remembering of historical episodes like this one has been a key issue for the opposition movement in Korea. It must be understood that in the Korean context, there is really only one movement – the *undong*. Before democratization in 1987, there were few relevant distinctions drawn between liberal democrats, Marxist revolutionaries, labor-rights proponents, or reunification advocates. All were lumped together in literal and figurative opposition to the repressive military regime. It was not until the 1990s that special-interest movements on topics such as women's rights or the environment began to gather strength, and so South Korea's civil society is as young as its democracy. Even today, the conventional understanding of what an activist does or what defines a movement largely mirrors the pre-1987 *undong*.

This original prototypical *undong* is a postcolonial, nationalistic movement. As such, the primary purpose of the *undong* is to represent the spirit of the everlasting Korean folk, the common people, the masses who at least spiritually are rural, traditional, and genuine. The word for these Korean folk, these genuine masses, is *minjung* (Wells 1995). Its closest translation is the Gramscian and postcolonial term "subaltern," because embedded in its meaning is the whole history of Korea's victimization at the hands of foreign powers and its betrayal at the hands of elite collaborators.

Opposition activists narrate a twentieth-century history that is constructed around a string of dates (Abelmann 1996: 14). The dates, stretching from 1919 to 1987, represent events in which the *minjung* spoke with the only historical voice they are allowed – the rebellion, the uprising. One such date is 3 April (*sa-sam*), the day in 1948 that Cheju Islanders first took up arms, representing just one episode in the epic struggle of the disempowered *minjung* to survive and resist the ravages of the powerful and corrupt, both foreign and native.

The irony, though, is that activists are typically urban, middle-class, and highly educated. They may be ideologically aligned with the *minjung*, but for most there is little or nothing in their personal backgrounds or daily lives to suggest an identification with anyone rural or traditional. Activists therefore constantly confront divisions between themselves and the victims of the injust-ices they work to undo. My informants often lamented that they belonged to "a citizen's movement without citizens." While this was partly a complaint about how hard it is to involve ordinary people in any type of political activity, it also underscored how widespread is activists' recognition of the gaps between the movement and the *minjung*.

As a result, people in the movement are often actively engaged in strength-ening their identification with a national folk culture. Music is one apparent favorite in this category; many rallies I attended included varieties of "farmer's music," performed by small clubs of students or housewives who meet regularly to learn and practice a particular style of drumming and dance. Others actually go to the countryside to help farmers bring in the harvest – many informants reported spending summer vacations in this manner during their university years. Abelmann discusses the awkwardness reported by some activists, who modeled their consciousness on the farming minjung, only to travel to the countryside and find themselves trying to raise the consciousness of the farmers themselves (1996: 156–157).

It is easy to see the new styles of hanbok clothing in the same light – a conscious attempt by urban activists to align themselves with a politically pure rural image. I often read or heard that certain of the new styles of hanbok originated in the democracy movement, adapted in the 1970s from rural costumes. One newspaper article overtly claimed that the new hanbok, from the mid-1980s until its mass popularization, were most often worn by students, artists, and those with (social) "consciousness" (Ko 1997).

Feminism in Korea, though – unlike the democracy or labor movement – is widely considered to be a baldly Western-derived ideology and not something indigenous or easily adapted to Korea. If feminists purportedly align themselves with an innately Western ideology, why then do they buy, sell, and wear the new hanbok? The answer has to do with the relationship between Korean feminism and the broader subculture of the Korean opposition movement, and also with the relationship between gender and nationalism in contemporary South Korea. I return to these matters later in this chapter.

Consuming and Co-opting the New Hanbok during a Crisis of Nation

First, however, it seems important to acknowledge that not all the clothing choices an activist makes are necessarily political. One component of why feminists wear the new styles of hanbok is its recent mass-market popularization. In just the last few years, these natural, comfortable, politically purer versions of traditional clothing have developed into a new and highly successful industry, one that kept growing through the recent economic crisis, when almost every other industry suffered (Shin 1998). Many shops that specialize in the new hanbok are located in particular neighborhoods known for offering a newly trendy traditional culture. But the clothing also is now being mass-marketed through major department stores and even in general clothing shops in the local markets and on street corners. In these mass-market settings, needless to say, the new hanbok is not described as politically subversive – rather, the major selling points are its comfort and convenience, and its capacity for reawakening Korea's national pride.

This comes through most clearly in the language used to name the clothing itself. A number of different terms have been used to describe nontraditional hanbok. While the terms are used by different people in often conflicting ways, due either to their incomplete knowledge of the field or to their ideological agendas, something like the following scheme emerged in my fieldwork.

In media discourse, all styles of nontraditional hanbok were at first called "reformed" (*kaeryang*), beginning around the end of 1996. The implication was that the recognizably traditional garments (skirt, jacket, trousers, etc.) had been modified to be more comfortable and informal – reformed to fit contemporary settings.[5] However, some protested that to call the new clothing "reformed" implied that the traditional style was somehow flawed (Kim Uk 1997), and about a year later, various newspapers began to replace "reformed" with the term "lifestyle" (*saenghwal*). Again, the stress was on its comfort or convenience, and hence its suitability for ordinary life.

This comfort and convenience bears some examination; a single term, *p'yeon hada*, encompasses both meanings, and this same term appears in nearly every description of the new hanbok that I found during fieldwork, whether it was in conversation, advertisements, or news stories. It was certainly the most common catchphrase used to describe "lifestyle" hanbok. In Korean, the term "lifestyle" is generally used to convey an abstract impression about the contours of the activities of a particular occupational group: a student lifestyle, a housewife lifestyle, an office lifestyle. But here its implications transcend any one group and are directed more to the sense of everyone's own daily life, ordinary activities, the real world. In such a context, describing this clothing as comfortable and convenient, read backwards, is a criticism of both traditional hanbok and, in a more veiled sense, of modern Western-style clothing as well.

Comparing new and traditional hanbok, the critique is fairly clear. Traditional hanbok is very expensive formal wear, nowadays primarily reserved for significant ritual occasions such as the wedding of a close relative, and worn even then primarily by older women. Brides wear traditional hanbok for engagement photos as well as for the most traditional part of their wedding – an arduously formal series of bows performed to their new in-laws. In a different kind of formal setting, a company or institution will often employ young women, unfailingly beautiful and dressed in brilliant traditional hanbok, to greet people arriving for a special event.

Wearing this type of traditional hanbok to school, to an office, or while grocery shopping, is almost unthinkable – it would be like wearing a lavish evening gown or tuxedo in broad daylight for the most mundane activities. This is partly due to custom but is also because the physical properties of traditional hanbok make such activities thoroughly impractical and inadvisable. The garments are too fine, too easily stained, too hard to clean, and too bulky for daily life. Also, my informants frequently pointed out that the design of a traditional woman's hanbok is too uncomfortable to wear often – the long skirt (*ch'ima*) that fastens around the upper chest has to be tied very tightly lest it fall off.

There is another sense, however, in which the new styles of hanbok are also a veiled criticism of modern Western clothing – and of Westernization in general. This is the thread to which I believe activists and other political actors are most attuned when they wear the new styles of hanbok. In the media and in mainstream discourse, however, this critique is mostly veiled as praise for the new hanbok as a way to embrace or honor Korean culture in a globalizing world.

The anti-Western shadow of this philosophy emerged most strongly at the height of the 1997/1998 economic crisis, which peaked in the early months of my fieldwork. The "Asian flu," as Wall Street termed this economic catastrophe, began in Thailand and a few months later caused the Korean currency – the *won* – to plunge as well. Once the fall started, over-leveraged conglomerates couldn't pay their loans, and the South Korean banking system – which had never been fully independent of the South Korean government – was on the verge of collapse. The only thing that saved the Korean economy from the financial equivalent of nuclear holocaust was the International Monetary Fund

(IMF). It rushed in at the invitation of the South Korean government and kept the banking system afloat, but on very strict terms – Korea had to institute massive and harsh economic reform. In the four to six months that followed, large corporations shrank and small firms died off by the dozens. The numbers of jobless and homeless soared visibly (Schlachter 1998; Ha and Lee 2001).

In this context, Koreans felt – and were encouraged to feel – that they were under attack by the outside world. The entire set of economic and social disasters was immediately termed the "IMF era" or "IMF crisis" – or more simply, the IMF. Everyone in Korea studies a little English, and so the common joke for a few months was that IMF stands for "I'M Fired." In the firestorm of public rhetoric that ensued during these times, Korean consumers were urged from all sides not only to help the Korean economy, by buying domestically made goods, for example, but also in various ways to protect and revive Korean culture and the Korean national spirit itself, such as by wearing hanbok.

Around this time, almost as often as they used the terms "reformed" and "lifestyle" hanbok, the media also used the term "our clothing" (*uri os*), which evokes other common phrases like "our country," "our language," and "we Koreans." This is a definite insider's term – no matter how fluently she speaks Korean, a foreigner cannot refer to "our clothing" or "our language" without causing uncomfortable laughter at the linguistic error. It is also one of the most common terms used in the hanbok industry, appearing on store signs and in promotional literature.

The nationalism encoded in the naming and marketing of the new hanbok became especially overt in the months following the economic crisis. Pro-Korean nationalist rhetoric in the media became noticeably heightened, and all kinds of products were marketed as IMF-era money-savers, as Korean-produced and hence morally superior to imported goods, or as a celebration of the Korean nation itself. Hanbok companies – especially those producing "lifestyle" hanbok – were uniquely positioned to take advantage of all three of these marketing tactics.

One aspect of the IMF rhetoric was the constant exhortation to limit spending and reduce consumption. Housewives in particular were bombarded with advertisements and articles vilifying wasteful practices and lauding any effort to become more frugal. A good example for our purposes is a short article in the *Tonga Daily News* announcing a series of sewing classes offered by the Women's Support Fund. For an unspecified fee, women could take a four-month course and learn to sew various kinds of "lifestyle" hanbok, with an eye to future employment. This was published under the clarion call, "Women, in the IMF era take up needle and thread!" (Hong 1998). Other hanbok stores in later months offered to convert old formal hanbok into smart new "lifestyle" outfits, in recognition of the economic travails of their customers and in honor of the traditional holidays of Autumn Festival or Lunar New Year. Other brands of hanbok stressed that their garments were made from Korean-produced fibers; this selling point was emphasized both for the product's superior quality and for its moral uprightness in preventing consumers' hard-earned cash from going to foreign companies.

The most commonly used marketing tactic, however, was selling hanbok as an overt celebration of the nation. In this respect, the hanbok industry was supported by parallel efforts in certain governmental units, in particular the Ministry of Culture and Sports and the National Folk Museum. At least from the end of 1996, the Ministry had launched a campaign to encourage people to wear hanbok more often, and while this campaign at first made no distinction between traditional and new styles of hanbok, the manufacturers of "lifestyle" and other new styles of hanbok were quick to adapt to this supportive political environment.

Soon after the government proclaimed the first Saturday of every month to be a "Day for Wearing Hanbok" (hanbok *ipneun nal*), newspapers ran articles informing the public that anyone wearing hanbok on the right day would be admitted free to certain museums and historical sites – specifically mentioning that "reformed" or "lifestyle" hanbok would be included (Kim Yong-seon 1997). Other articles reported that schools and government offices around the country were adopting "lifestyle" hanbok uniforms in cooperation with the government's call to revitalize the hanbok culture (Pak 1997; Yi Heon-chin 1997b).

Finally, in autumn 1998 a major exhibit opened at the National Folk Museum, titled "Globalized Images of the Hanbok" (although the exhibit's own English translation of this title omitted the word "globalized"). The first half of the exhibit traced a historical narrative of the transformation of Korean clothing from the early days of modernization through the decades of Japanese colonialism. The second half of the exhibit jumped to an extensive display of the range of contemporary hanbok designs, from moderately priced "lifestyle" outfits aimed at the average consumer, to office and school uniforms, to elegant and elaborate designs for special occasions, such as weddings and funerals.

The final display in this section was devoted to the high-fashion designer Lee Young Hee, whose incorporation of hanbok-inspired themes in her internationally acclaimed designs has earned her widespread popular recognition in the Korean media. Lee was one of the first Korean designers to have her work showcased in a major international fashion show, the 1993 Paris Prêt-à-Porter Collection. Her work includes highly stylized interpretations of the "line" of traditional hanbok; reportedly, Lee sees her designs as a statement about the potential for hanbok to be worn by "women all over the world" (Lee 1993). Given how deeply hanbok is embedded in nationalist discourse, however, I suspect the mental image of non-Koreans dressed in hanbok might not come easily to many Koreans.[6]

It is worth pointing out here that even though the government campaign to promote the wearing of hanbok preceded the economic crisis, once the IMF-era rhetoric was in full swing, both the campaign and the exhibit incorporated similar sentiments in their public presentation. An official of the Ministry of Culture and Sports wrote in her introduction to the hanbok exhibit:

Even though the hanbok, which has always been with our people over several thousand years, has gone through many changes, the original form of this representative cultural asset has emerged victorious up to the present day.

Many have feared that the hanbok might disappear due to the rapid importation of Western goods during modern times. However, since the establishment of "Day for Wearing Hanbok" two years ago, the number of people habitually wearing hanbok has seen a large increase. This fact, and the fact that even during these difficult economic times the hanbok industry has seen continuous growth and success, are truly a cause for happy celebration.

We opened the hanbok wearing movement in order to inherit our people's traditions and to revitalize cultural stagnation. As is well known, hanbok is laden with the spirit of our ancestors who valued propriety and righteousness. Its beautiful lines and colors contain a unique personality that cannot be found in any country's clothing tradition but our own.

The hanbok that is imbued with our people's pulse and soul is a clothing superior to that of any country in the world. Therefore, revitalizing our cultural product in daily life and for international pride is not merely a matter of revitalizing its spirit; rather, we also want to open new opportunities for the fashion industry as well. (Shin 1998 – my translation)

The dramatic rhetoric about glorious traditions, wise ancestors, and unique cultural assets sounds strange here but in fact is fairly representative of the terminology and hyperbole I found associated with discussions about hanbok and other nationalistic issues. I cite this particular passage at length, however, not only as an example of IMF-era rhetoric – the passage also underscores the cooperation between government and industry in promoting the new hanbok and demonstrates how their glorification of hanbok for national pride is usually tied to an indirect swipe at Westernization and the West in general.

Postcolonial Feminism, Sexuality, and Hanbok

Nonetheless, the veiled criticism of Western-style clothing was not fully apparent to me until I came across a pamphlet produced by Nature's Friend, a natural cosmetics and "lifestyle" hanbok company. At the end of a detailed description

Figure 3.2 Images from an advertising pamphlet by Nature's Friend. The woman
on the left is surrounded by bullet points detailing the unhealthy and
unattractive aspects of her Western-style dress and cosmetics. The
woman on the right wears "lifestyle" hanbok; the reader is exhorted to
"revive an image that reveals the self-respect and healthiness of
Koreans." Illustrations courtesy of Nature's Friend (Chayeon eui Peos).

of the products in their cosmetic line, the final pages of the booklet present two
contrasting images (Figure 3.2). The first shows a Korean woman trying to
resemble a Westerner, with numbered bullet points highlighting the unhealthy
and unattractive results of each alteration to her body, from her permed and
colored hair to her tight, high-heeled shoes. The second image shows a Korean
woman with pure and natural hair, skin, and clothing; the text reminds us that

the most beautiful woman has natural beauty and calls us to revive an image that reveals the self-respect and healthiness of Koreans.

What goes unnoted in the text but fairly leaps off the page at the reader is the contrasting body language of the two women and their corresponding connotations of femininity and sexuality. The proper Korean is turned at a slight angle, head slightly bowed and hands folded demurely before her. She is the very image of a good daughter-in-law or wife. The wanna-be Westerner stands squarely facing the page, long-nailed hands on her hips, with elbows and head at a jaunty, bold angle. In mainstream Korean terms, she is not quite a prostitute, but she is on that path. The contrast, I would argue, is meant to underscore not just the appropriateness of natural Korean cosmetics and clothing, but also the inappropriateness of supposedly Western displays of defiantly sexual femininity.

The question this leads me to, in considering the Korean women's movement, is with which of these two exaggerated opposites my informants would align themselves. This question involves the troublesome dialectic of sexuality and nation in Korean feminism and will point to the conundrum presented by feminist activists' use of the "new" hanbok.

Others have discussed the logic of colonialism and how it employs metaphors of gender and sex (Stoler 1995; Burton 1999; Clancy-Smith and Gouda 1998). Powerful nations are cast as masculine, against an image of weaker, effeminate, colonized races. Such metaphors accrue corporeal substance when foreign soldiers, encamped on colonized soil, contribute to the development of a military camptown subculture, with its own sex industry in which local men pimp local women for foreign soldiers while the two governments assume parallel stances of relative superiority and submissiveness (Moon 1997; Enloe 1990). Indigenous nationalists who seek to evict the colonial oppressors then fall into similar metaphors, casting themselves as the masculine protectors of the raped woman-nation – and calling collaborators "whores." In contemporary South Korea, this is the story behind the epithet "Yankee whore," commonly hurled both at camptown prostitutes and at Korean women who marry white men (Kim Hyun Sook 1998). A deeply rooted Confucian ideology valuing female chastity – as an item rightfully owned by their Korean fathers, husbands, and sons – above women's very lives heightens the debate. Most middle-class feminists were well indoctrinated in this brand of patronizing and misogynistic nationalism during their university years.

As the local promoters of an overtly Western ideology, Korean feminists thus find sexuality to be a risky topic. The leaders of the movement are mostly in their forties and fifties, and younger activists told me that the conservatism of that generation regarding issues like premarital sex or divorce was one of the biggest sources of conflict within the movement. Even at an organization that focuses on sexual violence, and that sees as its central goal the development of a healthier sexual culture in Korea, it is difficult to find statements that defend outright the open expression of women's sexuality. Regardless of the activists' personal views on this subject, such a move would probably be politically disastrous, opening their movement to charges of being overly Westernized and contributing to the corruption of Korea's cultural purity. In short, feminist activists have to sidestep potential charges of being intellectual "Yankee whores."

There are options for female identity beyond the polarized images discussed above, and Korean feminists are working to extend the territory that lies between "good wife/wise mother" and "Yankee whore." But how does occasionally wearing hanbok contribute to their project? To approach this question, I offer one more ethnographic example.

Hanbok and the Performance of Political Identity

The largest concentration of feminists wearing hanbok that I observed took place not in Korea but in Mongolia. The 3rd East Asian Women's NGO Forum was held in Ulan Bator in August 1998. The Korean delegation was organized by a coalition of women's groups, but as its main representative was also the president of the Korea Women's Hotline, much of the work was done by staff members at the Hotline. Furthermore, a full third of the delegates, while representing various groups, were also members of various Hotline branches across Korea. Early in the four-day conference, a Cultural Night was scheduled, as chance would have it, at a local Korean restaurant. Each delegation from the participating countries – Japan, South Korea, China, Taiwan, Hong Kong, and Mongolia – was to share its culture with the gathering after the meal.

In the late afternoon, the Korean group decided to gather before dinner to rehearse its performance. Upon meeting, we discovered that nine of the twenty delegates, with no prior discussion, had independently brought hanbok outfits to wear at the Cultural Night. Admiring each other's beautiful clothing, they decided on the spot to include a fashion show in the evening's performance. So, following a ten-minute excerpt of a traditional dance performed by one delegate (a dance professor), the hanbok-clad women promenaded onstage in groups while singing *Arirang*, the prototypical Korean folk song.

Of particular interest to me was the range of hanbok styles present at this event, and the correspondence of each to the age and political identity of the woman wearing it. The four oldest women wore the most traditional style, differing primarily in color scheme and accessories. Two other women wore quite different styles of "reformed" hanbok. One was a forty-ish professor of philosophy who was always elegantly dressed; her outfit had a long, slim line

Figure 3.3 The Korean delegation in Mongolia rehearses an impromptu fashion show; one member wears a "reformed" hanbok with waist-length jacket and calf-length skirt. In the background are women wearing "traditional" hanbok. Photo by Rebecca N. Ruhlen.

with collar and sleeve patterns reminiscent of the profusion of color in Korean temples. The other was the twenty-something daughter of a Christian minister from Pusan; her outfit was in traditionally brilliant pink and green hues and was "modified" from the traditional style primarily in that the jacket was longer and the skirt shorter (Figure 3.3). Two other women wore the simple cotton "lifestyle" hanbok that I most frequently observed among activists, in much more muted color schemes. The older of the two, also a professor and the president of a Hotline branch, was in a waist-length jacket and ankle-length skirt, while the younger, a twenty-five-year-old Hotline staff member, was in a longer jacket and trousers – essentially the garments a man could have worn. The final participant was the dance professor, whose shimmering white silk hanbok was specifically suited to her dance.

This grouping was no outsider's contrivance, for the fashion show presented the women in precisely that order. The oldest and most traditionally dressed appeared first, while the group sang a slow, formal version of *Arirang*; the two in "reformed" hanbok appeared next, with the music a bit faster; and the two in "lifestyle" hanbok followed, as the singing switched to a decidedly more upbeat and defiant version of *Arirang* – the tune used at many a protest rally, with verses often composed for the occasion. The leader of the delegation then took the microphone and explained the characteristics of each hanbok style for the rapt audience.

Given the discussion above about the overt nationalism associated with hanbok in Korea, it makes sense that the Korean delegates saw their impromptu fashion show as an appropriate vehicle for sharing their culture with the other Forum participants. It is worth noting here that among the other five delegations, only Mongolia's included anyone dressed in traditional costumes, and that was only a handful of women out of around three hundred, nowhere near the forty-five percent of Koreans in hanbok. There were no Japanese *kimono* or Chinese *qi pao* that night. This suggests that the South Korean discourse on nationalism, clothing, modernity, and gender may be unique in the region, the reasons for which would no doubt require another article to explore.

It is also worth noting the contrast between the Cultural Night in Mongolia, when half the Koreans wore hanbok, and the celebration of International Women's Day at Yonsei University that I described earlier, at which almost no one except the very visible master of ceremonies wore hanbok. In Mongolia, the Koreans were deliberately performing "Koreanness" for the benefit of foreign observers, while at Yonsei University, they were performing feminism primarily for the benefit of their own movement.

In a more general sense as well, the new styles of hanbok in particular often seem to be used as literal costumes in the overt performance of some aspect of one's identity, agenda, or political position. As I moved through various circles in the activist world and took note of the instances in which my informants wore the new hanbok, I found that it was usually for some sort of public appearance, something that took them out of the office or shelter and into the scrutiny of outsiders. Recall my opening anecdote about the senior activist who consciously acknowledged that a nice "lifestyle" hanbok outfit was the thing to wear to a fund-raising meeting. I saw a similar deployment of new-style hanbok at press conferences and parties. I cannot count the number of times that I showed up for a scheduled rally to find my friends – young women whose normal attire was jeans or khakis – wearing their one-and-only hanbok outfit that day.

If the sole goal for these public appearances was to appear nicely or professionally dressed, a Western-style suit or blouse and skirt would have done the job and, in many instances, probably would have been cheaper or more accessible for most of my informants. I suggest that other considerations guide the decision to wear new-style hanbok for public performances of feminist activism. On the one hand, because the clothing is associated with a "movement consciousness," wearing it among other activists is a way of stating solidarity with the broader *undong*. In a sense, feminists might use this clothing to say, "We borrow a lot of ideas from a Western ideology, but we are real Korean activists nonetheless." On the other hand, because hanbok on women's bodies in particular carries an encoded message about proper Korean womanhood, wearing it for the scrutiny of the general (non-activist) public might also be a way of saying, "We are feminists, but we conduct ourselves with propriety." Both strategies garb a potentially threatening political agenda (the feminist wolf) in softer, more reassuring clothing (the proper sheep's clothing).

It must be stressed, however, that feminist activists are by no means the only Koreans who consciously deploy hanbok in public performances of identity or political position. The aforementioned government-and-industry-sponsored campaign to promote the wearing of hanbok is explicitly aimed at strengthening the public's sense of itself as a body of nationalist citizens, in response to a growing concern that 1990s' globalization was eroding the average Korean's pride in national identity. Many schools, companies, and local government bodies in 1997 and 1998 were replacing Western-style uniforms with new-style hanbok uniforms or instituting new requirements regarding the regular wearing of hanbok on the job (see above; Yi Heon-chin 1997a; Yi Myeong-chae 1997). Equally significant is that these decisions were so often regarded by the media as being nationally newsworthy.

One more thread in this web of political performance involves the changing of the guard that was signaled by the presidential election victory of the former opposition dissident Kim Dae Jung, within days of the start of the national economic crisis. The same ruling party, with overt ties to the previous military regimes, had been in power since democratization in 1987. Their defeat for the first time in history by the opposition party was regarded hopefully by many as a sign that South Korean democracy was flourishing and that the new administration would better represent and heed the wishes of the populace. An editorial calling for Kim Dae Jung to wear hanbok for his inauguration, to demonstrate to the world Korea's pride in its culture and resilience as a nation (Yi Sang-man 1998), can only be seen as further evidence that hanbok is a powerful tool in the performance of political messages by a broad range of actors.[7] In fact, one wonders, if government ministries and department stores can join forces in deploying the new hanbok to such effect, have the protest roots of this clothing been co-opted to the point of irrelevance?

Conclusion

It is not a stretch, then, to see that the various styles of hanbok, as demonstrated by the contexts in which they are worn and the forums in which they are discussed, are deeply embedded in asserting and contesting Korean identity. As Korea's civil society outgrows the pre-democracy bifurcation of postcolonial collaborators and *minjung* activists, people are developing more flexible and multilayered ways of asking and answering the questions: Who is most genuinely Korean? Whose claim to the nation is most valid?

For feminist activists, meanwhile, this issue is complicated all the more by their unique position vis-à-vis gender, Westernization, and nationalism. Despite the fact that women, as those most closely associated with hanbok, bear the primary burden of enacting these assertions and debates about Korean identity, and despite the ways in which female subjectivity and sexuality are claimed as a sort of national territory, feminists have not yet tackled these issues in relation to hanbok and instead seem willingly to accept the rules of the hanbok game. As the young Hotline staff member insisted, when we were talking about these issues after the Mongolia trip, "Rebecca, you don't understand; wearing hanbok is just something we Koreans *do*."

Notes

1. My fieldwork in South Korea during 1998 and 1999 was funded by a dissertation research grant from the Korea Foundation and further supported by the Asia Women's Studies Center at Ewha Woman's University. During fieldwork, I was lucky to have capable and enthusiastic research assistance in the person of Choi (Talia) Sun Kyung. Earlier versions of this chapter were presented as papers at Indiana University Purdue University-Indianapolis and at the annual meetings of the Central States Anthropological Society, as well as the original panel at the 1999 Meetings of the American Anthropological Association. I owe special thanks to Clark Sorensen, Sue Kenyon, Susan Sutton, Seung-Kyung Kim, Nancy Abelmann, Roger Janelli, Eriberto P. Lozada, Jr., and the volume's editors. Their collegial generosity and encouragement in matters both intellectual and practical helped enormously.

The bulk of my dissertation research was located in Seoul and focused on the development and workings of the progressive women's movement, dealing primarily with activism on violence against women and other aspects of women's human rights. I worked closely with two primary organizations, the Korea Women's Hotline (*Hanguk Yeoseong eui Cheonhwa*) and the Korea Sexual Violence Relief Center (*Hanguk Seongp'okryeok Sangdamso*). My informants at each group asked me to name their organizations in my scholarly work, to help publicize their efforts. Ethnographic tradition and concerns for their privacy, however, leave me less comfortable with naming the individuals who patiently and steadfastly facilitated my work with them. I thank the many staff members, volunteers, and clients whom, regretfully, I must leave anonymous here.

2. A pseudonym.

3. There are exceptions to this rule. For example, even in 1990s Seoul, I often saw elderly men wearing white linen or ramie hanbok during the heat of summer. Also, babies (especially boys) would be dressed in fancy hanbok outfits for professional photographs and special ceremonies such as the feast marking their hundredth day of life.

4. Located off the southwest tip of the Korean peninsula, Cheju Island has long been viewed as a remote and exotic corner of the Korean nation, where inhabitants spoke an unintelligible dialect and the women were strong enough to do men's work, such as fishing and diving. The volcano at the center of the island, Halla-san, in myth and folklore marks the southernmost reach of the Korean world. Cheju Island's role in Korea's bloody postliberation history is largely unknown by the general Korean populace, who associate the island instead with its booming tourist industry.

5. There are other interpretations of this label, however. One designer told me that *kaeryang* was meant to indicate the "reform" of traditional hanbok not *forward* in time to modern society, but *back* in time to the clothing styles of pre-Choson dynasty and pre-Confucianized Korean culture. It is true, for example, that during the Three Kingdoms period and then under Unified Shilla (roughly 57 BC to AD 935), women's costumes often included a skirt that fastened at the waist and a jacket that fell to the lower torso (Yang 1997: 28–9, 56).

6. Months before the late-1997 economic crisis began, Korean newspapers announced that Lee had been selected by Mattel Corporation to design a complete hanbok outfit for the "Korean Barbie" in its line of internationally costumed dolls. Said Lee, "It was very difficult to select colors that suit [Barbie's] blue eyes and pink skin" (Kang 1997).

7. President Kim wore instead a Western-style suit to his inauguration; it was the First Lady who wore traditional hanbok, demonstrating the usual means by which the survival of national identity is cast as a burden to be borne by the female body.

References

Works in English

Abelmann, Nancy (1996), *Echoes of the Past, Epics of Dissent: A South Korean Social Movement*, Berkeley: University of California Press.

Burton, Antoinette (ed.) (1999), *Gender, Sexuality, and Colonial Modernities*, London: Routledge.

Clancy-Smith, Julia and Gouda, Frances (eds) (1998), *Domesticating the Empire: Race, Gender, and Family Life in French and Dutch Colonialism*, Charlottesville, VA: University Press of Virginia.

Eckert, Carter J., Lee, Ki-Baik, and Robinson, Michael (eds) (1990), *Korea Old and New: A History*, Seoul: Ilchokak, Publishers (for the Korea Institute, Harvard University).

Enloe, Cynthia H. (1990), *Bananas, Beaches, and Bases: Making Feminist Sense of International Politics*, 1st US edn, Berkeley: University of California Press.

Ha, Seong-Kyu and Lee, Seong-Woo (2001), "IMF and the Crisis of the Marginalized Urban Sector in Korea,"*Journal of Contemporary Asia* (Manila) 31(2): 196–213.

Kim, Elaine H. and Choi, Chungmoo (eds) (1998), *Dangerous Women: Gender and Korean Nationalism*, New York: Routledge.

Kim, Hyun Sook (1998), "*Yanggongju* as an Allegory of the Nation: Images of Working-Class Women in Popular and Radical Texts," in Elaine H. Kim and Chungmoo Choi (eds), *Dangerous Women: Gender and Korean Nationalism*, New York: Routledge.

Kim, Seong Nae (1989), *Chronicle of Violence, Ritual of Mourning: Cheju Shamanism in Korea*, Unpublished Ph.D. dissertation, University of Michigan.

Lee, Yoo-Lim (1993), "Local Designers Break into the Big Time," *Business Korea* (Seoul) 10(12): 56.

Mani, Lata (1998), *Contentious Traditions: The Debate on Sati in Colonial India*, Berkeley: University of California Press.

Moon, Katharine H. S. (1997), *Sex among Allies: Military Prostitution in U.S.-Korea Relations*, New York: Columbia University Press.

Moon, Seungsook (1998), "Begetting the Nation: The Androcentric Discourse of National History and Tradition in South Korea," in Elaine H. Kim and Chungmoo Choi (eds), *Dangerous Women: Gender and Korean Nationalism*, New York: Routledge.

Schlachter, Susan (1998) "Deconstructing South Korea," *Asian Business* (Hong Kong) 34(9): 36–41.

Stoler, Ann Laura (1995), *Race and the Education of Desire: Foucault's* History of Sexuality *and the Colonial Order of Things*, Durham, NC: Duke University Press.

Wells, Kenneth M. (ed.) (1995), *South Korea's* Minjung *Movement: The Culture and Politics of Dissidence*, Honolulu: University of Hawaii Press.

Yang, Sunny (1997), *Hanbok: The Art of Korean Clothing*, Seoul: Hollym Corporation.

Works in Korean

Articles below from the *Tonga Ilbo* (Tonga Daily News) were accessed by searching the paper's archives on their internet site: www.tonga.co.kr. In lieu of page numbers, the archives include the date and time of day at which each article was filed.

Hong Seok-min (1998), "Shilkwa paneullo pulhwameul kkwemaepshita," *Tonga Ilbo*, 5 April, 20:14.

Kang Sang-heon (1997), "Babi'inhyeong hanbok ipneunda," *Tonga Ilbo*, 1 August, 20:21.

Kim Uk (1997), "'Kaeryang hanbok' poda 'cheonseung hanbok' euro," letter, *Tonga Ilbo*, 12 December 08:09.

Kim Yong-seon (1997), "Hanbok'ipko kamyeon kokung muryeoipchang," Kihoik/Yeonchae section, *Chung'ang Ilbo*, 13 January.

Ko Mi-seok (1997), "Kaeryang hanbok, p'yeon'anham – koun pitkkalo taechung'e inki," *Tonga Ilbo*, 6 September, 08:14.

Pak Dong-uk (1997), "Chinchushi samhyeon yeoko, kaeryang hanbok kyobok seoncheong," *Tonga Ilbo*, 26 December, 08:12.

Shin Nak-chun (1998), "'Hanbokeui sekyehwa imichi,' cheon'e puch'yeo," in Kukrip Minsok Pakmulkwan (eds), *Hanbokeui sekyehwa imichi*, Seoul: Munhwakwankwangbu.

Yi Heon-chin (1997a), "Hanbokipko teungkyo An'yang p'yeongch'on 'purimch'o-teungkyo,'" *Tonga Ilbo*, 10 November, 20:02.

—— (1997b), "'Kongmuweon hanbokipko keunmu hacha' . . . Kyeonggido urios'ipki undong," *Tonga Ilbo*, 2 August, 07:28.

Yi Myeong-chae (1997), "Pasetwoireuyu'eop, 'hanbokkeunmu' imichi ch'abyeolhwa," *Tonga Ilbo*, 14 July, 08:01.

Yi Sang-man (1998), "DJ ch'wi'imshiktae hanbok ibeosseumyeon . . .," *Tonga Ilbo*, 21 February, 20:10.

4

Designing Diasporic Markets: Asian Fashion Entrepreneurs in London

Parminder Bhachu

This chapter examines diasporic cultural production of formerly ethnic clothes that have moved into mainstream fashion arenas in Europe and internationally. Based on fairly recent research on South Asian women, fashion entrepreneurs who have spearheaded these new national and transnational fashions, I examine the journeys of commodities, design, and images in local and global markets.[1] In these economic domains, British Asian women are, and have been, assertive cultural and commercial agents. They are global connectors par excellence, who transfer their designs and cultural expertise across the globe through a transnational clothes economy. I am referring to the production and marketing of the now ubiquitous Punjabi or *salwaar-kameez* suits (hereafter referred to as "the suits").

Tracking the emergence and popularity of the suit on London streets over the past thirty years is significant because, as I show, it has become both an important sign and medium of the changing postcolonial relations among racially and ethnically diverse communities in urban Britain. The suit has shifted from being a sign marking immigrant difference in 1960s London to being a sign of cosmopolitan chic in 1990s London. Tracking these changes not only confirms that the meanings of things, including clothing, are made in particular historical contexts, rather than adhering in their material existence, but also reveals how the continued re-making of those meanings has occurred around the issues of raced and gendered difference. Indeed, the history of salwaar-kameez is not only emblematic of the raced and gendered negotiations among groups in London, but has been a key mode of expression and political movement. In this paper I reveal how British Asian designers have encouraged cultural pride within their migrant communities and have stimulated the consumption and display of the suit by women who are not a part of that community, including high-profile white socialites and fashion models.

Salwaar-kameez suits, also referred to as *shalwaar-kameez*, are made in all kinds of fabrics. The suit is composed of a long tunic with slits (of varying length, but normally between 12 and 15 inches, depending on the fashion context) down both sides, loose baggy trousers, often with a cuff at the ankle, and a head scarf that is between two and three meters long. The length and width of all these components change with fashion styles, as do the shape and silhouettes. The basic three components remain fairly static but their interpretation varies.

Indian diaspora fashion markets have recoded national European and transnational cultural and consumer spaces, despite the odds, both racial and commercial. The innovative role of Asian women as cultural and commodity brokers is critical to the redefinition of these consumer spaces. Their command over economic resources, their design expertise, and their use of technologies that rapidly transfer commodities using modern communications are transforming and defining new global economic and cultural realms. They are savvy design agents in the new capitalist markets of the new millennium, as they assert their politically and culturally inflected fashion agendas. This is a story of niche markets, local, national, and transnational, created by entrepreneurial Asian women who are connecting the globe through their cultural and commercial work. This opening of new territories is done through many micro- and macro-dialogic design conversations between customers and entrepreneurs using global communications between London and their production sites in the Indian subcontinent.

Immigrant women and their daughters maintained their cultural confidence, including their ethnic clothes, despite the hostile racial contexts in which they found themselves in Britain in the 1960s and 1970s, a time when there was a dramatic increase in the immigrant population from the Indian sub-continent and its diasporas. The expanding critical mass resulted in a higher local profile for South Asians that was often negatively charged. For example, their salwaar-kameez were negatively referred to by the wider society as pajamas. Yet, the commercial economies of these same clothes have mushroomed since the mid-1980s. These have been spearheaded by the daughters of immigrant mothers; their innovative reinterpretations of the suit are taking place in different subcultural and class contexts in London and across the globe. They have redesigned and recontextualized the cultural and sartorial economies of their mothers, who were often from multiple migrant communities.[2] Their cultural and commercial interventions represent characteristic features of reflexive modernization, of design processes, and aesthetics (Lash and Urry 1994; Giddens 1991;

Beck et al. 1994). This fashion economy grows out of politicized cultural terrains that are negotiated through a multiplicity of identities, cultural locations, and biographical trajectories of movement and location. The women who create this economy include both fashion entrepreneurs in public commercial sectors and the domestically based seamstresses from diasporic cultures of sewing, most of whom are both consumers in and producers of this economy. In this chapter, however, I focus primarily on the former. I explore the cultural and commercial connections that are producing niche markets that are culturally and politically mediated through dialogic cultural and identity texts. These are innovative market circuits that disrupt and subvert established cultural and sartorial economies (Christensen 1999).

Before I go on to describe the cultural narratives of the suit, I should describe my own position within this fashion economy. As a resident of London for over thirty years, I have witnessed the suit economy grow and have observed its different developmental phases. I have observed and participated since I was a child in the domestic circuits of this economy, as well as the commercial markets that emerged in the 1980s. I have been a producer, consumer, and academic commentator. While I have not been part of the commercial markets of the suits – my participation there has been as a consumer – I sew proficiently and have stitched my own suits since my early twenties. I share this diaspora heritage of proficiency in sewing with the most innovative fashion entrepreneurs who opened up the new suit market in the 1980s.

The women who market and design the suit improvise and innovate using a negotiative style with their customers. They respond to their customers' requests and many co-construct designs democratically with their clients. Their ethos is in tune with the contemporary market moment of new capitalist processes that are about designing individually tailored products that take account of and respond to customers' desires. These improvisational sensibilities are translated into this fashion economy based on innovation similar to that of American pioneer women at the turn of the last century who were expert seamstresses. The source codes of their improvisations and their ability to capture the nuances of the latest trends and incorporate them into producing imaginative innovative suits are critical to the commercial enterprises in London markets. This background of innovation, combined with the marginal cultural and racial locations of their producers in Britain, makes them form the form. They create new cultural and sartorial forms in having to negotiate their cultural and identity styles all the time. They do not repeat and reiterate a form that already exists, though some make the already significant more significant. In fact, the most innovative British Asian entrepreneurs create new significations in new cultural and commercial arenas. It is this ability to respond to the moment, the cultural moment, the market moment, and the contemporary economic and political scene, through their racialized cultural politics that gives them an edge in the market. I am suggesting that the precursors of the suits marketed and co-constructed in commercial arenas are to be found in the very significant sewing economies to which second-generation daughters have given a new impetus using global communication and sophisticated production sites in the Indian subcontinent. There, their British Asian-negotiated aesthetics are translated into suits for the market. They are not necessarily expert seamstresses, although the ones I interviewed are, but they translate their hybrid influences into sewn garments for the market (see Bhachu 2003).

The translation of the aesthetics of domestically produced suits stitched by seamstresses is central to the development and style of the most innovative enterprises, especially those led by British-raised and British-born second-generation daughters who have asserted their voices through style and in many cases transferred this style into the market.

I have closely monitored the movement of the suit from its place as a marginal and denigrated signifier of immigrant women to the mainstream locations where they are now found. I have focused on London because it is the British city with the largest number of East Asians. In common with other cities where Asians are resident, London has a settled East Asian community with a substantial second generation. This critical mass of young people is asserting its cultural agendas and its version of British Asianness in a number of domains, specifically in the media, in political arenas, and in the ways in which they define their identities. The phenomenon of multiple identifications is wonderfully well captured in award-winning film director Gurinder Chadha's documentary entitled *I am British but* . . . Some of these young people are creating new markets as they negotiate local contexts and assert their grounded aesthetics in many symbolic and cultural economies of which the suit markets represent one facet. Some of the most innovative diaspora Asian music trends, from Bhangra to British Asian Reggae, and Ragamuffin, sounds of Asian underground, have their origins in England. These are internationally influential media and hybridized music trends that have parallels in other consumer markets, such as the Asianization of food, music, and clothing commodity markets. London is also generally known as a cutting-edge fashion capital for mainstream fashion and design markets, a global site in which many outsiders want to open markets and where they desire commercial success.

The Cultural Trajectories of the Suit Economy

In the 1960s and 1970s, a period when the majority of British Asians immigrated to the United Kingdom, Punjabi suits represented the clothes of immigrant women. These women were mainly working-class and those who were not were often considered by local whites to be so. Thus, these clothes were negatively charged in Britain. Upper-class Indians who had been in Britain for many years as a result of the British presence in India were not identified with the wearing of the suit but instead with the wearing of saris. These immigrant clothes, both suits and saris, were worn primarily by the wives and daughters of men who had been recruited as labor migrants after the Second World War to fill the labor shortages. They were recruited because they were resident in British colonies, and many had British citizenship rights and passports. The suit, however, was worn mostly by North Indian women, primarily Punjabi, but also women from other North Indian communities. Some of these women were multiply migrant; they had left India from fifty to a hundred years before migration to Britain (Bhachu 1993, 1996), and had lived in many other places, such as East Africa, for many years. Despite these histories, the clothes of the immigrant women represented a threat, in that the colonized had come to the land of the colonizers.[3] These immigrants had to negotiate their cultural and economic forms all the time in situations of disequilibrium. They have had to deal with dissonance on a daily basis. This experience has been to their cultural and commercial advantage since they moved to Britain (Thurow 1999) because they had the expertise to deal with dissonance. Many directly migrant women wore the suit. However, the commerce around the suit that has taken it into the realm of designed identity-coded products and the boutique commerce of the late 1980s and 1990s was spearheaded by the daughters, the second-generation diaspora children of multiple migrants. The markets for the suits are fundamentally connected to the diasporic aesthetics of previous communities (for example, settlements in East Africa where some Asians had lived for almost a century) and point-of-origin economies where these aesthetics were developed.

Immigrant women kept the suit economy alive because they adhered to their cultural base and their sartorial confidence despite the racial odds. They were told that they were wearing night clothes or pajamas. There were many racial slurs leveled against them. They were taunted and labeled "Pakis," the universal label applied to all suit-wearing women regardless of whether they were Pakistanis or not, and regardless of whether they were locally born or from the diaspora communities with children who had never been to either Pakistan or India. The older women migrants who kept suit-wearing alive, who maintained their cultural and sartorial confidence, are precisely the women who socialized their British-raised and British-born daughters into wearing the suit (Figure 4.1). They provided them with a cultural framework for these clothes through their own example of wearing the suit and through the emphasis on narratives of cultural pride. I write elsewhere (Bhachu 2003) about how my

Figure 4.1 Mother and daughter in salwaar-kameez, demonstrating the importance of generational transmission of the value of the suit. Photo by Parminder Bhachu.

own mother encouraged me to wear the suit. First, she set an example by wearing it herself; second, she sewed suits for me according to the styles I liked that were in tune with the fashion trends I subscribed to; and third, she socialized me to have confidence in my cultural background and clothes in particular. She always told me to be proud of my heritage and my culture and to wear "my national dress" with confidence. In fact, she tutored me using a pedagogy of cultural defiance, teaching me to be myself despite the cultural terrain.

Though this kind of socialization is not uncommon, it is also the case that second-generation daughters developed and interpreted the suit according to their own British subcultural and subclass locations, and according to styles, images, and fashion trends of their times. These women are precisely the ones who spearheaded the commercial economies of the suits. They inserted their culturally negotiated consumer products into the market by creating micro-markets on their own terms through their own design choices and personal interpretations of style. They developed the markets further through micro-design conversations about style that later were translated into fully realized clothes. These fashion entrepreneurs use global markets. The communicative relays and transferral agencies that these economies have spawned allow for rapid manufacturing of clothes in production sites in India and Pakistan using British Asian and local design templates.

This is a graded economy that includes other women with different biographical trajectories who are also connecting the globe through their cultural and commercial activities. However, on the British scene, second-generation women from multiply migrant families were the pathbreakers, followed much later by suit entrepreneurs who had different cultural and commercial trajectories, and who came from the Indian subcontinent to initiate their enterprises. They essentially entered the new commercial spaces that daughters of migrant women had pioneered in London, the site in which they were raised and that they knew intimately as local residents. This local residence gave them enormous market advantage compared to subcontinental elites who wanted to capture the London markets. These immigrant women and their second-generation daughters, by going about their clothing business in their local site of residence, captured new economic and cultural terrains by actually creating these markets.

Their cultural and commercial styles emerge from the contemporary cultural and market moment, though these also have sources in the transplanted diaspora aesthetics and migrant sensibilities of their parents' generation. They have redesigned and professionalized diasporic designs, the basis of cultural production in migrant communities, through their own expertise and their local subclass and subcultural locations and racial experiences in Britain. In doing this, the entrepreneurs are in sync both with new capitalist processes, including notions of flexible production, and with reflexive modernity and all its features of co-construction (Giddens 1991, Beck et al. 1994). They make connections through networks rather than nations, and they construct their biographical trajectories though their experiences. Most crucially, these are then projected through their transformative cultural and commercial activities in the market. Lester Thurow points out that market success comes to those who are able to deal with dissonance and disequilibrium in changing economic landscapes. He states, "New technologies means change. Change means disequilibrium. Disequilibrium conditions create high-return high-growth activities. The winners . . . have the skills to take advantage of new situations" (1999: 33). While most British Asian fashion entrepreneurs are not quite in the market situations that Thurow describes, his point about successful entrepreneurship being related to the ability to deal with disequilibrium certainly applies to them. They created new markets from the margins as a result of having to deal with dissonance and in having to formulate a cultural and commercial space first for themselves and later for mainstream customers. In innovating new markets through their racialized and politicized subjectivities and cultural locations (Petzinger 1999), they are pioneers from the margins. This marginal culturally mediated commerce has disruptive potential in bringing products to the market that were not previously significant and that were initially meant for small and peripheral minority populations. Such markets often initiate the new spaces of culture and commerce. Clayton Christensen states, in his book *The Innovator's Dilemma* (1999), "Disruptive technologies bring to the market a very different value proposition than had been previously available. Generally, disruptive technologies under perform established products in mainstream markets. But they have features that a few fringe customers (generally new) value . . . disruptive technologies typically are first commercialized in emerging or insignificant markets."

These new dynamics of identities through new cultural and commercial forms have created new ways of being British, new clothes aesthetics, and new sartorial economies. For instance, the fashion icon Princess Diana wore the suit many times in the last few years of her life (Figure I.1). She was influential in familiarizing people with the suit much beyond the circuits in which it was normally worn. More recently Cherie Booth (whose husband Tony Blair is the British Prime Minister) has been dressed by Bubby Mahil, a diasporic daughter about whom I write in greater detail below. Bubby represents the diasporic aesthetic par excellence through her dialogically designed suits. She was born in Kenya and moved to Britain when she was two years old. She is a locally raised British Asian from a multiply migrant background. I suggest that some of the mainstreaming of the suit has to do with the changing textures of what it means to be British as British Asians make their mark on their country of residence. In addition to Princess Diana, British royals such as Lady Helen Windsor, daughter of the Duke and Duchess of Kent, the Queen's cousins; media stars such as Academy Award-winning actress Emma Thompson; photographer and former girlfriend of Prince Andrew, Koo Stark; and supremely wealthy fashionable women such as Jemima Goldsmith-Khan, daughter of one of the wealthiest men in Britain and wife of the famous Pakistani cricketer Imran Khan, have all donned the suit between 1995 and 2000.

These dynamics represent their buying into and subscribing to the identity scripts that Asian women are generating. These trends have recoded the salwaar-kameez suit from its stereotype as a dress form of low-status immigrant women to that of a high-fashion and also couture garment. When fashion megastars Princess Diana and Jemima Goldsmith-Khan donned the suit, it was a potent moment, leading to its recoding. This recoding occurred because the cultural and commercial groundwork had been laid by immigrant women and their second-generation daughters who reinterpreted the suit design styles on the British scene according to their culturally determined racialized politics. The suit is no longer an immigrant thing. It was recontextualized in the late 1990s as high-fashion garb, now worn by the most fashionable women in Britain as well as remaining an important part of street style.

Movements of the Suits

As we have seen, in the late 1990s these suits were worn by the most fashionable women in London. They are globally available through many distributive agencies. These include upmarket designer boutiques in prestigious mainstream locations in central London, as well as the many market stalls and ready-to-wear designer boutiques in mainly ethnic areas catering to a different clientele. A whole range of women-initiated marketing niches have produced a plethora of boutiques run by women entrepreneurs who act as designers, redistribution agents, tailors, embroiderers, professional service providers, and media presenters of fashion shows.

There are many cultural and commercial actors in this economy of clothes. First, there are the fashion entrepreneurs who are locally born or raised, who have the most politicized design aesthetics and whose racial and cultural politics are played out strongly in their clothes and commercial agendas. Second, there are those who fall into the category of suit marketers who are direct contextualizers; they essentially transfer clothes made in the subcontinent to many locations globally without having any design input. Third, there are the home-based seamstresses who sew for the public for money and, fourth, the domestic producers who sew for themselves and their families. The latter is the oldest of all the suit-making groups and the ones who kept the suit economy alive in the 1960s and 1970s, despite the racial and cultural odds.

All these groups made possible the remarkable breakthrough of the suits into mainstream markets in the 1990s. The designing, marketing, and distribution of these suits has rapidly become part of different diaspora economies. Global markets and related modes of communication, such as faxes and courier services, have catalyzed the rapid availability of these clothes in international arenas, as has Asian women's travel back and forth to home countries from various diaspora locations to which they have migrated. This form of consumption facilitating the international transferability of designs of this essentially ethnic material culture is a new phenomenon of the 1990s and the early 2000s. Thus, suit retailing and designing represent a "gendered commerce" (Mort 1996), mostly controlled by Asian women entrepreneurs.[4] These are currently profitable and culturally powerful "female aesthetic communities" (Goldstein 1995) in which the circulation, production, design innovation, distribution, and consumption of goods is controlled, managed, and consumed by women, both within subcontinental centers and also in diaspora locations. Commercially savvy – some trained at leading design and fashion schools in India, Europe, and the United States – these design and marketing personnel have entered this fast-growing market. They transformed the production of the suits from essentially domestic economies, often situated within the domestic domain with generationally developed diasporic sewing cultures, into commoditized global economies of the new millennium. These clothing economies are governed by all the codes of locality, transnationality, and diasporic aesthetics that are fundamentally recoding British consumer spaces.

Cultural Brokerage through Design Markets

An important tool in facilitating the kind of proliferation and flexible hybridity I am describing has been the use of emerging technologies to connect markets. Global markets[5] are determining the fashion styles of these suits with multiple and simultaneous cross-flows of information from the major cities and design centers around the world. Fax machines transfer the designs, cutting instructions, shapes, embroideries, and *chuni/dupatta* (headscarf) styles. Although there is an exclusive market of designer suits, there is also a great degree of standardization of these clothing forms through global markets. For example, often the same wholesalers in India and Pakistan design and manufacture similar clothes and then supply them globally to major diaspora Asian markets, leading to easy availability of these clothes in all the major cities of South Asian settlement. However, their interpretation is fundamentally determined by the local context of subclass and subcultural styles and the cultural baggage of migration of their wearers. The localization of these suits, a globally available commodity form, negates this standardization, because of the interpretation of these clothes through local and regional styles and cultural codes. For instance, notions of multiple Britishnesses are inscribed in the interpretation of these dynamically changing and potent sartorial forms, thus contesting British sartorial hegemonies. These artifacts also are strongly encoded signifiers of the material and symbolic economies of global, national, and local class styles. British Asian entrepreneurial women have fashioned highly politicized domains and are using markets and colluding with capitalist processes in complex ways much beyond the simple mechanisms of economic exchange in markets. The diaspora daughters who created these new markets are selling identity products, co-constructed and designed with their customers, a demo-cratic design-production exercise. The design is faxed to India where the clothes are manufactured and then brought onto British markets. The process is essentially reproducing the diasporic migrant aesthetic inheritances, cultural baggage negotiated by previous generations in dissonant landscapes where they had to formulate and negotiate their cultural forms despite the odds. These are the cultural apparatuses and politicized social frames into which they have been socialized as diasporic products from migrant backgrounds. They have redesigned and dedesigned these aesthetics to produce new politically and culturally inflected design economies and consumer products that are sold through the new markets they have generated.

The production of these clothes has been greatly professionalized through the market, and they are now products of multiple sites of production and design expertise, both local and global. This is obvious from the wide range of ready-to-wear clothes boutiques catering to different class markets that have mushroomed in the 1990s in all the major centers of Asian population in Britain and other parts of the world, as well as the most upmarket mainstream high-fashion areas in London (Figure 4.2). In the late 1990s, they were to be found in exclusive central London locations such as Mayfair, Knightsbridge, and Baker Street in Marylebone. The ready-to-wear outfits sold in these shops cost anything from 25 to 35 pounds sterling in local Asian markets in ethnic areas, and from 400 to 8,000 British pounds sterling for the designer suits both in local and central London locations. These exclusive designer shops represent a retail economy run by Asian women entrepreneurs who feed many other diaspora clothes markets. Some of these entrepreneurs are locally born, while others either are raised in London or are from India with excellent Indian connections and a proven record of commercial success there. For example, the shop established by the renowned revivalist India-based designer Ritu in

Figure 4.2 An example of a hybrid salwaar-kameez, featuring shortened tunic and stretch fabric leggings, as envisioned by a British Asian fashion entrepreneur Komal Ravel, owner of Bombay Connexion, for sale to discerning consumers. Photograph courtesy of Bombay Connexion, 1992.

North Audley Street, Mayfair, provided the customer with exclusive Indian-made goods and access to services on the subcontinent. This shop, like some of the other exclusive boutiques opened by subcontinent-based design professionals, closed in the late 1990s. However, her clothes are available to an exclusive clientele through exhibitions organized by her London-based partner in grand London hotels. India- and Pakistan-based fashion entrepreneurs have been less successful in keeping their enterprises open in comparison to locally based immigrant daughters who were the pioneers in these local, though transnationally connected, markets. I write elsewhere (Bhachu 2003) about why the design and commercial agendas of elite subcontinental designers do not succeed often in London markets. They are national elites in their own countries but outsiders to globally connected local London markets. The success in London markets of locally based design professionals is fundamentally tied to their residence in London, a site they know well and one that produced them.

Among these London pioneers, the first to open a designer boutique in London was multiply migrant diaspora design professional Gita Sarin, who now owns two exclusive shops. Her first shop, called Rivaaz (trend), is in Wembley in West London and caters to a predominantly Asian clientele. It is located amidst a large East African Asian population. Her second shop opened in November 1995 in Beauchamp Place in Knightsbridge, the street where established mainstream designers are located. Other designer boutiques include Chiffons in Green Street, East London and Soho Road, Birmingham; Yazz in Baker Street in Marylebone; Libas of the fashion magazine *Libas*, selling exclusive Pakistani-style suits in Berkeley Street, and also the shop Ritu in North Audley Street, both in Mayfair. The Knightsbridge-based boutique EGG[6] opened in 1994, a politically correct/ecologically friendly and supremely upmarket enterprise, which has an art gallery on the premises and produces beautifully crafted almost art-suits in cottons and natural fabrics in Kinnerton Street. It is a commercially successful joint venture of Asha Sarabhai, of the Indian textile dynasty that has followed Gandhian traditions of cloth and craft production, and Maureen Doherty, the former style supremo for the chain of trendy Joseph shops. All these female commercial spaces constitute a gendered economy run by women entrepreneurs primarily based in Britain, although some have partners resident in India.

Diaspora Fashion Globalizers

To exemplify how vibrantly the suit has figured in the significance of Asian styles on the London fashion scene, I will now discuss two specific cases of diasporic designers. Two diaspora London-based fashion globalizers are Gita Sarin of Rivaaz, who is now in her fifties, the first to open a designer boutique described above, and Bubby Mahil, who is in her mid-thirties. Bubby is from the younger generation of British-raised Asian women. She is the owner of two innovative boutiques named Chiffons, located in London and Birmingham. She became very well known in the late 1990s as the woman who designed the Punjabi suits of Cherie Booth (see above, p. 146). These two designers are both Punjabi Sikhs from East Africa. Both are products of elaborate immigrant sewing cultures developed over two generations in East Africa that they transformed into a professional skill in the context of increasingly global fashion in London. They are both "time-space" compressors par excellence (Harvey 1989) in transferring designs and patterns with enormous speed from London to India, where their clothes are made. These are inserted back into the London markets for local consumption within three weeks for the elaborately embroidered and beadworked suits, and four days for the simpler non-embroidered ones in interesting rich fabrics and designs. The rapid speed of circulation is facilitated by the many courier companies that have sprung up to service this massive increase in clothes traffic.

Entrepreneur Gita Sarin of Rivaaz worked with leading Parisian designers and was the first to produce the now defunct mail-order catalogue of the salwaar-kameez suits called Rivaaz in 1986. She pioneered this type of marketing of designer Indian clothes. She opened her first shop, also called Rivaaz, with her own label in Wembley, in the famous Ealing Road in West London. Her second shop in Knightsbridge captured a more plural customer base including American film stars and other famous media personalities. She says her white European/American market constitutes 80 per cent of her clientele in her Knightsbridge shop, which also includes wealthy locally born second- and third-generation Asians. Surprisingly, her clientele also includes transnationally based subcontinental Asians who have easy access to the best designer-suit markets on the subcontinent, but who prefer to buy in high-status fashion capitals like London, befitting their high-status reference groups. For example, in September 1996, when I interviewed Gita Sarin, she said that she was working on the wedding outfits of a well-known Pakistani politician's daughter-in-law. Gita uses rapid communication networks such as faxes to get garments from India into London markets. This easy flow of information, the collapsing of space and time and the interchangeability of market sites, in which her designs, patterns, and stitching instructions are faxed to India and garments are manufactured according to her very professional requirements, is a market development led by London-based Asian women designers. This was a new phenomenon in the 1990s.

A Savvy Diaspora Design Negotiator

Bubby Mahil of Chiffons shares Gita Sarin's East African Asian diaspora background. These shared contexts are reflected in the design vocabularies they negotiate, the silhouettes they stock, and in their relatively egalitarian retail interaction styles with their customers in Britain. She represents the new breed of savvy design-conscious Asian fashion entrepreneurs, who are similar to the clientele with whom they share a subculture and to whom they sell their clothes. She closely monitors mainstream fashion styles, seasonal colors, fabrics, and silhouettes, especially those in vogue among the young, the 20- to 35-year-olds with money to spare. She responds to these trends and translates them into British-Asian style clothes rapidly. For example, in 1996 lime was a dominant fashion color and was reflected in the outfits Bubby designed and sold in her shop. Her shop window displays were also interpreted in different shades of lime.

Bubby Mahil is also a democratizing design negotiator as reflected in the dialogic way she produces suits with her customers. She negotiates with her customers in a dialogic style – a body dressed rather than a dress embodied – that represents a different process from the design vocabularies innovated by other designers and one that cannot be negotiated by their regular customers. Bubby represents a British diaspora context of a young locally raised Punjabi British woman. She captures the market of young consumers who share her biographical trajectory, British experiences, and commodity contexts. She is quite egalitarian and open to comments from her customers, who regularly give her suggestions and state their preferences about what she should stock in her shops. She listens with attention and often responds to the input, which comes from all age groups. Her British diaspora design aesthetic is different from that of some other boutiques, many of which will indeed get outfits made in India for their British customers on a made-to-measure basis by copying outfits already in their shops in different sizes and colors. However, most shops sell from their available stock of standard-size merchandise already in the shop, even though they are open to suggestions and closely monitor popular trends. In contrast, Bubby facilitates a subversion of design. One need not wear what is already designed and stitched, but one may create an individually produced suit by contributing one's own ideas in collaboration with a design/retail professional. Bubby makes salient diaspora voices through design, thus valorizing Asian women's voices through a sartorial design discourse around a material culture of clothes situated amidst global commercial spaces.

By engaging with a client in this fashion, Bubby is a democratic design innovator who dynamically produces a design syntax together with her customer. I witnessed an incident in her Green Street shop in East London that made this clear. Such interactions were common. A tall, plump Asian woman who regularly buys from Bubby wanted an outfit to wear at a wedding. She did not choose or like any suits from the merchandise already in the shop. She and Bubby came up with a grey outfit. They went through fabric samplers to choose the fabric, and then selected the neckline, the type of beadwork and area of the outfit to be embroidered, and the general shape, using a bit of this and a bit of that from existing outfits in the shop together with Bubby's own preference for what suited her. Bubby did a rough basic sketch based on her customer's suggestions and choices while giving her own experienced input. Bubby later refined and elaborated the basic sketch, with more detailed drawings of sleeves, necklines, trouser shapes, areas to be embroidered or beadworked, and general pattern instructions. Later on that day she faxed the detailed sketches to India. I saw the resultant garment – an individually chosen outfit that was dialogically produced through many arenas of expertise – back in the shop within three weeks for the customer to wear within her London social scene. This dialogic production of design and the stitching of these clothes with global and local inputs epitomizes the suturing of cultural land-scapes through clothes in global markets. Bubby creates a market drawn from the margins; by collaborating with her customer she can create designs that reflect both of their voices, even as the clothes retain Bubby's signature style.

Culturally Mediated Design Economies

These innovative processes result in new material and symbolic economies, and are products of the transformative agencies of ethnic and cultural entre-preneurs who are part of new forms of connectedness and flow. These new cultural forms neither are products of static sites nor are they generated in single sites. I am dealing with more fluid patterns that emerge out of different sites of production and that are multiply produced and consumed, but that fundamentally reflect the specificities of their interpretation, according to the codes of locality and regionality. These highly charged consumer cultures, governed by the codes of locality, transnationality, and diasporic aesthetics, are fundamentally transforming many British consumer and cultural spaces.

These new European spaces are not class-specific phenomena restricted to the upper classes or to a transnational elite – both Asian and European – but are processes that are to be found in every class and subcultural group. They reflect the influential cultural and commercial agency of Asian women in global markets. They are generating new geographies of fashion and style that subvert mainstream national style, a process that is redesigning European fashion landscapes. These new cultural textures and fashion geographies represent the politically inflected diasporic aesthetics generated by Asian fashion entrepreneurs that play a transformative role in the new cultural and commercial spaces in fashion markets. Such cultural production through clothes is catalyzed by the commodity contexts generated by such retailing outlets. Harjit Samra, who has a shop called Sheba and is one of the few male entrepreneurs in the suit markets, says that these processes and the donning of suits "strengthen our cultures, makes our cultures strong" – a positive reaffirmation of ethnic identities. At the same time, there are many depoliticizing consumer cultural moments through such commodity dynamics in global cities such as London and its markets that facilitate the appropriation of the salwaar-kameez suits by upper-class English women, by many other women from white and black groups, and by powerful mainstream designers with access to enormous powerful markets. Nonetheless, these new trends and the presence and influential cultural agency of these Asian women in various British niches play a strong role in shifting European cultural and consumer textures. They generate new culturally connected fashion styles, many of which are strongly inflected through their racial politics as played out in the market. I have examined the political subtexts involved in establishing these diaspora fashion markets that have recoded national European and transnational cultural and consumer spaces, despite significant racial and commercial obstacles. These new landscapes are products of complex and often difficult negotiations of the identities of Asian women and their battles to assert their diasporically produced British Asian cultural contexts and politicized voices through style and the new global economies of design in clothing markets.

I have suggested that markets are complex mechanisms of cultural and commercial exchange, and are about much more than straightforward sites of economic transaction. They are constituted by women doing politically grounded cultural work of identity through a national and transnational economy of formerly ethnic clothes that have entered many mainstream domains through market permutations from the margins. In this chapter, I examine the market and the impacts of people on the borders who are asserting their cultural agendas within many cultural and commercial spheres, inside and outside markets. I point out that capitalist processes are not devoid of the gendered and racialized cultural inputs of people on the margins who are asserting their subaltern voices in the market. The cultural and commercial inputs of immigrants and their second-generation children are coming into their own in these globalized domains, transforming both cultural and commercial landscapes, the market, and capitalist processes. By transferring and translating a clothes economy through their interpretative and design interventions, they are recoding both the clothes and capitalist processes with which they collude, and are creating and transforming according to their culturally mediated, often subversive agendas. Asian women are using the market in innovative and disruptive ways, not just as mechanisms of economic exchange but as potent instruments of their transformative cultural and consumer politics that code and continue to recode British landscapes. They are influencing and contesting mainstream capital and establishment conventions through their highly politicized cultural agendas encoded in their culturally tempered commercial sites. These pioneering women on the margins are redefining markets, which they are creating innovatively through the marketing of services and products as cultural texts that are generated through culturally produced, identity-negotiated products. These clothes-as-cultural-texts, pioneered by migrant women and their second-generation daughters, have spearheaded new local and global, cultural and commercial narratives.

Notes

1. My work on Punjabi salwaar-kameez suits constitutes research ongoing since 1989. In my book, *Dangerous Designs* (2003), I narrate a more detailed story about Asian women in Britain: their consumer niches, the role of design professionals and retail entrepreneurs who are professionalizing these formerly domestic economies in global markets, and the domestic seamstresses who remain vibrant in these transnational economies of clothes.

2. I use the term "multiply migrant" as opposed to direct migrants for those migrants and settlers who have moved repeatedly from one site to the next before settling in their destination economy. Multiple migrants are more experienced at the game of migration, at the management of their minority status, at the reestablishment of the infrastructure of their communities, and at the reproduction of their cultural base. These diasporic experiences give them an edge over direct migrants for whom migration is a first move. A longer discussion about multiple migrants is found in Bhachu 1993, and Bhachu 1996.

3. The negative coding of the suit also applied to the turbans worn by Sikh men. They fought with British employment agencies to be allowed to wear turbans when they worked in jobs such as bus conductors, or in banks and post offices, and for their sons to have the right to wear turbans in private schools. Many of them cut their hair and gave up the turbans until the times changed in the 1970s and 1980s when they donned them again as the communities became culturally confident with a critical mass of people, developed community infrastructures, and religious institutions. The suit story has some similarities.

4. See Frank Mort's analysis of the transformations in and the politics of masculinities as produced through consumption and fashion styles in "gendered commerce" driven by innovative style entrepreneurs and design professionals (1996).

5. The globalization of the Punjabi suits through commoditization has led to the rapid increase in networks of distribution. Women-led retail niches, the designer

boutiques – the high-status ones in Mayfair, St John's Wood, Wembley, Knightsbridge, etc., as well as those in Southall, East Ham, Romford, and the many market stalls – have mushroomed. A whole range of women-initiated marketing niches has produced a plethora of boutiques run by women entrepreneurs who act as designers, redistributive agents in this economy, tailors, embroiderers, professional service providers, etc. There are also the transnationally trained designers whose global networks give them the power to distribute these garments in various diasporic niches as well as to make them available to trendsetting Sloanes and various upper-middle-class circuits. Notable examples include highly trained and established designers, such as Zandra Rhodes in the late 1980s, Tarun Tahiliani, who has a designer suit shop in Bombay and who designed the dress for Jemima Goldsmith's wedding in Paris in June 1995, British designer Catherine Walker, who designed the powder-blue silk crepe Punjabi suit for her evening wedding reception, and many others who are emerging from various design schools in London, New York, Delhi, Bombay, Paris, etc.

6. This boutique results from a partnership between style supremo Maureen Doherty and Asha Sarabhai (see major article on them in *The Sunday Times*, 27 February 1994: 32–5). Asha Sarabhai states:

> "We talked about the idea of a shop for a long time because we were both tired of the way that the whole point of retailing seemed to persuade people to buy things they didn't really want,' says Sarabhai, a Girton graduate. She has dedicated her career to the protection of crafts and skills that are under threat from high-tech mass-production . . .
>
> Quality is the essence of Egg, and Sarabhai's clothes and fabrics succinctly embody its philosophy. They are seasonless and labor-intensive, made to last and even improve with age . . . The labor, of course, is relatively cheap. A full-length evening coat, cut like a kimono and finished to couture standard, is 700 pounds, a natural indigo cotton tunic 40 pounds . . .
>
> In terms of fame, Doherty's partner Sarabhai has a head start as an established designer of textiles and clothes. She has a one-man exhibition of work at the V&A to her credit and a cult following that includes serious aesthetes such as the painters Frank Stella and Robert Rauschenberg, the writer Gita Mehta and Issey Miyake . . .
>
> Sarabhai's career in textiles began in 1975 when she married a man from a respected and wealthy Indian textile dynasty. Its headquarters, a compound at Ahmedabad, north of Bombay . . . It was at Ahmedabad that the plan for Egg was hatched. As the frantic consumerism of the 1980s gives way to a new appreciation of lasting quality, Doherty and Sarabhai appear to have captured this new spirit (*Sunday Times*, February 1994: 35).

References

Beck, Ulrich, Giddens, Anthony, and Lash, Scott (1994), *Reflexive Modernization: Politics, Tradition and Aesthetics in the Modern Social Order*, Stanford: Stanford University Press.

Bhachu, Parminder (1993), "Twice versus Direct Migrants," in Ivan Light and Parminder Bhachu (eds), *Immigration and Entrepreneurship*, Rutgers, NJ: Transaction Press.

—— (1996), "Multiple Migrants and Multiple Diasporas," in Pritam Singh and Shinder S. Thandi (eds), *Globalization and the Region: Explorations in Punjabi Identity*, Coventry, UK: APS Press.

—— (2003), *Dangerous Designs*, London and New York: Routledge.

Christensen, Clayton M. (1999), *The Innovator's Dilemma: Why New Technologies Cause Great Firms to Fail*, Boston: Harvard Business School Press.

Giddens, Anthony (1991), *Modernity and Self Identity: Self and Society in the Modern Age*, Stanford: Stanford University Press.

Goldstein, Judith L. (1995), "The Female Aesthetic Community," in George Marcus and Fred R. Myers (eds), *The Traffic in Culture: Refiguring Art and Anthropology*, Berkeley: University of California.

Harvey, David (1989), *The Condition of Postmodernity*, Cambridge, MA: Blackwell.

Lash, Scott and Urry, John (1994), *Economies of Signs and Space*, London: Sage.

Mort, Frank (1996), *Cultures of Consumption: Masculinities and Social Space in Late Twentieth-Century Britain*, London: Routledge.

Petzinger, Thomas, Jr. (1999), *The Men and Women Who Are Transforming the Workplace and the Marketplace*, New York: Simon & Schuster.

Thurow, Lester C. (1999), *Building Wealth: The New Rules for Individuals, Companies, and Nations in a Knowledge Based Economy*, New York: Harper Collins.

5

National Colors: Ethnic Minorities in Vietnamese Public Imagery

Hjorleifur R. Jonsson and Nora A. Taylor[1]

The year 2000 marked a number of Vietnamese national celebrations. On 3 February the Communist Party commemorated its 70th year; 30 April was the 25th anniversary of the Hanoi victory over the Saigon government; and on 19 May Ho Chi Minh would have turned 110 years old. Throughout the country, the government drew attention to these national milestones by commissioning artists to make posters, billboards, stamps, statues, and paintings and placing them in public view. These works of art were intended not only to commemorate a historical event but even more importantly to unite the Vietnamese population through common national images. They were designed to present the Vietnamese people as a unified group, joined under a single flag, cause, and/or identity. The content of these representations of the nation, most of which feature images of women and ethnic minorities, points to ways in which Vietnamese national identity is constituted. The cases we discuss include images of women in ethnic dress, those of ethnic-majority *Kinh* (Viet), and some of the fifty-three other ethnic groups comprising Vietnam's population. The relationship between ethnic dress, identity, and the state is key to this discussion.

Along with its material function of facilitating human adaptations to a diverse range of environments, dress has long served as a symbolic code to mark people as particular kinds of individual. Societies have brought out different ways of marking identity and difference through dress, emphasizing features such as gender, status, and age within a system of codes that draw on color, fabric, and cut (Sahlins 1976; Turner 1980). Dress is communicative, and it elaborates a set of basic features into a system of relations and differences that people embody as members of socially recognized categories or groups. Dress fashions people into particular individuals who relate to larger worlds in specific ways.

Contemporary Western culture tends to assume that dress serves primarily to express individuality, but various social entities are marked through category-specific outfits, such as nurses, police, military staff, and so on. Different social frameworks bring out or reinforce particular ways of dividing up a social universe. Like language, dress simultaneously defines who shares a communicative code and who stands outside it. Because of this communicative function, dress can stand on its own and signify in the absence of a person embodying it. The same item of dress can encode a range of messages depending on the context of its use. There is no intrinsic relationship between dress and what it communicates, so the communicative properties of dress are symbolic rather than those of a sign (Leach 1976). It follows that the meanings of dress are intimately linked to specific and changeable frameworks for socially recognized categories or groups.

The focus of our chapter is on what is communicated through the traditional dress of Vietnam's highland ethnic-minority women. Many of the highland ethnic minorities in Southeast Asia use dress to distinguish men from women and children from adults at the same time as they mark one ethnic group off from others. Dress in these societies communicates membership in particular networks of exchange and other social relations. Our examination is not meant to explore the local meanings of dress within a particular minority society. Rather, we focus on the public life of its representations within the modern nation state, in museums, paintings, billboards, and propaganda posters. The topic of our chapter is thus the national appropriation of the symbolic dimensions of ethnic-minority women's dress for particular statements about identity and difference.

Contemporary representations of ethnicity through dress, however local they may appear such as in the case of Vietnam, may be viewed in the global context of nationalism. The nation, as a historically specific form of connecting people into lived social orders, has provided a general framework for reorienting identity and difference. The contributors to *The Invention of Tradition* (Hobsbawm and Ranger 1983) provide many examples of how fundamentally new forms of ceremony, dress, sports competitions, and public spectacle provided social and cultural frameworks for emerging national communities. The rise of national communities was a transnational process, and new nations could be modeled on preexisting ones (Anderson 1983). Of particular relevance to our case about ethnic-minority dress from the highlands of Vietnam is the rise of museums and related exhibits as public sites for displays of identity and difference through dress.

Since the nineteenth century, museums and expositions have displayed peoples through dress and other material culture. The logic of these displays suggests a tension between two ways of conceptualizing group identity, which dress has often been made to stand for. One is the nationalist emphasis on any one "people" ("*Volk*" in German) as unique, and their folk dress being a signifier for their identity. The other framework assumes an evolutionary or progressivist narrative, where the objects and dress of "a people" indicate their position within a global scheme of ranking groups in terms of postulated stages of evolution. American and European World's Fairs in the late nineteenth and early twentieth centuries frequently included "primitive" representatives in their displays, as integral components in these attempts to visualize and materialize processes of progress and civilization (Bennett 1995; Mitchell 1989; Stocking 1987; Taffin 2000).

Vietnamese depictions of ethnic minorities, in which dress serves as the fundamental signifier of identity, do not necessarily resolve the tension between the two views of identity, the nationalist emphasis on "a people" as unique versus the universalist notion of peoples as manifesting different stages of evolution. In part, this ambiguity has to be seen as a product of the nation's ambivalent relationship to its ethnic minorities as acting reminders of internal difference. This ambiguity is manifest, for instance, in a recent Vietnamese book on the textiles of ethnic minorities in the country's northern region (Diep 1997). The author states, "Textile patterns are truly the most vivid expressions of Vietnamese traditional culture . . . The designs express traditional cultural identity, the historical and cultural developmental process and of cultural interaction between ethnic groups (*sic*). The textile patterns thus preserve the culture of ethnic groups" (1997: 2). The author does not resolve the issue of whether to view the ethnic dresses as national or as markers of unique identities that are independent of the nation, but proposes that in spite of all the markers of difference, "The woven products of its 54 ethnic groups are valued cultural treasures of the entire Vietnamese nation . . . Wearable textiles and utilitarian fabrics play an indispensable role in the historical and cultural evolution of Vietnamese peoples" (1997: 1).

Neither is the tension between an evolutionary approach and one that sees each "people" as unique resolved in this work, and ethnic-minority dress stands for this problematic relationship of the modernizing nation-state and its internal Others. This tension remains unresolved in Vietnam, but the alterity that ethnic-minority dress signifies has in fundamental ways been nationalized. Further, this nationalization of difference is predominantly, if not exclusively, projected through images of women.

Women, Difference, and Nation

On visits to the countryside in northern Vietnam during the summer of 2000, we noticed several posters that portrayed the nation of Vietnam to itself. In one of them, placed on the outside wall of an ethnographic museum in the administrative center of Bac Thai Province, four women are shown standing in a semicircle, facing the other way (Figure 5.1). Each is dressed differently from the others. Three of the women carry flowers and the fourth a colored ribbon. The path they are on is depicted as a bright yellow line, and they are headed toward factories and construction materials that lie at the horizon. The four women are on the path toward industrialization and progress. As they head in that direction, they seem to be offering the flowers and banner to Ho Chi Minh whose face, in conjunction with four doves, appears in the sky above them. To the right of Uncle Ho is the image of the Vietnamese flag, a gold star on a red background. Also in the sky are dates, two marking the birth and the 110th anniversary of Ho Chi Minh and one marking the successful takeover of Saigon in 1975 that ended the American War (as it is locally known) and brought the country under a single government.

This official poster conflates the biographies of Ho Chi Minh and modern Vietnam in a specifically national manner. The date of his birth and the 110th anniversary of his birth several decades after his death come together with an image of the national flag and the visual markers of industrialization and peace, along with the date of the military takeover of Saigon. The poster's assemblage of images implies the destiny of the nation as tied to the life of Ho Chi Minh. But if the image is intended as a statement about modern Vietnam as a unified country, the dresses of the four women seem to speak to another reality. The women's dresses are neither modern nor national. Rather, they index "traditional" and ethnic or regional realities that seem at first glance to contradict the modern, modernist, and nationalist message of the poster. What makes traditional, ethnic and/or regional women's dresses suitable to the official portrayal of national destiny that includes military victory, an industrialized future, and the national emblems of the flag and the founder's life?

The representation of "traditional" Vietnamese (*Kinh*) and highland ethnic minorities through images of people in "ethnic" clothing is a fundamentally modern phenomenon. It draws on a nationalist gaze within which a select few ethnic markers stand as references to the multiethnic composition of the Vietnamese nation. Images of women in minority-ethnic dress are posted as celebratory. The intent of the images is not a move back to imagined or historical roots of ethnic diversity, or a multiculturalist celebration of difference for the sake of difference, but, and without exception, an appropriation of the markers of difference for the project of national unity and progress. Traditional

Figure 5.1 Banner outside an ethnographic museum in Bac Thai Province, that juxtaposes Ho Chi Minh and national temporality with women in outmoded ethnic and regional dress on the road toward industrialized progress. The text on the banner simply says "Socialist Republic of Vietnam." Photo: Hjorleifur R. Jonsson.

Vietnamese and ethnic-minority women are depicted, through the visuals of their dress, as analogous indexes of national unity. In their portrayals in the public sphere of postage stamps, billboards, etc., visibly non-modern women perform an iconic service to the nationalist cause, through both their dress and their femininity. The picture presented in this poster is one of harmony among different types of Vietnamese women who have been chosen to stand for the nation. But what is this picture about? Why does its subject matter make sense to an audience that is commemorating both the birthday of the founder of the nation and national reunification? In other words, why do women wearing traditional dress stand as national emblems?

In Vietnamese art, women and their clothing are portrayed to illustrate national symbols that have been invented or created for political purposes. As Ann Marie Leshkowich describes (in Chapter 2 of this volume), the *ao dai* (Vietnam's national dress) was designed by a painter as a means of capturing the essence of the modern Vietnamese woman and is often used by national propagandists to convey the modernity of the ethnic *Kinh*. When depicted in works of art utilized by a national organization, the dresses worn by minority women highlight the non-modern qualities of the ethnic minorities. Both kinds of dress are signifiers for the nation's peoples, the modern and the non-modern, and as such they problematize modernity and progress. As signifiers for kinds of people, the national majority and its internal Others, they focus the attention on peoples and erase traces of the state's involvement in defining peoples and national agendas.

The women in the Bac Thai poster are adornments in an artistic rendering of the nation and therefore we must consider their semiotic position and question whether ethnic-minority women in Vietnam are being represented or transformed as they become pictorial and national subjects. Also, how does art become a terrain where issues of ethnicity, gender, and nationalism get played out? In this particular poster, the four women are identified by their dress or costume. Their nonindividual identities are equally manifest in the dresses that stand for particular ethnic or regional collectivities and in the fact that their faces are not emphasized. The women's outfits tell the viewer who they are, where they come from, and which segment of the population they stand for. The woman on the far left is wearing a precolonial outfit called an *ao tu than*. Currently, this outfit is most familiar from performances of *cheo*, a folk opera associated with the Red River Delta in Vietnam's north, where Hanoi is located. At her right is a woman in an outfit that identifies her as one of the indigenous minorities of the Central Highlands region. The dress could be from Ede, Jarai, Bahnar, or another of the many ethnic groups in the region, but the reference of the dress is regional. The woman "stands for" the Central Highlands (Tay Nguyen) that lie in the hinterlands adjacent to the border with Cambodia and Laos. Next to her is a woman in a shirt worn over black trousers, an outfit that associates her with the rice farmers of the Mekong Delta region that includes the city of Saigon. To the "southern" woman's right is the last of the four, wearing the colorfully dyed and embroidered skirt, blouse, and scarf that define her as belonging to one of the Tai ethnic groups in the northern part of Vietnam bordering China and Laos.

Through their non-modern dresses, the four women stand for the four traditional components that have come together through Ho Chi Minh's contribution to the nation. As representations of traditional collectivities, the four women hide as much as they reveal about the constitution of the modern nation of Vietnam. What they reveal through their dress is a reference to "the people" as fundamental to the modern nation. It is made obvious in this and other propaganda posters that Vietnam is made up of several kinds of people. At the same time, the conceptual workings of defining "the people" (through regional and ethnic identities) are hidden. What is in view and actively promoted in official imagery is the nation as various kinds of people who are all united in their gratitude to their leader, in their fight against foreign aggression, and/or on the way to progress.

An aspect of this nationalization of difference is evident on the fourth floor of Vietnam's Women's Museum in Hanoi, which displays mannequins in ethnic dress. The first three floors of the museum are devoted to important women from Vietnam's history, who have contributed to the nation's struggle against foreign enemies. In the context of the various war heroes, the mannequins of ethnic Viet and minority women appear incongruous. Some are posed as weaving or embroidering, but most as simply standing in their ethnic dress. The text panel at the entry to this exhibit suggests how inactive or domestic women belong to the official commemoration of the nation:

Fine clothes are made to beautify women of various ethnic groups who, at the same time, are the creators of the cultural values in dressing. Through clothes, we can understand the diligent work of women, their creative mind, their optimistic spirit, their responsibility toward the family and the community. Efforts of women are expressed through the different kinds (*sic*) of cloth they have woven, the forms of dress they have designed, the colors they have chosen, the decorations they have made, and through each of their stitches. In fact, those women (*sic*) clothes have contributed importantly to creating the cultural characteristic of each ethnic group and the whole Vietnamese nation.

These statements from the museum and the book on textiles are nontrivial semiotic appropriations of women's work. Whatever significance women's weaving and embroidery has had in the (re-)production of identity and difference, marking individual, gender, household, region, and/or ethnicity, the meanings of this work as a whole have been nationalized. At the same time, and equally important, through this appropriation of the values of their work, women have been defined as the makers of tradition. Given the overarching modernist project of the Vietnamese government, this symbolic classification of women as the source of tradition has to be viewed in part as a patriarchal disenfranchisement of women within the nation. In lowland Vietnamese society, women have long remained in the shadows of their fathers, brothers, and husbands professionally, and subjected to Confucian moral codes of behavior. In art, women have been the subject of paintings since the colonial period and most often appear as dutiful and elegant wives and mothers. In painting, women are expected to look beautiful and represent the cultural ideal that is repeatedly propagated in magazines and newspapers as the proper Vietnamese woman (Taylor 1996).

If tradition resides so unequivocally with women and their work, then progress, national and otherwise, is the realm of men. Women, like ethnic minorities, can only be led to progress, as their essence resides squarely within the domain of the traditional. Lowe's (1996) analysis of the imagery of gender and nation in North Vietnam from the 1960s to 1975 brings out the same themes:

> In the iconography of the revolutionary nation-state, the peasant woman plants the roots of Vietnamese identity deep in the national soil, and tends their growth, displaying the signs that establish difference: her dress and her class. This division of labor frees the male worker and soldier to devote themselves to the forward-looking tasks of nation building, modernization, and integration into the communist brotherhood (Lowe 1996: 45).

After 1975, subsequent to the war against the United States and for national unification, images of women in (outmoded) regional and/or ethnic dress have continued to convey "traditional" realities to the nation. Public imagery in postindependence Vietnam is not confined to notions of gender and class. The modernist, national project has repeatedly presented ethnicity, gender, occupation, and class as analogous markers of identity. But, as we discuss below, the modernist appropriation of the markers of identity and difference is also a legacy of the colonial era. During that time, ethnicity and dress were redefined in relation to emerging political realities and new forms of subjectivity. This reworking of identity and social relations served to undermine the resonance of precolonial states as well as the practices of difference that sustained highland people's autonomy from state control. Colonial and postcolonial depictions and enactments of ethnic-minority identity through dress and customs share a concern with naturalizing state control of social reality. Using dress as a signifier, Vietnamese artists have played an important role in conveying ethnic and gendered realities to the general public in ways that reinforce the nationalist project. While our main concern is with this twentieth-century reality, we start the following section by charting dimensions of the reality that the colonial system undid.

The State, Ethnic Difference, and the People

A historical examination that attempts to chart majority–minority relations in Vietnam toward the present may implicitly project the territorial and ethnic dimensions of the contemporary postcolonial state onto a historical terrain where the bounded nation-state does not belong and where a majority–minority discourse may be fundamentally alien. Our intent here is not to map a Vietnamese space on the landscape of the past, but to highlight the historical specificity of twentieth-century ethnic relations and the period's imagery of ethnic and national identity.

Precolonial Vietnamese courts tended to be indifferent to the internal affairs of hinterland villages, while relations for trade and tribute were common. Ethnic identity was a feature in these dynamics, in that hinterland populations reproduced cultural schemes that were largely independent of state-centered, lowland society. Dry-rice farming (swiddening, slash-and-burn) was beyond the reach of the state's taxation schemes, and from the state's perspective these hinterland populations were uncivilized. Vietnamese courts, and society more generally, used terms such as *man* (Chinese, "barbarian") and *moi* (Vietnamese, "savage") for highland peoples. While the courts might strike deals with their leaders for warfare, tribute, and allegiance against a rival court, there is no indication of an attempt to integrate highland peoples into Vietnamese society. In this, highland–lowland relations in Vietnam are analogous to those in other parts of Southeast Asia. "Society" assumed a state with a court that integrated settlements and people through its control over trade and tribute and assigned identities in a hierarchic fashion. Lowland wet-rice farmers were as central to the economy of this state-centered society as they were low in its hierarchy.

Among populations that subsequently came to be defined as minorities in the northern region of Vietnam, there was commonly a local elite whose status depended on its relations with Vietnam's courts (and sometimes those of northern Laos). Many of these settlements, of Muong, Thai, Tay, Nung, Cao Lan, Yao, and other peoples, were engaged in wet-rice cultivation, and were thus within (while often marginal to) the civilized realm of the state. Within the state's framework of society, there was nothing questionable about these settlements, while their distance from the court may have contributed to cultural autonomy and the perpetuation of differences (in language, ritual, and dress) from Vietnamese society (see Condominas 1990; MacAlister 1967). In theory, highland dry-rice farmers stood outside this court-centered vision of society. The status of settlements vis-à-vis the state was not determined in ethnic terms, but through relations and positionings that were as likely to divide as to coalesce people who shared an ethnic reference. Discussing the early nineteenth-century law code of the Nguyen ruler Gia Long (r. 1802 to 1820), Hickey notes that while it allows Vietnamese men

> to enter the frontier areas and settle in one of the military colonies, it was forbidden . . . to remain in the milieu of the highlanders, for in doing so [a man] would be contaminating himself. Article 109 of the Gia Long Code specified that any Vietnamese who contracted marriage with a person "of barbarous races" would be subject to one hundred blows with a rod. (Hickey 1982: 165–6)

One of the few statements concerning the significance of dress within this bifurcated social environment is in a decree from another Nguyen king, Minh Mang (r. 1820 to 1841). He attempted to "civilize" the leaders of highland peoples, who occasionally presented tribute to the court, by providing them with tunics appropriate for the occasion rather than their appearing for the court in what to him was "bare skin." The outfit that the highland leaders were given for the occasion was that specified for "mandarins of the second class of the seventh degree in the civil service" (Hickey 1982: 172–3). One delegation of thirty-three highland leaders offering submission to the court in 1842 was summarily executed, which effectively cut the court's relations with highland peoples for some time (Hickey 1982: 182). Woodside (1971) characterizes the court's relations with highland peoples as "quasi-tributary, quasi-bureaucratic, [noting that] the Tho, the Nung, the Man, and the Meo highlanders [in the north] all lived under their own local chiefs," some presenting their tribute through the Lao rulers of Luang Prabang (1971: 244). Woodside shows further that the Nguyen court's emphasis on proper attire did not extend only to tribute-bearing highlanders. During his reign, Minh Mang twice issued "long edicts commanding [lowland] northern women to change from skirts to trousers" (1971: 134).

The French colonial takeover of Vietnam in the nineteenth century gradually extended to neighboring Laos and Cambodia, and the French called their domain Indochina. Colonial rule brought a new model of state and society, one that took ethnic-cum-racial identities as axiomatic, and ethnographic classification became an important aspect of the colonial strategy. Henri Roux's (1924) ethnographic account on northern Laos, for instance, insisted on the correctness of a racial classification of ethnic categories in terms of language families. Roux complained (1924: 373) about the laxness of local categorizations, where people's identity could change along with changes in livelihood and social relations.

The French colonial effort to identify peoples as "races" was in terms of the evolutionary theories of the time, and assumed that people could be ranked on a scale of progress (Blanckaert 1988). There was no inherent agreement on the policy implications of such classifications. French administrators debated whether the indigenous peoples of the Central Highlands were better off "protected" by the French from Vietnamese lowland populations or if they "vanished" as a "race" because they were too primitive (Salemink 1991: 254–6). In the Central Highlands, French administrators established themselves as the legitimate rulers through ceremonies where leaders of highland populations paid allegiance to them in a "traditional" way and wearing their traditional (highland) garb (Hickey 1982: 306–7; Salemink 1991: 252). This manipulation of tradition, including the explicit use of traditional dress, for the purposes of rule and expropriation draws on the colonial-era (and proto-nationalist) notion of "the people" as the basis for rule. Herein lies the drive behind the French colonial zeal to identify and classify all the "races" in Indochina and their ethnic components (see for instance Bonifacy 1919; Aymé 1930).

As was the case with other colonial regimes in Southeast Asia, the French rulers of Indochina became the collectors and defenders of traditional cultures and ways of life once they had quelled various forms of local resistance to their rule. This is one aspect of the colonial-era shift away from rulers and their courts and toward "the people" as the defining feature of "society." In Vietnam, other aspects of this shift drew on nationalist and anticolonial ferment in the early twentieth century that was decidedly antiroyal and antitraditional. Markers of a Chinese-influenced hierarchy in dress and hairstyle, as well as the Chinese-derived *Nom* script that was unique to Vietnam, became the targets of nationalist movements (Marr 1971). The state was identified with feudal and colonial oppression, and the nationalist making of Vietnam was expressly in the name of "the people" whose historical destiny was shaped by the struggle against foreign aggression. The Vietnamese term *dan toc*, analogous to the Malay *bangsa* and the Thai *chonchat* (all mean "the people"/ "nationality"), indexes a historically specific formulation of the nation that assumes an ethnic essence as the defining feature of community and identity.

In official documents, modern Vietnam is said to consist of fifty-four ethnic groups. But aside from a very recent Vietnam Museum of Ethnology and its publications, and a set of one-inch-tall porcelain figures of women in ethnic dress (Figure 5.2), public notions of Vietnam's ethnic diversity assume a smaller number of peoples. The four women in the poster in Bac Thai are one example. Others depict figures standing for the three (lowland) geographical regions of north, center, and south, and the division of the population into members of five language families. The latter is common in museum displays. There is not a single predominant definition of the components of the national population in Vietnam as there is in Laos. In the Lao case, the notion of High, Mid, and Low Lao (*Lao Sung*, *Lao Thoeng*, and *Lao Lum*) has become a very resonant model of the national population. This tripartite categorization is depicted,

Figure 5.2 A box of ten miniature porcelain images of women in ethnic dress, from a set that depicts all of Vietnam's ethnic groups. The figurines are of unified national space (e.g. "Bana, Vietnam") with the exception of majority Kinh for whom there is one each for "North Vietnam" and "South Vietnam." Photo: Hjorleifur R. Jonsson.

for instance, on currency notes through a representation of women in ethnic dress (Trankell 1998: 48). The three women refer to components of the nation both through ethnicity and region, Hmong highlanders in the north, Lao lowlanders in the central region, and Mon-Khmer-speaking mid-slope dwellers in the south.[2]

In Vietnamese public art, depictions of "kinds of people" are not fundamentally ethnic in character. Rather, ethnicity is one of the features that constitute kinds of Vietnamese. Examples of this include billboards that portray a doctor, a factory worker, a soldier, a peasant woman, a child in a school uniform, and an ethnic-minority woman as together making up the peoples of Vietnam (Figure 5.3). In these depictions, ethnicity and occupation stand as analogous markers of identity, and the most commonly implied reference of these pictorial assemblies is how all the kinds of people contribute (in their different ways) to the nation. Identity, whether ethnic, occupational, gendered, or otherwise, has been nationalized. Our understanding of the position of ethnic minorities in these depictions is that they stand as a measure

Figure 5.3 A billboard image showing representatives of the various sectors of the modern nation as in a family photo. Note the spatial division of men, women, and children, and the symmetry of the women in traditional ethnic minority dress (far left) and the modern ao dai (far right). Drawn on the margins are the outlines of the electrified urban future (left) and a flower garden (below). In official pronouncements, Vietnam's ethnic diversity is often described as a garden of scented, colorful flowers. Photo: Hjorleifur R. Jonsson.

of the progress of the Vietnamese nation. In their traditional, non-modern ethnic dress, they are an indication of the inclusiveness of the national community and at the same time of how far all other segments of Vietnamese society have moved from this condition of non-modern-ness.

The Vietnamese Propaganda Poster

The art of the Vietnamese propaganda poster draws equally on colonial encounters, nationalist politics, and the experiences of war for independence. Artists who had studied painting and drawing under the French colonial regime from 1925 to 1945 at a school established by the French painter Victor Tardieu, the Ecole des Beaux-Arts d'Indochine, joined anticolonial forces and began to create art that served the rising nationalist movement (Taylor 1997b). This included paintings of landscapes, Vietnamese villages, farmers, and ethnic minorities. Artists used their drafting skills to fashion images of the Vietnamese in their native environment, drawing attention to the characteristics of the Vietnamese nation. Depictions of people served to encourage Vietnamese citizens to consider themselves national subjects. Landscapes were the most common genre that served to incite pride in the Vietnamese land and reinforce viewers to imagine the nation as a geographic entity, where "land" and "people" were aspects of the same essence. Posters utilized these ideas and simplified them for the average viewer.

As national art that contributed to a national understanding and sentiment, this art was "popular" in the sense of being nonelite and being aimed at nonelite public spaces. The posters also addressed an international audience in order to project images of an independent Vietnam in the face of colonial opposition. The first poster created for the independence movement read in English "Vietnam for Vietnamese" and consisted of a lineup of historical figures meant to evoke past struggles against foreign aggression. This first graphic depiction of the nation of Vietnam and its people, created by Tran Van Can in 1941, served as a model for many subsequent posters. The image of a heroic Vietnamese standing at the helm of an abstracted outline of the Vietnamese map was utilized throughout the independence period, the revolution, and the war against the United States. Posters often show Vietnamese nationals standing on maps of Vietnam as a way to legitimate Vietnamese rule over the entire territory of Vietnam, north and south.

The nationalist depictions of Vietnam had a political project, toward the shared signifiers of a national community and away from alternative configurations such as the French colonial creation of Indochina (Goscha 1995). This shift, as well as the focus on "the people," contributed to a conceptual reworking of space and identity in terms of a shared struggle against foreign aggression, and posters then broadcast this vision with their combinations of "Vietnamese subjects" and the outlines of the national space.

While paintings were used to imagine the essential traits of the Vietnamese nation in an ideal or romantic form, posters spoke more directly of the Vietnamese fight for nationhood. In the early 1940s most of the population of Indochina was illiterate and posters served to draw attention to the anticolonial struggle and to combat illiteracy. Using the ancient art of woodblock printing, artists drew images of women learning to read and peasants wielding pens instead of hoes, thus simultaneously encouraging the population to learn to read and join the revolutionary forces. Painting materials were expensive and scarce, but paper was easily made and images easily reproduced through basic printing processes. Graphic arts did not just serve poster making but also helped to create stamps, currency, and political logos. Artists participated in the making of medals, stationery, banners, and pamphlets. Portraits of the revolutionary leader Ho Chi Minh were also created during this time. In fact, Ho Chi Minh figured more prominently in posters than in paintings.

Posters reduced complicated political ideas to simple, iconic messages. A mother and child, a rice farmer, or a soldier standing beside a flag, a historical relic, or brandishing a weapon, projected the concept of the people fighting for Vietnamese autonomy. References to history were combined with present concerns, such as poverty and illiteracy, to illustrate the need to modernize for the sake of national well-being.

> A number of posters mixed modern and traditional images and symbols to highlight the timeless character of the spirit of resistance to foreign invasion: a traditional Dong Son design, a modern map of Vietnam, and images of different ethnic groups armed with modern and traditional weapons . . . Placed together, modern, traditional and linguistic signs echoed specific patriotic messages: patriotic traditions; the goal of national reunification; national defense; commemoration of war heroes; contribution to national construction; military victory; territorial integrity; national reunion; and regenerative patriotism. (Vasavakul 1997: 4)

Ethnic minorities were included among the symbols of patriotism, history, and/ or tradition in these posters. In poster art, ethnic minorities are visual signifiers of national unity and yet they are historically non-Vietnamese and live in areas removed from modern development and political authority, in the mountainous regions bordering China, Laos, and Cambodia.

One reason for their inclusion is that the seat of the independence movement was located in the highlands north of Hanoi. This was also where the art school was relocated after it closed down during the Japanese occupation, and the French withdrawal and subsequent return to Indochina after the revolutionary leader Ho Chi Minh declared independence in September of 1945. Posters were not made at the art school in Hanoi. But when an art school reopened in the region of Viet Bac where the independence movement was stationed, To Ngoc Van, a graduate of the Ecole des Beaux-Arts d'Indochine, was put in charge and there he conducted classes in art and politics. Influenced by movements in the Soviet Union and China, artists in Viet Bac were encouraged to think about ways in which art could serve the state and the process of nation building. Posters became the popular vehicle for expressing national identity and encouraging the population to join the national struggle. The art school remained in the region of Viet Bac until the Viet Minh (Independence League) victory against the French at the valley of Dien Bien Phu, northwest of Viet Bac, in 1954. During the nine years that the revolutionary movement was stationed in the hills, artists were greatly intrigued by the ethnically varied highlanders residing in the northern regions of the Red River Delta and were inspired to sketch them and include them in their posters depicting the nation of Vietnam (Taylor 1997a).

Posters made after 1954 consistently included one or more ethnicities when referring to the Vietnamese "people." Part of the reason for this has to do with vocabulary and Vietnamese definitions regarding ethnicity and nationalism. Ho Chi Minh first used the term *dan toc Viet Nam* or Vietnamese nationals in his 1945 declaration of independence. By *dan toc Viet Nam* he meant that all the people of Vietnam were to define the nation. In subsequent use, the term *dan toc* is less inclusive, as ethnic minorities are persistently marked in speech as *dan toc thieu so* or *dan toc it nguoi*, "small-group people."

In poster and billboard art, ethnic minorities are essentially an Other within the Vietnamese population, they never stand for average Vietnamese. In posters made during the war against the south, ethnic minorities were portrayed in arms. The combat for national unification was depicted in posters as a struggle for the entire Vietnamese population against the United States and imperial aggression. In posters, therefore, ethnic minorities appear concerned with national causes and are placed on equal terms with the Vietnamese in national affairs. Yet, the fact that minorities are represented in their traditional clothing negates that equality. Unlike the *ao dai* that is worn by Vietnamese ethnic nationals and connotes modernity and urban sophistication, the dresses worn by Hmong, Yao, or Tai women have no modern counterpart. They did not undergo a transformation during or after the colonial period in response to the "new" independent nation. It is as if the posters are still locking the ethnic minorities in time and refusing them full participation in the modern Vietnamese nation. Their participation in the national struggle, the process of nation building, and Vietnamese society are recorded through their dress. Presenting the ethnic minority in art as an item of ethnic clothing is more than an identification symbol, it projects an image of backwardness. The ethnic-minority dress is the symbol that legitimates Vietnamese authority over the ethnic minorities within the national borders.

During our visits to the ethnic-minority areas in the north and the south of the country we discovered that ethnic-minority dress is not commonly worn. Conversations with minority people suggest widespread Vietnamese prejudices regarding ethnic-minority cultures as "backwards," and partly for this reason ethnic-minority peoples wear market clothes[3] in an attempt to avoid these prejudiced connotations. Official policies have aimed at eradicating backward practices and have emphasized progressive changes in livelihood, culture, and rituals (Evans 1992). Recent efforts at the "selective preservation" of minority cultures (Salemink 2000) therefore seem aimed more at sustaining enough markers of ethnic difference to maintain the notion that Vietnam consists of fifty-four ethnic groups than at any interest in these minority cultures or identities as such.

The official notion of ethnic diversity, that the country contains fifty-four ethnic groups, is presented as an achievement. As such, it belongs with other statistical markers of national acheivement such as gross domestic product. But most importantly, the "achievement" implied in the cliché of fifty-four ethnic groups concerns the success of unifying such diverse peoples. It is in this context that the markers of alterity must be retained through the visuals of diverse ethnic dress. If this diversity disappears, then the great achievement of national unification is no longer apparent. What the posters declare, in their propagandist fashion, is not far from the reality of ethnic diversity in contemporary Vietnam; difference is officially sanctioned only insofar as it contributes to the image of the nation. Within this framework, as in the posters, the more locally oriented practices of ethnic-minority livelihood, culture, and rituals simply have no place.

The Bac Thai poster of Vietnam's population through four kinds of women in traditional dress can be viewed as portraying some of the regional and ethnic divisions with which the making of modern Vietnam has been confronted. The representation of lowland ethnic Vietnamese as "north" and "south" speaks to a particularly twentieth-century predicament, not only in the dismissal of the previously predominant central region of the Nguyen courts in Hue, but also and more importantly concerning the 1954 division of the country into North and South Vietnam following the nationalist victory at Dien Bien Phu, and the subsequent American War. Both the nationalist victory in the north and the struggle over the south involved contest over the loyalties of highland ethnic minorities, and this is what poster depictions of people in ethnic-minority dress variously commemorate or attempt to stimulate. The importance of women in these posters appears informed by many of the same concerns as Gladney (1994), Schein (2000), and others have noted for the visual portrayals of ethnic minorities in southern China. The other is repeatedly presented as feminine and backward (colorful and exotic). Not only does this convey the "unmarked" majority as masculine and progressive, in important ways it makes it possible to imagine and experience the national majority as a coherent subject.

The depiction of Vietnam's internal Others as traditional, diverse, and feminine is a projection that conveys uniformity on lowland peoples, erasing ethnic and other divergence. That is, the imagery of highland minorities as the national Other conjures up the national Self as modern, uniform, and masculine. This projection of diversity through images of ethnic-minority women is clearly an example of internal Orientalism. But whether it is primarily about ethnic-minority peoples in the hinterlands is another issue. There are sizeable populations of ethnic Chinese, Khmer, and Cham peoples in the lowlands, for instance. The portrayal of national diversity in posters, billboards, and the like serves to sanction and routinize particular ways of imagining and experiencing diversity. Diversity is depicted in relation to national goals, which serves to insert national hegemony into the imagery of the nation's Others. As such, the propaganda function of the images may lie in what they leave out as much as in what they make implicit. Among the features of diversity that are erased from view are frameworks of lowland social life that vary by class and region as well as ethnicity, the limited success and ultimate failure of collectivized farming, and Vietnamese masculinity as concerned with household matters or private pleasure as opposed to the relentless contribution to national defense and progress that is on view in posters and billboards.

Ethnic-Minority Clothing in Art

Artists found the highland peoples interesting to sketch and draw. There was also a political motive for including them in the art of the period. The Viet Minh knew that it needed the support of the peoples in the highlands to fight against the French. In the preparations for the battle of Dien Bien Phu, ammunitions, food, water, and other supplies had to be carried through areas inhabited by highland minorities. Not only had the highlanders to physically help the Viet Minh in offering food and water, but also the Viet Minh had to secure their friendship and alliance. The French had traditionally viewed the hill peoples as "primitive" peoples who could be manipulated to benefit the colonial economy more easily than could the more sophisticated Annamese urbanites. During the interim period between 1945 and 1954, the French also may have hoped to promote a "divide and conquer" policy and set the highlanders against the Vietnamese in order to weaken Viet Minh forces (Salemink 1991). It was in the interest of the Viet Minh to uphold a unified front and join forces with ethnic groups living within the contested geographic area of Vietnam. And after the Viet Minh victory at Dien Bien Phu, Vietnamese scholars maintained the idea of a Vietnam with a harmonious population and dissolved any notion of ethnic tension. As Patricia Pelley writes, "(t)o repudiate the colonial claims that Vietnam was fragmented along ethnic lines, post colonial scholars vowed to write national history from an inclusive, multi-ethnic perspective" (Pelley 1998: 377).

Sketches made of ethnic minorities during the 1940s and 1950s served as models not only for future billboards and posters but also for paintings and drawings made by artists and graduates of the various national schools and colleges of fine arts after independence. It has become standard practice even today for art students to travel to the mountainous regions of Vietnam and sketch portraits of the different ethnic groups. These sketches turn into paintings that are sold on the tourist market and in galleries in Hanoi and Ho Chi Minh City. While these portrayals of ethnic minorities have an appeal as curiosities or exotica, they originally served a political agenda similar to that of (propaganda) posters and billboards. Artists from the 1960s through the 1980s often painted themes revolving around the education of minorities by Vietnamese soldiers or government workers, the development of the highlands, and other assistance projects provided by the state to less modernized regions of Vietnam. In these paintings, the Vietnamese are shown in their worker or soldier uniforms helping their fellowmen. Women are dressed in indigenous clothing to delineate the nation's diversity and yet emphasize the collaborative efforts of majority citizens and others.

Some artists who trained during the resistance period in the hills of Viet Bac have continued to paint minorities almost as a reminder of that period. Artists such as Mai Long and Linh Chi have made paintings of highland ethnic minorities their trademark (Figure 5.4). Furthermore, part of their success as painters is due to their ability to portray minorities in a realistic and yet idealized fashion with an emphasis on minority dress and textile patterns. Minority clothes provide artists with artistic and aesthetic material, enhancing a portrait with color and texture. Paintings of farmers and soldiers in their simple uniforms appear bland and drab compared to the brightly embroidered leggings, skirts, jackets, and headdresses of the Yao, Hmong, and Tai. Through portraits made by Vietnamese *Kinh* artists, minorities become commodities, signifiers for sale that add another layer to how minorities are appropriated for Vietnamese agendas.

After graduating from the art school in Viet Bac during the period of resistance against the French, Mai Long and Linh Chi developed their artistic skills while sketching minorities in the mountains. Though their intent never was to sell paintings of minorities in particular, their reputation as painters of minorities helped to establish them as artists first in the immediate postindependence period and more recently in the development of the international art market. Mai Long lived in Son La province northwest of Hanoi near the border with Laos for eight years after the Viet Minh victory at Dien Bien Phu. He grew very familiar with the Tai groups living there, eating their food, living in their houses, and raising his children with theirs.

Mai Long's presence in a highland village was part of a program of educating minorities in the Vietnamese language and political theory to incorporate them into the nation. He was not sent as an educator but rather as an observer, a body, an influence on the local population. Somewhat like an American Peace Corps volunteer, he was there to help spread the goodwill of the government's

Figure 5.4 Mai Long's painting of a Black Thai woman. Private collection, photo by Hjorleifur R. Jonsson.

literacy campaigns to the mountainous regions. The influence that he and others would exert on the highlanders would help the process of socialization reach the border areas. He and his family grew fond of Tai customs and habits, and in conversations with us they suggest that the stay there had a greater impact on them than on the highland Tai. Mai Long's paintings of minorities show signs of his affection for the Tai, but they are also emblematic of the Vietnamese intervention in the highlands and the national appropriation of ethnic-minority dress as a signifier.

Nationalizing Difference, Naturalizing the State

Dress as a marker of ethnic groups is a particular legacy of the colonial period and nationalist ferment during that era. This is not to say that prior to the colonial era ethnic differences were not marked through dress and fashion. Rather, notions of difference were reworked. For the region that became Vietnam, dress marked status and relations to the state, for instance, and changes in status could be manifest through dress, such as when a ruler made his mark on his subjects with a new dress code or provided leaders of hinterland populations with outfits adequate for royal visits. During the colonial period, dress became a signifier for a different classification of identity, one that assumed ethnic uniformity in the place of shifting positions within a political landscape. There is an element of continuity in spite of these apparent changes, in that dress as a marker of identity still depended on the state's classificatory scheme. This scheme, rather than the state's role, is what changed; people were now to be identified in terms of assumed ethnic essences.

The colonial-era making of dress as an ethnic index served to redefine pre-existing markers of community, tradition, and political affiliation, and the anticolonial nationalist movement drew on this colonial legacy of "peoples" to problematize internal Others in relation to national agendas. Pervasive notions of ethnic-minority clothing as a marker of backwardness have led hinterland peoples to wear market clothes. Meanwhile, these essences of assumed backwardness have been repeatedly appropriated by agents of the state, in a varied global context, for celebratory statements of the ethnic and regional unity of the nation.

Earlier, we stated that locally oriented practices of ethnic-minority livelihood, culture, and rituals had no place in Vietnamese propaganda posters or within national imagery more generally. But ethnic-minority practices and markers of local identity have not been erased. Instead, they have been reoriented to the extralocal. It is as such, as they bear on national goals, that ethnic-minority dress and cultural practices have been endorsed. The public commemoration of alterity has in fundamental ways been about the nation. There are numerous parallels to this process in other settings (Muratorio 1993; Adams 1997; Jonsson 2000), where national authorities engage in celebrating markers of difference such as ethnic (minority) dress at the same time as national policies have effectively undermined any of the practices of difference that the dress previously signified.

The most recent example of such dynamics of reorientation occurred in the context of widespread unrest in the Central Highlands of Vietnam, in January and February 2001, where thousands of ethnic-minority people staged demonstrations protesting religious persecution and outsiders' encroachment on their land. Authorities sent in the military to quell the protests, and arrested at least twenty people (*New York Times*, 8 and 9 February 2001). A few weeks later, according to the Vietnamese media, over two thousand ethnic-minority youth in the region assembled for a:

> two day annual festival aim[ed] to preserve and develop minority groups' cultural identities and to welcome the 70th founding anniversary of the Ho Chi Minh

Communist Youth Union and the 26th anniversary of national reunification. A folk song singing contest, costume show and musical instrument performance, and introduction of local culinary arts are included in the festival. (Vietnam News Agency 2001)

The emphasis on markers of local identity (dress, music, and food) in the Central Highlands festival of national loyalty, several weeks after ethnic-minority peoples staged public protests against their current predicament, shows clearly how the nation-state appropriates signifiers of local identity and reorients them to a national public sphere. As in billboards and museums, this indexing of diversity as celebratory and fundamentally national in character thrives on notions of the state's agents as leading the peoples of Vietnam toward modernity and progress, and/or in sustaining their traditions. The success of that notion depends on depictions of the people as in need of guidance and leadership, which is what the recurring portrayal of "the people" (ethnic-minority or not) as feminine and traditional so persistently conveys. Dress is fundamental to these portrayals and enactments of the people. As an appropriated signifier, ethnic-minority dress serves as a vehicle for defining national unity and for sanctioning the state's power to define the parameters of the social landscape.

Through various policies regarding livelihood and cultural practice, Vietnam's authorities have effectively stigmatized ethnic-minority traditions as backward and incompatible with national goals. Within this national scheme of identity and difference, ethnic-minority peoples may reproduce some of their cultures outside the official gaze. But any public manifestation of minority peoples through dress or other features is likely to be a statement about national essences, a display of the successful insertion of national agendas, and definitions into the fabric of ethnic-minority identity.

The Vietnamese appropriation of their internal Others is in many ways an inheritance from the French colonial regime, and it is within that process of global/local interactions that we situate the emphasis on the visual markers of alterity: traditional, ethnic, or regional dress. Both the French colonial state and the modern nation-state of Vietnam have staged rituals of ethnic-minority allegiance, where the use of traditional dress has played an important part. In both cases, the endorsement of alterity has closely followed the suppression of protests. The repeated embrace of internal Others in their traditional dress can be seen as an attempt to erase from view the disruptions that various forms of warfare and state control have brought upon the peoples of Vietnam since the nineteenth century.[4] The fundamental contribution of globalization to dress as a signifier in Vietnam may be that it has facilitated the image of "local" (ethnic-minority) identities as timeless. At separate historical moments, this state-endorsed image of the Other's timelessness has placed colonial and postcolonial state regimes within the traditional and natural order of things, at the same time as it has removed state-produced violence and inequality from view.

Notes

1. This chapter is a revised version of our "Other Attractions in Vietnam," published in *Asian Ethnicity* (3, 2), copyright Taylor & Francis 2002, and is used with permission. Our research in and on Vietnam and its art and ethnic minorities draws on several stays and visits since 1992 (Taylor in 1992–94, 1995–96, 1998, and 2000, Jonsson in 1996, 1998, and 2000). We are each indebted to the Center for Asian Studies at Arizona State University for separate A.T. Steele Grants, and the College of Liberal Arts and Sciences at Arizona State University for separate Faculty-Grant-In-Aid Fellowships, that made possible our most recent research. Our collaboration draws also on separate strands of previous research in Vietnam, Cambodia, and Thailand. Nora A. Taylor thanks Fulbright-Hays for a research grant, and, for another grant, the Joint Committee on Southeast Asia of the Social Science Research Council and the American Council of Learned Societies, whose funding came from the Andrew W. Mellon Foundation, the Ford Foundation, and the Henry Luce Foundation. For support of his research, Hjorleifur R. Jonsson thanks the National Science Foundation, the Wenner-Gren Foundation for Anthropological Research, the Nordic Institute of Asian Studies, and the Walter F. Vella Scholarship Fund.

2. Trankell (1998: 49) states that Lao Thoeng refers primarily to Khmu. The banknote representation of mid-slope Lao does not show Khmu, however. Khmu (Kmhmu) are northerners. Frank Proschan (2001) states that the striped dress of the Lao Thoeng woman is that of one of the southern groups. The ethnic-as-regional division of national space in the Lao imagery has parallels in Vietnamese depictions of the nation through kinds of people. See Proschan's (1996) discussion of the ethnic label *Kha* (that is analogous to the Vietnamese term *Moi*) for an account of the tripartite division of the peoples of Laos.

3. By "market clothes" we mean the standard, store-bought shirt and pants that do not mark people as local in the sense of having a sub-national ethnic or regional identity. This is not to say that such store-bought clothes are neutral as signifiers of identity; they tend to mark people in national terms as rural or urban and further to be a marker of class position.

4. Such processes of erasure are also evident in the designation of the indigenous peoples of the Central Highlands of Vietnam as "proto-Indochinese" and "Montagnards," both of which "suggest a virtual reality of transparent concepts uncorrupted by the shifting terrain of history that has local, national, and transnational dimensions" (Jonsson 2001: 63).

References

Adams, Kathleen M. (1997), "Touting Touristic 'Primadonnas': Tourism, Ethnicity, and National Integration in Sulawesi, Indonesia," in Michel Picard and Robert E. Wood (eds), *Tourism, Ethnicity, and the State in Asian and Pacific Societies*, Honolulu: University of Hawaii Press.

Anderson, Benedict (1983), *Imagined Communities: Reflections on the Origins and Spread of Nationalism*, London: Verso.

Aymé, G. (1930), *Monographie du Vᵉ Territoire Militaire, Indochine Française* (Exposition Coloniale Internationale, Paris 1931), Hanoi: Imprimerie d'Extrême-Orient.

Bennett, Tony (1995), *The Birth of the Museum*, London and New York: Routledge.

Blanckaert, Claude (1988), "On the Origins of French Ethnology: William Edwards and the Doctrine of Race," in George W. Stocking (ed.), *Bones, Bodies, Behavior: Essays on Biological Anthropology*, Madison: University of Wisconsin Press.

Bonifacy, Auguste (1919), *Cours d'ethnographie indochinoise*, Hanoi-Haiphong: Imprimerie d'Extrême-Orient.

Condominas, Georges (1990), *From Lawa to Mon, From Saa to Thai*, Canberra: Department of Anthropology, Research School of Pacific Studies, Australian National University.

Diep Trung Binh (1997), *Patterns on Textiles of the Ethnic Groups in Northeast of Vietnam*, Hanoi: Cultures of Nationalities Publishing House.

Evans, Grant (1992), "Internal Colonialism in the Central Highlands of Vietnam," *Sojourn*, 7(2): 274–304.

Gladney, Dru (1994), "Representing Nationality in China: Refiguring Majority/ Minority Identities," *Journal of Asian Studies* 53(1): 92–128.

Goscha, Christopher (1995), *Vietnam or Indochina: Contesting Concepts of Space in Vietnamese Nationalism, 1887–1954*, Copenhagen: Nordic Institute of Asian Studies.

Hickey, Gerald C. (1982), *Sons of the Mountains: Ethnohistory of the Vietnamese Central Highlands to 1954*, New Haven: Yale University Press.

Hobsbawm, Eric and Ranger, Terence (eds) (1983), *The Invention of Tradition*, Cambridge and New York: Cambridge University Press.

Jonsson, Hjorleifur (2000), "Yao Minority Identity and the Location of Difference in the South China Borderlands," *Ethnos* 65(1): 56–82.

—— (2001), "French Natural in the Vietnamese Highlands: Nostalgia and Erasure in Montagnard Identity," in J. Winston and L. Ollier (eds), *Of Vietnam: Identities in Dialogue*, New York: Palgrave.

Leach, Edmund R. (1976), *Culture and Communication*, Cambridge: Cambridge University Press.

Lowe, Viviane (1996), *Women in Arms: Gender and Nation in the Democratic Republic of Vietnam*, MA Thesis, Australian National University.

MacAlister, John T. (1967), "Mountain Minorities and the Viet Minh: A Key to the Indochina War," in Peter Kunstadter (ed.), *Southeast Asian Tribes, Minorities, and Nations*, vol. 2, Princeton: Princeton University Press.

Marr, David (1971), *Vietnamese Anti-Colonialism*, Berkeley: University of California Press.

Mitchell, Timothy (1989), "The World as Exhibition," *Comparative Studies in Society and History* 31(2): 217–36.

Muratorio, Blanca (1993), "Nationalism and Ethnicity: Images of Ecuadorian Indians and the Imagemakers at the Turn of the Nineteenth Century," in Judith D. Toland (ed.), *Ethnicity and the State*, New Brunswick, NJ: Transaction Publishers.

Pelley, Patricia (1998), "'Barbarians' and 'Younger Brothers': The Remaking of Race in Postcolonial Vietnam," *Journal of Southeast Asian Studies* 29(2): 374–92.

Proschan, Frank (1996), "Who are the Khaa?" *Proceedings of the Sixth International Conference of Thai Studies*, Chiangmai, Thailand, Theme 4 (Traditions and Changes at the Local Level).

—— (2001), personal communication.

Roux, Henri (1924), "Deux tribus de la Région de Phongsaly," *Bulletin de l'Ecole Française d'Extrême Orient* 24.

Sahlins, Marshall (1976), *Culture and Practical Reason*, Chicago: University of Chicago Press.

Salemink, Oscar (1991), "*Mois* and *Maquis*: The Invention and Appropriation of Vietnam's Montagnards from Sabatier to the CIA," in George W. Stocking (ed.), *Colonial Situations: Essays on the Contextualization of Ethnographic Knowledge*, Madison: University of Wisconsin Press.

—— (2000) "Sedentarization and Selective Preservation among the Montagnards in the Vietnamese Central Highlands," in Jean Michaud (ed.), *Turbulent Times and Enduring Peoples: Mountain Minorities in the South-East Asian Massif*, London: Curzon.

Schein, Louisa (2000), *Minority Rules: The Miao and the Feminine in China's Cultural Politics*, Durham, NC: Duke University Press.

Stocking, George W. (1987), *Victorian Anthropology*, New York: Free Press.

Taffin, Dominique (ed.) (2000), *Du Musée Colonial au Musée des Cultures du Monde*, Paris: Maisonneuve & Larousse.

Taylor, Nora A. (1996) "Invisible Painters: North Vietnamese Women Artists from the Revolution to Doi Moi," in Dinah Dysart and Hannah Fink (eds), *Asian Women Artists*, Sydney: ArtAsia Pacific.

—— (1997a), *The Artist and the State: The Politics of Painting and National Identity in Hanoi, Vietnam, 1925–1995*, Ph.D. dissertation, Cornell University.

—— (1997b), "Orientalism/Occidentalism: The Founding of the *Ecole des Beaux-Arts d'Indochine* and the Politics of Painting in Colonial Vietnam, 1925–1945," *Crossroads* 11(2): 1–34.

Trankell, Ing-Britt (1998), "'The Minor Part of the Nation:' Politics of Ethnicity in Laos," in Ing-Britt Trankell and Laura Summers (eds), *Facets of Power and Its Limitations: Political Culture in Southeast Asia*, Uppsala: University of Uppsala, Department of Anthropology.

Turner, Terence (1980), "The Social Skin," in Jeremy Cherfas and Roger Lewin (eds) *Not Work Alone: A Cross-cultural View of Activities Superfluous to Survival*, Beverly Hills, CA: Sage.

Vasavakul, Thaveeporn (1997), "Art and Politics: Nationalism in Vietnamese War Posters," *The Asia Pacific Magazine* 8.

Vietnam News Agency (2001), "Minority Youth Cultural Festival in Central Highlands," Electronic document, http://www.vnagency.com.vn/Public/Readnewse.asp?FileN=frav2003.010, Accessed 20 March 2001.

Woodside, Alexander (1971), *Vietnam and the Chinese Model*, Cambridge, MA: Harvard University Press.

6

Dress for Sukses: Fashioning Femininity and Nationality in Urban Indonesia

Carla Jones

On a hot afternoon in Jakarta in June of 2000, I listened carefully to one of Indonesia's foremost "experts" on professional dress and lifestyle explain her reasons for worrying about Indonesian middle-class women.[1] Eileen Rachman, owner of a nationally renowned self-improvement course for women, writer of a syndicated magazine column, and expert in a traveling workshop series on dress and manners, explained her reason for the need for these programs thus, "Carla, I must confess that sometimes I am embarrassed by Indonesian women's lack of appreciation of 'lifestyle.' I see Indonesian women, especially when I am traveling abroad, who make me feel ashamed because they don't know how to interact with others, they dress awkwardly, and they just don't seem world class. They just don't have a lifestyle. I feel it is a kind of responsibility for me to help them become more developed." Her comment was telling for its frankness, but also as an indication of how seriously the appearance and manners of Indonesian women were understood to be to a larger national debate on the future of Indonesian national culture.

In this chapter I suggest that a significant site for the contest over the terms of modernity in contemporary Indonesia is women's bodies, particularly through their dress and manners. I describe how middle-class women in the central Javanese city of Yogyakarta strove during the late 1990s, through a private course of personal development, to educate themselves and others on the appropriate ways of personal appearance and presentation. The course instructors and students were involved in cultural production, by distinguishing themselves from and with other class and status groups both within and without Indonesia, through consumption.[2]

As many scholars have argued about the link between dress and national identity, it is not uncommon for postcolonial nationalists to embrace a form of self-Orientalizing that represents the national collective through women's "traditional" dress in ways that make both the particular outfit and the connection between women's bodies and the national body appear to be natural and timeless (e.g., Chatterjee 1989; Comaroff 1996; Smith 1995; Schein 2000; Schneider and Weiner 1989; Taylor and Jonsson, Chapter 5 of this volume). As a result, while male citizens have been encouraged to attempt to pass as unmarked by wearing the increasingly global uniform of the suit, women are encouraged to become more marked through the donning of local outfits that become nationalized. In many cases this has been the outgrowth of racialist colonial techniques that emphasized the importance of dress and comportment as a mode of rule and superiority (Cohn 1989; Murra 1989). In the post-colonial context, such outfits then become glossed as traditional precisely because they are deemed to be the very antithesis of fashion, because they appear not to have changed over time. Yet what makes such outfits currently serve nationalist motives may contradict what Western definitions of fashion demand, that is, constant change. So the question then remains, what are the effects of a push for national fashion on citizens? And how do these effects vary according to gender?

Strikingly, many of the instances of such gender-specific nationalist self-Orientalizing are of women's "traditional" clothes that are typically worn infrequently, often for rituals or official functions that emphasize the sacredness of the outfit (e.g. Ruhlen, Chapter 3 of this volume; Leshkowich, Chapter 2 this volume). In the case of Indonesia, John Pemberton has argued that the Suharto regime's celebration of such traditional dress was part of a larger political project to link the regime's designs on national development to an apparently ancient and sacred Javanese culture (Pemberton 1994).[3] In general, less attention has been paid to the ways in which national identities are refracted through and invested in forms of women's style that are not ethnically marked or that seem like contemporary Western styles, and yet that are increasingly the norm for women from a wide cross-section of classes in many postcolonial contexts. This is certainly the case in many of the urban centers in Asia. It is possible that the invisibility of this phenomenon on the global fashion stage is because these clothes appear to be inauthentic, unmediated imitations of styles originating outside the country.[4] Yet in the case of Indonesia such an interpretation would misinterpret the motivations behind the development of national fashions. The cultivation of an indigenous Indonesian fashion industry, which celebrates neotraditional styles as well as Western-style clothing, has been a key element of national development strategy, development that has been figured as not only economic but also cultural. National elites have considered fashion, or "*fesyen*" as it is called in Indonesian, to be one component of national cultural growth. Indonesian designers who have trained in Europe and the United States have local celebrity status within Indonesia, fashion shows are covered in close detail in women's magazines, and women who cannot afford their designs still know and track collections. It is possible that this kind of consumer awareness is a continued effect of the colonial concern with using dress as a marker of difference. During the nineteenth century, as Patricia Spyer has argued, Dutch colonizers in the Aru Islands of the East Indies used knowledge of fashion, acquired through both its production and its consumption, to negotiate rule there. While Dutch traders collected luxury items, such as pearls and exotic feathers for the European fashion market, they simultaneously criticized local tastes. Islanders were considered unaware of the inherent appeal of their commodities, yet were mocked as failed mimics when they wore European-style clothes. "[L]ike history and time, fashion belonged to colonizers and not the colonized" (Spyer 1998: 169). For contemporary elites in Indonesia, arriving on the global stage involves having local fashion. For Jakarta taste-makers and designers, having local fashion means not simply pride in and use of neotraditional women's clothes, although that is important, but also the knowledge and enjoyment of clothes that are appropriate to white-collar work (as opposed to manual labor or factory work). Showing that one can locate knowledge about local fashions' position in a global chronology of fashion references, revealing the ebbing and waning of trends specific to an Indonesian cultural context, all the while maintaining cultural authenticity, have been as important to producing developed citizens as other sectors of national development.

I situate my discussion of how Indonesian women citizens learned to value and consume fashion in a larger history of national development strategy in Indonesia. I make two separate but related points in my argument. First, I analyze how new forms of expertise, manifested most explicitly in private personal-development courses, educated women citizens into consumers of Indonesian *fesyen*, through knowledge about both the "traditional" uniform for women, the sarong and lace blouse ensemble called the *kain kebaya*, and the more apparently Western-styled professional skirt-suits and other outfits. The effect of these new discursive forms of expertise was that women instructors and students in the courses I studied learned to perform femininity in ways that created new gender and class identities. Following the work of Judith Butler (1990), and by extension Michel Foucault (1995 [1977]; 1990 [1978]), I suggest that such performances disciplined women into normative femininity but also allowed women consumers to see their performances as providing important cultural and material effects. Second, I argue that the women I knew considered their consumer work to be just that, cultural work essential to personal progress in the public sphere, rather than merely pleasure located in the private sphere of the home. The argument that women's consumer activity is often undervalued or made invisible, by imagining it as self-indulgent pleasure, has been an important contribution in American feminist research (see, e.g., di Leonardo 1987; Conroy 1998; Hochschild 1989a, b). However, there is still little research on the ways in which new class and gender formations outside the United States interpret women's consumer activity.

Class-ifying Women in Yogyakarta

In the late 1990s, women in Yogyakarta who could afford to do so chose to find information on how to achieve a modern feminine lifestyle through private personal-development courses. I base my argument in my fieldwork on one such course on personal development, where women strove to educate themselves and others in the appropriate techniques of personal appearance and presentation. Ubiquitous attention to personal grooming and fashion choices was evidence of how the feminine self was increasingly under siege in the later years of the Suharto New Order regime, which began in 1965 and ended in the Asian Economic Crisis in 1998. Women were not to appear too rich, too backward, too poor, or too un-Islamic. Women therefore used their surfaces or "social skin" (Turner 1980) as a communicative palette through which to negotiate their social worlds. Terence Turner argues that decoration (or lack thereof) of the body is a universally "symbolic stage upon which the drama of socialization is enacted" (112). However, I show that it is within particular histories and relations of power that dress and decoration can become a dominant element of the moral self. This is particularly interesting when there are forces actively trying to sell commoditized elements of this self to a target population, as was the case during the intensive advertising and marketing period of the heady last years of the Suharto regime. Indeed, a shared value of the importance of appearances, which the course I studied exploited, was in fact not new to Indonesian men or women. However, what the course did was to emphasize this value in new ways that were related to the history of the preceding thirty years.

Theoretical approaches to the study of consumption have often focused on the domestic sphere, because consumption seems to occur in private and for apparently personal reasons. Yet in making these assumptions, such approaches have also often dismissed consumer choices as either personal expression or imitative, strategic gestures designed to manipulate a viewing audience. For example, Thorstein Veblen's analysis of consumption argued that clothing choices were attempts of particular class members to emulate the styles of the classes just above them (1994 [1899]). In part because of the emphasis theorists of Marx have placed on the role of production in forming class positions, until recently consumption has been understudied as a significant site for cultural work. Yet consumption can be a site for collective negotiation, as in the case of national debates on culture, while still offering a limited but material space for creating individual identities. This is particularly stimulating to consider in the context of women's uses of fashion. Veblen's critique of consumption interpreted the consumption of fashion as a uniquely feminine foible and plight. According to Veblen, women are trapped in a larger social system that forces them into meaningless attention to tasteful display. Fashions are particularly rich sites for such display, then, for it is through the clothing on women's bodies, and the fact that women seem to be so magically enamored of the allure of that clothing, that women can come to be seen as victims of a system that prevents them from producing.[5] The display of status, often through clothing, ultimately serves to enhance the image of the man who produces the income supporting that consumption. Women in Veblen's analysis are thus limited by an economic and gendered system that turns them into consuming servants for men. In short, a man only looks as good as his wife's "look."

By contrast, more recent work on consumption suggests that Veblen's approach ignored the important cultural and personal meaning generated through consumption, particularly in the face of changing social conditions. This new attention to consumption has emphasized the possibility for a variety of alternative functions of consumption, including political resistance, kinship work, and identity formation, even as those changing social conditions create new class inequalities.[6] Indeed, women in the course I studied did acquire techniques of display that equipped them to perform their femininity competitively, sometimes even above their material class positions, but such performances could, on occasion, also reveal the borders of gender and class identities. As a result, women's consumer choices in general, and fashion choices in particular, were not simply secondary manifestations of urban public culture in 1990s Indonesia. Rather, women's appearance choices were culturally productive acts central to creating that culture.

An important element of how this cultural work was made and circulated was the role of local and national elites. The global/local gap that globalization theories have cast as abstract was a much more complicated dichotomy for local elites in Yogyakarta, one which they mediated by offering fashion information to their fellow women citizens. For example, although foreign styles were visible on imported television programs, the personal development course I studied offered locally esteemed women a forum to inform students on how to adjust and correct such styles for the Indonesian context. In so doing, local elite women transformed their prestige into a form of noblesse oblige, securing their own positions, while introducing qualities they valued, such as national or religious identity.

The parallel use of the idea of development as both personal and national is not surprising to those who are familiar with the Suharto New Order state. Development was the explicit goal of the Suharto regime, which Suharto called the New Order to contrast with the perceived chaos of the previous regime of President Sukarno. In the context of gender in contemporary Indonesia, this is especially interesting. Indonesian citizens were constantly exhorted to focus their energies on the goal of development. Yet the kinds of people into which Indonesians were to become transformed were gendered. While to Americans this may seem natural, given anthropological discussions of gender roles in the region it is surprising. This is a region where women have enjoyed financial power, and access to divorce and property and inheritance rights; a region where conceptions of gender difference emphasize complementarity over hierarchy (e.g., Errington 1990).

National rhetoric about development did not emerge in a vacuum, however. The language of development and enforced order was shaped in part by international discourses about development, through which the Suharto regime benefited directly. By ensuring stability through political repression and endorsing the story of Indonesia's development as the creation of an emerging market, the last fifteen years of the regime saw considerable economic growth, averaging annual growth rates of over 7 per cent. In addition, while the elite grew fantastically wealthy, urban areas also saw the growth of a class of working poor and a growing middle class. As a result, the 1990s in particular in urban Indonesia were marked by considerable foreign and local investment dedicated to increasing Indonesian consumption, evidenced by the construction of large air-conditioned malls, traffic jams on city streets due to increasing car ownership, and generally conspicuous consumption. Yet while consumption was increasingly located in private homes, homes that were gated and locked from contact with neighbors, it was simultaneously one of the central symbols of public life in this period. Increased consumption was the sign that Indonesia had arrived on the world stage. As a result, consumption was not simply a secondary part of social life. Rather, it was generally acknowledged that consumption was one of the important sites for negotiating meanings and identities. From its foundations, then, this new middle class was marked by anxieties and struggles over the role of gender in the formation of a uniquely Indonesian form of modernity. Being middle-class meant more than just access to financial resources, but was a symbolic position as well, requiring self-surveillance and display, much as Pierre Bourdieu has argued (1989: 254–6). Being middle-class was more than access to the means of production, it meant access to the means of consumption.

One characteristic of both men and women in the new bourgeoisie was the sense that the future of Indonesian national social life would be shaped through the efforts of self-cultivation and self-fashioning. The sense that the individual should be a personal project, almost a career, was linked to broader goals of social transformation. Although the specific visions of the future varied, depending on the particular group, most shared the opinion that self-discipline, manifested in confident, responsible citizens, would be the building blocks for Indonesia's collective future. Unfortunately, the reverse logic was difficult to bear when the economic crisis hit, because then the enormous social devastation was experienced by almost everyone I knew as both a national disaster, but most acutely as personal failure and shame.

However, the rhetoric of self-sacrifice for the common good was directed much more clearly at women citizens than at men. Indeed, the sort of disciplinary practices that the women I knew enthusiastically sought out were significant because they were in most instances the sort of practices that are almost invisible in Western society. The tools for achieving a successfully disciplined and gendered body were not only available for purchase for those who chose to attend the course, but collectively and consciously valued by both the instructors and students. This contrasts with the sort of class-exclusive hoarding of expertise that Bourdieu describes as one way that privilege is reproduced (1989). Because the privileged classes make the rules of social interaction appear natural, while not revealing those rules, members outside the class group are often prevented from full participation. In contrast, instructors of the femininity course I studied considered it their obligation to share this knowledge with women who aspired to be like them.

The New Order

The New Order's program to define what it meant to be an Indonesian woman became an explicit state project during the 1970s, as President and Mrs. Suharto developed their vision of the hoped-for national culture. More significantly, however, in 1974 the Panca Darma Wanita, or Five Women's Duties, were articulated by the state, just as women were increasingly entering the industrial workforce. According to the Darma Wanita, a woman's role in national development was to be exercised in the context of the family. Interestingly, then, while the Suharto regime was reaching out internationally to multinational investors through promoting their inexpensive female labor force, on the domestic front the Suhartos were promoting a vision of domesticity to Indonesian women. The ideal Indonesian woman's role was identified first and foremost as a loyal supporter of her husband; second, as caretaker of the household; third, as producer of future generations; fourth, as a family socializer, particularly of children, and last of all as an Indonesian citizen (Sullivan 1983:

171). What has come to be called "Ibuism" (from the Indonesian term for mother, *Ibu*) is based in Darma Wanita organizations, one of the only women's organizations sanctioned by the state, and organizations that channeled state values to families through the role of the mother as housewife.[7] Women in particular were therefore asked to make sacrifices and exercise self-discipline for the common good. As a result, the New Order image of the ideal modern Indonesian woman combined Western ideologies of bourgeois domesticity with local, so-called traditional ideologies of femininity and bureaucratic images of dutiful citizenship.

Interestingly, many older women I knew credited Darma Wanita for teaching them the importance of appearance in general, and the specifics of national style over ethnic style in particular. Ibu Tita, the 65-year-old wife of a retired military officer, reminisced with me about how she had learned to become a fully "Indonesian" woman in the 1970s and 1980s. She remembered her personal style before starting to attend Darma Wanita meetings as ethnic. Until then, she recalled, she thought it was appropriate to wear the lace blouse/batik sarong (kain kebaya) every day. Like most Buginese woman of mid-level status she had a limited but rich assortment of lace blouses and sarongs she would mix and match for everyday wear, in addition to Buginese silks she reserved for special occasions. Her wardrobe style had been, in her opinion, very Buginese. But through wearing the Darma Wanita uniform of pink blouse and skirt, she came to realize that kain kebaya was to be reserved only for the most special occasions, such as formal Darma Wanita events or weddings. She found the sarongs and lace blouses, which she had always worn with the family's savings in the form of her gold jewelry, to be signs of the status and ethnic identity of the wearer. In contrast, she found the Darma Wanita everyday uniform a much more up-to-date and refreshing equalizer of women, since Darma Wanita women all looked the same when wearing the uniform: Indonesian. For the same reasons that she had found the national language Bahasa Indonesia to be less hierarchical than Buginese, and had therefore insisted with her husband that they speak only Indonesian with their children, she likewise found the Darma Wanita uniform to be an important tool in creating egalitarian relations among women. It was through the habit of wearing the pinkish blouse and skirt uniform that she slowly put away her kain kebaya into mothballed cupboards and started to wear other blouses and skirts on a daily basis. She and her now adult daughter, both admired by their extended family and neighbors for their personal appearance, also credited Darma Wanita for teaching them their makeup application skills. There they had learned how not to appear too backward or rural, by reducing the amount of gold jewelry they wore and by applying rouge and lipstick subtly. Through the instruction and performance of Darma Wanita meetings, they felt they had learned to move beyond older, ethnic models of hierarchy and adopt a national identity that minimized differences.

Yet the other popular image of Darma Wanita, during the period of my fieldwork, was of the highly restrictive interpretation of the kain kebaya. The official version of the kain kebaya featured a batik design specific to Darma Wanita and furthermore represented to many of the women I knew the oppressive control of tradition over the body. The version of the kain kebaya that Darma Wanita made dominant was not the timeless tradition that it appeared to be. Rather than the more casual and loose version of the outfit which Jean Gelman Taylor describes as dominant in the mid-colonial period, before the boundaries between colonizer and colonized become more delineated (1997), the outfit that was the "national dress" for women had morphed into a far more constrictive form with Darma Wanita. The regular use by President Suharto's wife of a very tight interpretation of the kain kebaya, complete with lacquered hairbun (*sanggul*), dark sunglasses and large handbag, became the signature look for the Darma Wanita woman and the accepted interpretation of the "traditional" dress for women.[8]

While official development organizations like Darma Wanita offered instruction on appearance and housewifery, by the time of my fieldwork most of the women I knew found Darma Wanita meetings unappealing. Rather than domesticity, they associated personal development with a professional lifestyle. Instead of being sites for helpful instruction, Darma Wanita meetings were increasingly thought of as arenas for local political maneuvering. In addition, the once equalizing uniforms worn at such meetings by then seemed like examples of bad taste. As one instructor in the course I studied liked to say, "Be careful with wearing batiks, like the women at Darma Wanita. It is easy to end up giving the impression you are a tablecloth or curtains."[9] Nonetheless, the general sense that the world is made up of populations of more and less developed peoples still held explanatory power for Yogyakarta women. The idea that movement between these levels was available to those who so strove was therefore attractive.

Indeed, it was precisely in a general sense of moral social decline in the later years of the New Order, frequently symbolized by the excesses of women who either consumed too much or incorrectly, that the crack in the New Order ideology of development was most visible. The gap between the promises of development and the limits young middle-class women faced in realizing those desires, frequently because of corruption, had created a middle class that not only felt left behind in the wave of consumerism but also was casting about for alternative ways to transform themselves and their society. In particular, upper-middle-class women in Yogyakarta, instructors and managers of the local venues of expertise for correct femininity, saw their roles as vital to assisting lower-middle-class women to negotiate this gap.

However, while this course was often seen as an alternative to official women's groups designed to teach housewifery, the effects did not directly conflict with state goals for development but rather existed in dialogue with them. Similar political work to the official women's groups was involved in the world of private femininity courses and the consumption skills they taught. It would therefore be a mistake to see the role of this femininity course, and the world of self-improvement education regarding women's bodies and behavior in Indonesia, as simply reactive to official state ideologies. Indeed, the model of modern womanhood on offer in the self-improvement discourses both resisted and reinforced state ideologies.

New Cultures of Expertise: The Private Femininity Course Industry in 1990s Indonesia

In the decade prior to the economic crisis a small industry of instructional femininity courses flourished in many Javanese cities, as well as on Sumatra and Bali. The national expert quoted at the beginning of this chapter is one of the best-known femininity instructors, whose particular expertise is focused on white-collar career fashions and manners. However, the course I studied was offered by a small private business college run by a modernist Islamic institute (Achmadiyah) in a prestigious part of Yogyakarta. Like many such colleges, it offers short courses on business presentations, public relations techniques and public speaking, in addition to a course called "Personal Development" (*Pengembangan Pribadi*). I use the term femininity course to describe these courses because, although it is not based on the Indonesian term for the course, it conveys the gender-specific content of the course.[10] However, the Indonesian course title is instructive. The course uses a different term to refer to development than the more ubiquitous term "*pembangunan*." In part because *pembangunan* referred to state-sponsored national development projects, such as large concrete edifices and the national car and airplane projects, it seemed ill suited to describe personal change. Rather, the private course in Yogyakarta used *pengembangan*, based on the verb *kembang* meaning to bloom or flower, as a more poetic and appropriate term to describe self-realization, and because it felt a step removed from the term that had been colonized by official definitions.[11]

Based directly on the early twentieth-century American finishing program John Robert Powers, the course title suggested that the class concerned general self-improvement, and therefore might be helpful to both male and female students.[12] However, closer reading of the course themes revealed that the information conveyed was oriented to women. For 350,000 rupiah each (approximately $175.00 (US) or about one month's income for many students) approximately twenty students would meet two evenings a week for six weeks. Students came from a variety of backgrounds, but often were the daughters of low- to mid-ranking civil servants or teachers.[13] They were instructed on subjects such as personal grooming and how to select and apply makeup, put together day and evening outfits, engage in polite conversation and eat Western-style meals.[14] In general, two concerns seemed to motivate both the instructors and the students of the course: 1) the need to not be "left behind the times" (*ketinggalan jaman*) in an era of globalization and 2) to distinguish class and status differences, in particular to not appear "*kampungan*" or literally "village-like" or backward.[15]

Goals for most students included career and social advancement, which they couched in terms of desire for increased self-esteem, the sort of self-mastery and sense of identity that was appealing at a time of social flux (*percaya diri* or literally "belief in oneself"). Instructors in the course measured student self-esteem through vocal and carriage skills. Particular emphasis was placed on appropriating fashions and personal skills from expert sources (such as local and foreign magazines, television, and motivational philosophies such as Stephen Covey's) in ways consistent with what was considered Indonesian and feminine. The course I studied had been open for five years, although similar courses had been successfully operating in the capital city Jakarta since 1982.

The Jakarta courses featured nationally respected designers and fashion consultants, both male and female, some of whom traveled to offer weekend one-day intensive seminars in smaller cities. Local variations on the course, including the Yogyakarta course I studied, incorporated the expertise of these same designers and experts through magazines.[16] Eventually the Jakarta courses expanded to cover a wide variety of lifestyle and consumer subjects beyond fashion, including one-day seminars on interior decorating, cooking, and etiquette. Full courses had appeared in Solo, Surabaya, Denpasar, Medan, and Yogyakarta by the early and mid-1990s.[17] During the first few years of the course's operation in Yogyakarta, the students were primarily middle-aged wives of advancing civil servants. The skills taught at such courses were thought to be useful to women in their forties and older, helpful in finding ways to keep their husbands faithful, especially as their husbands advanced professionally and their careers required increased public socializing. By the time I conducted my fieldwork from 1996 to 1998, the majority of students in the course I studied were young women, aged 25 to 35, who were preparing to graduate from various levels of post-high school education and were seeking employment. The same skills taught earlier to keep husbands faithful were then deemed useful for young potential employees in getting work or keeping a boss content. In general, the economic advantages for students in taking the course appeared clear. Graduates of the class were successful in getting jobs at the various offices, banks, and retail outlets in Yogyakarta. Indeed, the Matahari department store, anchor store of the main Yogyakarta mall, sent all its new retail assistants through a version of the course before formally hiring them. The most high-profile success stories from the programs were cases of graduates who had gone on to careers as presenters on local television programs.

Yogyakarta as an urban site is in a unique position. As a secondary city, it is thought to be not as exposed as Jakarta is to the cultural influences of globalization, but neither is it insulated, in large part because of increasing international tourism to the city and some multinational companies producing there. In addition, the women who ran the course often saw themselves as the first line of education for women arriving from rural settings just outside the city. The instructors therefore imagined themselves negotiating among good and bad taste. Good taste came from international influences acquired from personal travel to Australia, Singapore, or Europe and America, foreign magazines acquired through friends and family abroad, and Jakarta-based mass media. These sources were used to counteract the influences that students were perceived to bring to the classroom, such as rural backwardness and nouveau riche enthusiasm for displaying new wealth through flamboyant fashion choices, such as wearing brands or logos visibly on one's clothing. As a result, the instructors served as intermediaries in the often theoretically abstract global–local dichotomy. As mid-level elites and as women of considerable local respect, some with family or other personal ties among the *priyayi* or aristocratic class of the Yogyakarta sultanate, they served as vehicles of expertise on self-cultivation. Rather than simply reinforcing the model of Javanese power relations in which junior-status citizens seek the advice and blessings of royalty, the instructors' appeal and cachet was a hybrid of appeals to both their Javanese prestige and their reputations as people who move around the world. Travel and access to international standards of good taste was just as important in determining their prestige as ties to the Yogyakarta royal court.[18]

The instructors therefore felt a responsibility to the students, and their own developmentalist agendas, and were consequently highly attuned to global trends. Although they clearly profited from the course, all the instructors insisted that they were involved in the course because they did not want Yogyakarta to lose out in an era of globalization.[19] Consistent with this, instructors intentionally kept the fees at the same price throughout the economic crisis (thereby, because of the drop in the value of the rupiah and dramatic inflation, effectively cutting the cost of the course by two-thirds) in order to keep it available to precisely those students who "needed" most what the course had to offer – i.e., tools for social mobility. In other words, if lower-middle-class women could most benefit from the content of the course, then

the fees should be kept within range of that clientele. This decision also prevented the course from closing altogether, as its many local competitors did
during the economic crisis.

The course's explicit goal was to transform women's tastes and manners
and as a result, transform their personalities (*kepribadian*) and their social
status. At base, both students and instructors shared the opinion that personal
development was the result of recruiting information, such as what styles are
current or on the way out, in the service of change in social position. The goal
of self-transformation was to be achieved through self-discipline. The basic
assumption was that one's inner life is shaped if not determined by surface
performances. Disciplining one's appearance would therefore result in alteration of the self. In fact, every student learned that the only way to fully know
herself was to see herself in the eyes of others. Instructors frequently exhorted
students to internalize the instructions from the course, stating after explaining
various rules on dress or makeup, "you should really just make these rules your
'*common sense*,'" using the English phrase that communicated global cachet.
Instructors also reminded students that the transformation might not be
immediate, but students should be patient for the benefits to accrue.

The primary contrast to a polished, up-to-date woman was the "*kampungan*"
woman, a negative identity associated with both rural backwardness and
nouveau riche tackiness. One of the reasons why the label "*kampungan*" was
so threatening was that, increasingly, young village women were earning
income through wage factory and domestic work. Economically, national
development was to be achieved through neoliberal policies aimed at producing a successful export-oriented economy, based in large part in producing
garments for sale in developed economies.[20] The production of textiles and
clothing, which are among the most labor-intensive industries in modern
economies (Dicken 1998: 296), have been increasingly moved offshore to low-
wage countries, including Indonesia. Textile-production factories have been
key sites for entry-level work for rural women migrating to cities. Indeed,
development rhetoric outside Indonesia, particularly in response to the anti-
sweatshop movement in the United States, has argued that garment-factory
jobs are a first step on a ladder of economic development.[21] Throughout the
late 1990s, Indonesia's textile and clothing exports were third behind oil/gas
and wood exports, comprising roughly 12 percent of GDP, and 28 percent of
total foreign exchange exports (approximately $12.6 (US) million) (*Europa
World Year Book* 1999: 1772–78). Textile production was therefore central
to the economy. However, in public rhetoric on development, the New Order
state did not focus on the material importance of textile production in
the national progress narrative, instead promoting the accomplishments of
heavy industry and high technology projects. In contrast, factory women were

frequently symbols for a national struggle over what would be Indonesia's national culture.

As Aihwa Ong has described for Malaysia (1990: 385–422), young women leaving parental surveillance to work in factories often face public criticism for their consumer behavior. Islamic groups in particular expressed concern that young women earning income away from parental control become negative elements in the wider culture. Similar rhetoric circulated in Yogyakarta. A frequent example of this was cited by young men whom I knew in Islamic student groups in Yogyakarta who complained of extravagant consumer behavior among factory women and domestic helpers returning from overseas. These women were accused of returning to their villages wearing jeans or Nike tennis shoes, signs that were interpreted as proof of inadequate control over their appetites or lack of moderation. As a result, women who dressed in a *kampungan* way were not simply revealing their bad taste, but also revealing their failure to exercise self-control in general, including the sexual arena. As one young male academic confidently assured me, "Factory workers and domestic maids returning from abroad wearing those expensive tennis shoes, you know, they are usually having free sex." Understanding the link between appearance and sexual propriety better explains the mandate of the femininity course to create "good women." Frugality and sexual modesty as attributes of Islamic identity were key elements of such a woman. As a result, the stakes were high for women to give evidence of their grasp of middle-class propriety and good taste.

One of the other key distinctions between fashions recommended to students was based on a temporal scale, i.e., that left to their own designs, students might select "looks" that were out-of-date but about which they did not know they should feel embarrassment. As a result, the instructors felt their role was to explain the many choices available to women in selecting clothing that was attractive, current, yet proper. A strong sense of timelag shaped this assumption, a gap of both development and time between global cities, such as Paris or New York, from which good taste emanated, and its arrival in Indonesia. In this way, consumer goods such as fashion and makeup told a story about oneself to oneself and to others. Goods communicated one's position in a world of either more or less developed people (cf. Wilk 1990). Staying on top of trends required vigilance, and failing to inform oneself of what was "in" or "out" would reveal one's proximity to or distance from centers of power. Although access to communication from such perceived centers had increased through mass media and the internet, the women I knew still perceived themselves to be in a system in which Yogyakarta was a marginal site, second to Jakarta and global cities.

Similarly, students might be inclined to choose fashions that were direct imitations of Western fashions. But with instruction, students could learn what was wrong with Western fashions (that they are too sexy), while acknowledging the fact that Western fashions are clearly the international standard. As one celebrity explained in a magazine interview:

> If an Indonesian woman is seen walking in the mall in a miniskirt, . . . or dressed without even a bra! Even if this esthetic [*esthetik*] is beautiful and sexy, she is undoubtedly immediately going to be thought of as a "naughty woman." If an Indonesian woman is so unfortunate as to acquire that label, there are many consequences that follow . . . [E]ven for special parties one must think a thousand times first [before selecting an outfit]. (Asokawati 1998)

This concern with appearances seems to confirm broad Western stereotypes of Asian cultures in general, and Asian women in particular, as obsessed with "face," or outward appearances as linked to prestige or shame (cf. Hevia 1995). Dorinne Kondo argues that the perpetuation of this stereotype ignores the fact that the stakes involved in personal appearance can be high, not only for some imaginary group of Asians, however, but for most humans (1997). In fact, students' motivations should not be misunderstood as evidence of women who were either vain or gullible, but rather of women who fully grasped the importance of bringing into line all elements of their lives in order to achieve "*sukses*." After all, real jobs were gained or lost and husbands really did threaten to or did leave wives for younger women. Moreover, the question of whether or not to take such a course, or to avail of Darma Wanita meetings, was always couched in terms that the information was just too important to risk ignoring.

Course Instructors' Goals

Although the course material appeared to focus on the manipulation of the surfaces of women's bodies, through fashion, hair styling, or etiquette, teachers insisted that the course was really one part of a whole transformation of students' personalities. The most explicit theme of the course was self-confidence. Teachers repeatedly mentioned that this was the most challenging part of instruction also, because they were working against what they perceived to be thousands of years of "tradition" in which Javanese women were valued for being demure and shy (*malu*). The force of generations felt to the instructors as though they were struggling against an impenetrable wall of backwardness. The section of the course on public speaking in particular was important in this regard. Instructors struggled to get students to speak up and enunciate clearly, based on a model of speech designed to train television anchors.

Yet if the goal of the course was to change women on a personal, even psychological, level, why the focus on dress and appearance? The notion that the changes one made could be life-altering was central to understanding the popularity of the course. Students described the course as a way of altering one's *sikap* or character. The acquisition of knowledge and taste necessary for pulling off a look involved a change in one's mode of thinking, and such change could not come without focus and dedication. The director for the John Robert Powers franchises in Asia, during a visit to Jakarta in 1997, emphasized the importance of self-discipline in achieving the goals of the course, saying, "The most important thing is the desire to change."[22] Several women in the class explained to me that one could not expect to become an attractive and modern woman without cultivation. As one student explained, "It isn't just going to happen . . ." ("*Tidak akan terjadi saja*"). Transforming oneself into a woman whose image is current and attractive and conceals any backward roots, requires learning. Another student explained, "This course gives me the theory, but if I am going to be successful, I have to apply this theory in practice. I will have to constantly remind myself throughout the day how to stand and how to smile. It's hard these first few weeks, but hopefully it will become a habit."

Instructors also encouraged students to see themselves as being observed and assessed, aware constantly that they were being watched by others. The goal was for students to internalize the feedback they received from all of their encounters with others, until they learned to see themselves as others saw them. As one expert was quoted as saying in *Femina*:

> In Eastern culture, including that of Indonesia, the value of what is appropriate or not appropriate is highly connected with a woman's "image" (*imaj*) in the eyes of society . . . "Fashion" is a form of nonverbal communication. If a woman chooses to appear or wear clothes of a certain style, it is a way for her to indirectly say that she wants to state who she is and her point of view on life, what her personality is, her character, and much more. . . . (Asokawati 1998)

The course therefore offered not only the tools for learning how to construct one's appearance but also for learning how to look at each other. In this regard, students were taught to focus the gaze they were learning to apply to themselves on others as well. Instructions on how to assess someone in social interactions were part of the rules, such as "If a person wears glasses, they are probably in the category 'intellectual'" or "If you want see if someone is neat, look at her shoes. If her shoes aren't clean or appropriate, it doesn't matter what else she is wearing." However, this strategy gave students the impression that they should in fact be able to achieve the "looks" exemplified by the

Figure 6.1 Instruction scene during personal development course. Photo by Carla Jones.

instructors, even though they did not have financial or local access to the cosmetic products used in teaching. Consistently, the name-brand consumer goods used for teaching aids were not available for sale in Yogyakarta. To purchase those products, the prices for which were far beyond what most students could afford, students would also have had to travel to either Jakarta or Singapore.

Nonetheless, students were regularly asked to identify themselves by work type and personality type from a predetermined list of choices when selecting hair, makeup and wardrobe styles. Women who saw themselves as being a "librarian" selected a certain style, while women who selected "swimmer" or "artist" were given different style advice. Interestingly, rarely did students work as artists or librarians (see Figure 6.1). The desirable jobs the students sought were in banks, hotels or administration. But the students were not just expected to find an identity and then enact its style. While this may appear as a simple transfer of expertise on various looks from the instructors to the students, I suggest there was more agency involved. Instructors offered these identity choices as explicitly universal, arriving from America but true generally for any woman. The language in both the courses and the fashion magazines that were consulted were peppered with English-language-derived fashion terms. Tips on *"gaya jaket"* ("jacket style"), *"memilih vest"* (picking a vest), or *"kesempatan memakai jins"* (occasions for wearing jeans) might indicate that

Indonesian fashion and language are relying on global references for what were local creations (Figure I.2, page 4).

However, instructors in the course told the students that these labels were to be applied loosely, and suited to the lives of Indonesian women. Instructors sought to point out that "looks" do not have naturally fixed meanings. "Modernization does not just mean techniques, but an adaptation of modes of thinking," said one instructor. "It is hard to separate the technology of the clothing from the meaning that can come with it. We have to fill these fashions from the West with our own interior meaning" (*batin*). Instructors reminded students that Western fashions had particular meanings appropriate to their original contexts. An example of this was the Western value of wearing comfortable footwear which was unattractive to the instructors, but which they interpreted as an effect of Western practicality. Likewise the Western power suit, with large shoulder pads, was too aggressive for Indonesian women but was appropriate for American women who are in positions of power. To make an outfit appropriate to the Indonesian setting meant not just a shift in the outfit itself, but an understanding of why this was necessary. For example, fabric colors were to be adjusted to maximize the Indonesian ideal of fairer skin. White fabric was explicitly forbidden, as it contrasted with dark skin, making one look even darker. Off-white fabrics were recommended instead to maximize the local value for fair skin. Matching shoe color to handbag color was of particular importance. In addition, one instructor stated that even though "power suits" were to be the global trend for 1998, it did not mean they could be worn in Indonesia, or Yogyakarta especially, without at least some modification, usually meaning longer skirts or higher necklines in keeping with the fact that "we are Muslim women." Students were told that their greatest concern should therefore be with changes in trends. Careful attention to styles should precede any fabric purchase or garment design. Women were encouraged to exercise a critical eye in assessing fabrics, avoiding the temptation to purchase just because something was on sale. Instructors encouraged students to select natural-fiber textiles (often imported) over abundant and inexpensive synthetics (usually locally made). Fabric for outfits should be sewn into garments within two months of purchase, or the fabric would be out of style. One instructor enjoyed making this point by showing a piece of fabric that was a year and a half old, calling it "antique."

Disciplined Students, Gendered Students

Dress, therefore, as a method for forming one's personality, was also an indication of one's success as a gendered person. This position confirms claims by theorists such as Judith Butler (1990) and Dorinne Kondo (1997) who argue that appearance and clothing are more than simple attributes of gender subjectivity but are in fact constitutive of it. Butler in particular claims that performing gender *is* gender, that there is no natural, authentic performer behind the act. A similar value on performance seemed to guide much of the advice in the femininity course. Although instructors frequently referred to various "laws of nature" (*hukum alam*) that dictate women's lives, such as "all women want to be beautiful," or "women like to shop," simply being born as a genetic female by no means guaranteed a successful woman. Rather, to fully realize one's potential as a woman required effort, and could perhaps be achieved through taking a personal-development course. One instructor described the success the course could have by pointing out a recent graduate. "When she arrived here for the course, she was a guy (*cowok*). Really a guy. The way she stood, the way she dressed. The change has been amazing. Since she took the course, she has become a woman." In contrast, women who refused to take their personal appearance seriously as a feature of their social position were not fully female. One woman friend who had married a doctor but continued to go around her house in a housedress, rarely leaving the house or dressing up, was described by her husband's family and friends as "not a woman." "Just because she has given birth doesn't make her a woman," one acquaintance said, proposing that she should take a personal-development course. Indeed, her mother-in-law, who felt her son was being shamed by his wife's behavior, offered to pay for enrollment, but she refused. The fact that her son eventually no longer chose to live with his wife and children was therefore understandable considering that his wife's personal appearance was inconsistent with her gender and class status.

It was in the context of New Order gender ideology that the importance of class distinctions, in particular the contrast to being *kampungan*, was most clear. In the context of late New Order Indonesia, an environment saturated with selling the joys of being modern, any sign of less-than-modern taste was what students were paying to erase. While most students knew that they would probably never use the same brands of skin cleanser or hire the same tailors as the instructors, because of their different access to financial resources, the instructors nonetheless insisted that creative and attentive students could achieve similar results at a lower cost. A theme of the college was "looking good doesn't mean doing more shopping." Techniques emphasized savvy shopping instead. Students understood that they could appear to be more professional or wealthy than they might in fact be by striving for a complete "look." For example, the wardrobe rules in the course included ways to assess a tailor, evaluate fabrics and choose styles appropriate to one's body type. The final exam for the course required the students to model day- and evening-wear

Figure 6.2 Students in their evening-wear selections during a final exam. Photo by Carla Jones.

outfits that they had commissioned (see Figure 6.2). The instructors, in order to assess whether the students had in fact selected good tailors, inspected the inside seams and hem stitching of the garments in deciding if the student had paid too much for the outfit. So prevalent was this value of succeeding at the appearance game at as little cost as possible that I knew several women who could have enrolled in the course but chose not to, not because of lack of interest or funds, but because they felt that they could acquire the same knowledge through careful attention to women's magazines and soap operas on television.

The emphasis on frugality was a feature of middle-class propriety in New Order Indonesia. Just as Darma Wanita seminars instructed women on how to run a household on cottage-industry income, or make ends meet in creative ways, so did this course offer ways to achieve an upper-class look without spending a lot of money. Extravagant displays of wealth were discouraged. As Pierre Bourdieu has argued, this pattern is typical of social distinctions made between new middle classes and a more established bourgeoisie (1989: 254–6). According to Bourdieu, the newly rich distinguish themselves from the working class by showing their ability to purchase more than simply day-to-day necessities yet still appearing hardworking, rigorous, and clean, through purchasing frugally. However, to the bourgeoisie these same expressions of new wealth may appear tasteless. Similarly, students in the course I studied found themselves torn between a desire to use the course as an excuse to purchase a new wardrobe or makeup ensemble and their instructors' more bourgeois, aristocratic desire for understated fashion choices. For example, students were advised that should they wish to spend a lot on a particular consumer good, items should not bear the brand logo on the outside, as this was evidence of being *kampungan*. Rather, the satisfaction of owning and wearing an expensive bag or dress should come from inside, inside oneself and inside the item (which is where the label ought to be, not displayed on the outside of the item). Indeed, one of the most common ways students lost points on their final exams was to have the examiners deem their garment choices too flashy or loud.

Another example of the class tension between instructors and students involved accessories, especially gold jewelry. Although the course was designed to teach students how to display wealth, that did not mean students were encouraged to accessorize with gold jewelry. Like Darma Wanita meetings which sought to minimize local social difference by replacing those hierarchies with new state-based uniformity, similarly the instructors also discouraged the excessive use of gold jewelry. However, instructors had different motivations than had been at work in the Darma Wanita context. For them, gold did not simply communicate wealth. Rather, it identified one with a rural or merchant background.[23] Indeed, one of the most counterintuitive changes women in the course were told to make was to minimize the amount of gold jewelry they wore. The general rule was that women were to count the pieces of gold they were wearing before they ever stepped out of the home, including gold-colored buttons or belt buckles, never exceeding a total number of seven pieces. Students were informed that wearing a lot of gold at once was a sign of being *kampungan*. Instructors said that telling women they should wear no more than seven pieces of gold at a time invariably evoked groans from the class. As one instructor stated, "Women just like to add a ring every day." Students complained to me that limiting their jewelry was the hardest adjustment to make. For merchant and rural women in much of Indonesia, family wealth is often concentrated in a woman's gold jewelry and in part to safeguard this wealth a woman is to wear all of her jewelry at once.[24] Moving into middle-class status for the students in the course meant shedding this understanding of family wealth, instead endorsing the value of keeping savings in a bank account. Jewelry was to be seen as decoration rather than family financial responsibility.[25]

A final point of tension between students and instructors centered on their often generational differences in interpreting Islam. Instructors in the course, who viewed themselves as faithful Muslims and in many cases understood their role in the course with an almost missionary-style zeal, nonetheless increasingly found themselves faced with students who had chosen clothing styles associated with pious Islamic practice. The use of *baju muslim* or long, loose-fitting clothes, and the fitted headcovering (*jilbab*) had become an alternative but significant mode of dress for young urban women in Java during this period. Yet just as the instructors interpreted their use of white-collar professional dress as a counterpart to the Darma Wanita styles glossed as traditional, so too did students who had chosen baju muslim interpret their acts as resistant to styles, including apparently Western styles, that they felt were associated with corrupt upper classes.

Research on young womens' motivations for wearing jilbabs reveal that class position influences unique reasons for what might seem like a general increase in the use of baju muslim in Indonesia. Suzanne Brenner has analyzed how young lower-middle-class women in Central Java used the jilbab to make critical personal and social statements of the general moral and social decline in the New Order (1996). To them, the veil was a political sign, a claim to a pious alternative modernity rather than a feudal and co-opted past. In contrast, Johan Lindquist has argued that poor migrant workers to the island of Batam wore jilbabs for strategic performative goals. For these women, wearing a jilbab in a sometimes hostile and threatening labor context can provide both a sense of personal pride and physical protection (2002). However, because it is a marked sign, Lindquist argues that wearing a jilbab can also invite critical speculation about a woman's sexual activity.

In the context of the femininity course, perhaps because most students were of a class position to be able to afford the course, those who chose to wear baju muslim did so out of a desire to enact a critique of corrupt representations of femininity. To these women, Western-style dress was corrupt, not because it came from some place called the "West," but because it had become the style of an older generation of Indonesian women whom they felt had embraced a secular pursuit of personal enrichment. Differing interpretations of Islam were therefore a source of polite negotiation between instructors and students in the course. The decision to wear a jilbab was neither discouraged nor encouraged by the instructors. Students frequently asked etiquette questions on how to handle introductions between men and women, so as to avoid physical contact between the sexes. Instructors sometimes perceived students' questions around issues of Muslim clothing as a subtle critique of an instructor's choice to not do so. Students who chose to wear the jilbab were therefore carefully informed that their decision would entail additional steps of self-maintenance, including extra salon trips and hair treatments to manage skin and hair subjected to the effects of heat and damp fabric on the skin. What the instructors and students shared, however, was a commitment to personal self-transformation through self-discipline, a theme that generally overcame the particular details of how to achieve that transformation.

Consumption of fashion, as appearance work, was therefore a way of performing and thereby producing gendered social difference in the late 1990s Indonesia. Although the importance of appearances was a shared value among both instructors and students of the course I studied, the details of what styles said about the self, and more importantly, what styles constituted the self, required instruction. As a result, middle-class women in urban Indonesia were not simply consumers limited to the private sphere, but producers engaged in contests over meanings and identities in late New Order Indonesia. While claiming that the search for self-improvement was purely for personal success and happiness, and indeed in many cases in fact acquiring a degree of the self-confidence and identity they sought, these women endorsed development ideology in ways that often had unintended personal and social consequences. Many of the women I knew perceived of their self-cultivation as a conscientious attempt at reconfiguring the dominant relations of power they felt the state was inscribing on them. They imagined themselves to be rejecting an official model of femininity for a more appealing and liberatory version that embraced attractiveness and women's professional work. Indeed, there were some key differences in content and motivation between Darma Wanita's rhetoric and the personal-development courses. While Darma Wanita focused explicitly on domesticity and a rather frumpy uniformity among women, the personal-development course mixed appeals to global cachet and style with the promise of potential professional success. By choosing the latter model over the former, many of the women I knew imagined their choices to be a small act of resistance against a state agenda that they did not endorse. However, both models of femininity shared key assumptions about the nature of progress and change, assumptions that positioned women as an unproblematic index of national development and thereby as the subjects of their own discipline. In conceiving of themselves as needy of personal development, as continual works-in-progress, the instructors and students in femininity courses such as the one I studied engaged in practices that both produced new individual subjects and reinscribed them into a larger community of citizens nonetheless participating in the persuasive project of a nation in development.

Notes

1. My title clearly borrows from the popular American business-dress bible, *Dress for Success*, by John T. Molloy, New York: P. H. Wyden (1975).

2. This chapter is the result of a panel on nationalism and dress at the Association for Asian Studies, which Ann Marie Leshkowich and I organized in 1999. This research was conducted as part of doctoral dissertation fieldwork from 1996 to 1998 (Jones 2001), for which I benefited from the material and logistical sponsorship of the University of North Carolina, Chapel Hill, the Fulbright Educational Foundation in Jakarta, the Pusat Penilitian Kebudayaan dan Perubahan Sosial at Gadjah Mada University and the Lembaga Ilmu Pengetahuan Indonesia. I am grateful to Sandra Niessen, Ann Marie Leshkowich, Joanne Eicher, and one anonymous reader for detailed advice on this chapter.

3. Pemberton's research did not focus primarily on the sartorial elements of the New Order's celebration of tradition and ritual; rather, he includes dress as one cultural form that the Suhartos found malleable to their goals. A number of studies have focused more closely on Indonesia's rich and diverse textile traditions (e.g., Gittinger 1989; Heringa and Veldhuisen 1997; Niessen 1993).

4. This may also be related to continuing Orientalist tendencies within the fashion industry itself, as Lise Skov's Chapter 7 in this volume clearly reveals. Western-style fashions designed anywhere other than in Europe or North America can, in this logic, only be imitations, while authentic Asian fashion must bear evidence of essentialized, Orientalist elements of a nostalgic "tradition."

5. See, for example, Abelson 1989 and Pinch 1998, for research on how women in Victorian England were imagined to be so desirous of luxury goods, fashions in particular, that they were driven to marginal mental states and shoplifting.

6. See, for example, Abu-Lughod 1990, Breckenridge 1995, Comaroff 1990, de Grazia and Furlough 1996, Freeman 2000, Hannerz 1996, Howes 1996, McCracken 1988, and Rutz and Orlove 1989.

7. This term was first coined by Julia Suryakusama in 1996. See, e.g., Suryakusama 1996.

8. Interestingly, within months of the fall of the Suharto regime it became fashionable for young urban women to wear a *kebaya* in a casual style, thrown loosely over a camisole and paired with jeans or informal sarongs. I consider this to be an example of the loosening connections between what citizens had felt was a strong grip on cultural expressions deemed "traditional," mixed with new self-Orientalizing motivations that reconfigure neotraditional dress as mutable, trendy and thereby fashionable.

9. In contrast, many of the older women I knew credited the early version of Darma Wanita, held for wives of military officers in the 1960s, with teaching them that everyday dress should not be the kain kebaya. It was there that they said they learned the kain kebaya should be saved for special occasions such as Darma Wanita meetings and family events.

10. Identical programs did not exist for men, although courses on self-esteem and business skills were offered for men and women at John Robert Powers. However, appearances were nonetheless linked to masculine identity. An example of this was a computer-training institute's slogan in Yogyakarta as the "school for people who wear ties" (*sekolah orang berdasi*).

11. Johan Lindquist (2002) found similar notions of personal development to echo national official rhetoric among migrants to the Indonesian island of Batam, although they used another term. Migrants, coming from Java and Sumatra in particular, described their motivations for moving to Batam as a desire for *kemajuan* or personal advancement, which was ideally achieved by earning income from multinational factory jobs but could also be acquired through newfound religious piety if their financial dreams did not materialize. Similarly, Tom Boellstorff's research among lower-middle-class gay men found that these men imagined themselves as personal projects, or what he calls "personhood-as-career," working to achieve an upwardly mobile subjectivity that was profoundly written onto the self (Boellstorff 2000).

12. The courses are successful across the Pacific, operating in Thailand, the Philippines, Singapore, Korea, Guam, Australia and Japan. It is also still in operation in the United States, with a focus on modeling training. The American courses are mixed-sex, offering training for aspiring male and female models.

13. Since the economic crisis of mid-1997, the course has not materially raised its fees. In the summer of 2000, the course still cost 400,000 rupiah ($50 (US)), which, because of the dramatic devaluation of the rupiah over the intervening years, actually represented a decrease in cost.

14. The need to know how to politely navigate the arrangement of utensils and plates at a formal Western-style meal was the by-product of increasing multinational corporate presence in Indonesia. Many office jobs required that employees be comfortable at evening receptions at hotels at which the menu was presented in a continental style.

15. There has been considerable romanticization of rural life in contemporary Indonesian public culture, through a nostalgia focused on images of lush green rice paddies, carefree children and women in "traditional" dress, i.e., kain kebaya. That positive nostalgia has been associated with the term for village "*desa*," whereas the more derisive term "*kampung*" more closely describes either urban poor or those nouveaux riches who overdisplay their wealth.

16. The magazine instructors especially found useful was *Femina*. This is not surprising considering the magazine's deep structural and economic ties to the best-known experts and courses. Experts had regular columns in the weekly magazine, and the courses in Jakarta were richly and regularly advertised, even though much of the readership did not live in Jakarta.

17. The course I studied was the only such course in Yogyakarta to survive the economic crisis. All others in the city, more than 25, closed due to the inability of potential students to afford the fees in a time of economic duress. The Jakarta John Robert Powers has survived the crisis nicely, recently opening a new expansion on their building, and upgrading the program to the prestigious "Five Level System."

18. The fact that some of the instructors had ties to the royal court is not surprising considering the court's historical role. During the colonial era, it was precisely the members of the royal court who held audiences with foreign visitors and used imported commodities (see, e.g., Taylor 1997). Their role as diplomats and mediators of outside influences was established well before the development of the personal development

industry. Indeed, members of the Yogyakarta royal court are still considered unique precisely for their cosmopolitanism and experience with foreigners, both from foreign travel and in hosting foreign visitors to Indonesia.

19. This attitude sounds similar to missionary talk justifying religious expansion. Some instructors were members of modernist Islamic groups, like Achmadiyah. These experiences might have instilled a passion and sense of desire to aid and educate fellow citizens. Lizzy van Leeuwen observes a similar connection between personal and interior decoration and religious zeal among wealthy Jakarta wives who give praise to God by beautifying themselves and their surroundings (1997: 340).

20. Textile industries typically employ inexpensive, unskilled female labor. For more on this pattern, see Chapkis and Enloe 1983.

21. For an example of this evolutionary logic in transnational garment production, consider Phil Knight's response to anti-sweatshop movement targeted at Nike in a *Washington Post* story on development. "Working in a shoe factory doesn't take much education and is very labor intensive . . . (countries) grow that way until they get to wages of somewhere around $10,000 a year, by that time there is a basic infrastructure built, and the workers can go across the street and start making computers and cars, and the shoe industry begins to fade" (Swardson and Sugawara, 1996).

22. His comments were translated into Indonesian, "*Yang penting keinginan berubah*."

23. This attitude was particular to the interests of instructors. Before the economic crisis, some of the new super-wealthy in Jakarta regularly rotated their jewelry as a gesture of praise to God for their good fortune (cf. Van Leeuwen 1997: 340).

24. Suzanne Brenner has described how women merchants of Solo invest family wealth in gold jewelry, women whom she describes as considered distinctly "unmodern" (1998: 184–9).

25. Interestingly, selecting and trusting a bank in Indonesia was a tricky proposition even before the economic crisis. An abundance of bank brands made selection challenging, and it was nearly impossible to find a bank that was not publicly known to be the property of a Suharto family member or crony. Indeed, by the end of 1997, instructors in the course had joined the long queues of citizens to claim their funds from bank accounts. Cash seemed a safer proposition than trusting a bank that IMF deregulators might close without warning. Sadly, though, gold was also no longer a secure investment either. Families needing cash flooded local markets with gold jewelry, causing gold prices to plummet.

References

Abelson, Nancy (1989), *When Ladies Go A-Thieving: Middle-Class Shoplifters in the Victorican Department Store*, New York: Oxford University Press.

Abu-Lughod, Lila (1990), "The Romance of Resistance: Tracing Transformations of Power Through Bedouin Women," *American Ethnologist* 17(1): 41–55.

Appadarai, Arjun (1993), "Consumption, Duration and History," *Stanford Literature Review* 10(1–2): 11–33.

Asokawati, Okky (1998), *Femina*, 1–7 February.

Boellstorff, Tom (2000), *The Gay Archipelago*, doctoral dissertation, Stanford University.

Bourdieu, Pierre (1989), *Distinction: A Social Critique of the Judgement of Taste*, London: Routledge.

Breckenridge, Carol A. (ed.) (1995), *Consuming Modernity: Public Culture in a South Asian World*, Minneapolis and New York: University of Minnesota Press.

Brenner, Suzanne (1996), "Reconstructing Self and Society: Javanese Muslim Women and 'the Veil'," *American Ethnologist* 23(4): 673–97.

—— (1998), *The Domestication of Desire: Women, Wealth and Modernity in Java*, Princeton: Princeton University Press.

Butler, Judith (1990), *Gender Trouble: Feminism and the Subversion of Identity*, New York: Routledge.

Chapkis, Wendy and Enloe, Cynthia (1983), *Of Common Cloth: Women in the Global Textile Industry*, Amsterdam and Washington DC: Transnational Institute.

Chatterjee, Partha (1989), "Colonialism, Nationalism, and Colonized Women: The Contest in India," *American Ethnologist* 16(4): 622–33.

Cohn, Bernard (1989), "Cloth, Clothes, and Colonialism: India in the Nineteenth Century," in Annette Weiner and Jane Schneider (eds), *Cloth and Human Experience*, Washington: Smithsonian Institution Press.

Comaroff, Jean (1990), "Goodly Beasts and Beastly Goods," *American Ethnologist* 17: 195–216.

—— (1996), "The Empire's Old Clothes: Fashioning the Colonial Subject," in David Howes (ed.), *Cross-Cultural Consumption: Global Markets, Local Realities*, London and New York: Routledge.

Conroy, Marianne (1998), "Discount Dreams: Factory Outlet Malls, Consumption, and The Performance of Middle-Class Identity," *Social Text* 54(1): 63–83.

De Grazia, Victoria and Ellen Furlough (eds) (1996), *The Sex of Things: Gender and Consumption in Historical Perspective*, Berkeley: University of California Press.

Dicken, Peter (1998), *Global Shift: Transforming the World Economy*, 3rd edn, New York and London: Guilford Press.

Di Leonardo, Micaela (1987), "The Female World of Cards and Holidays: Women, Families, and the Work of Kinship," *Signs: Journal of Women in Culture and Society* 12(3): 440–53.

Errington, Shelly (1990), "Recasting Sex, Gender, and Power: A Theoretical and Regional Overview," in Jane Monnig Atkinson and Shelly Errington (eds), *Power and Difference: Gender in Island Southeast Asia*, Stanford: Stanford University Press.

Europa World Year Book (1999), volume 1. London: Europa Press.

Foucault, Michel (1995 [1977]), *Discipline and Punish*, New York: Vintage.

—— (1990 [1978]), *History of Sexuality*, volume 1, New York: Vintage.

Freeman, Carla (1993), "Designing Women: Corporate Discipline and Barbados's Off-Shore Pink-Collar Sector," *Cultural Anthropology* 8(2): 169–86.

—— (2000), *High Tech and High Heels in the Global Economy: Women, Work and Pink-Collar Identities in the Caribbean*, Durham, NC: Duke University Press.

Gittinger, Mattiebelle (1989), *To Speak With Cloth: Studies in Indonesian Textiles*, Los Angeles: University of California.

Hannerz, Ulf (1996), *Transnational Connections*, London and New York: Routledge.

Heringa, Rens and Veldhuisen, Harmen (1997), *Fabric of Enchantment: Batik from the North Coast of Java*, Los Angeles: Weatherhill.

Hevia, James (1995), *Cherishing Men from Afar: Qing Guest Ritual and the Macartney Embassy of 1793*, Durham, NC: Duke University Press.

Hochschild, Arlie (1989a), *The Second Shift: Working Parents and the Revolution at Home*, New York: Viking.

—— (1989b), "The Economy of Gratitude," in David D. Franks and E. Doyle McCarthy, (eds), *The Sociology of Emotions: Original Essays and Research Papers*, Greenwich, Conn.: JAI Press.

Howes, David (1996), "Introduction: Commodities and Cultural Borders," in David Howes (ed.), *Cross-Cultural Consumption: Global Markets, Local Realities*, London and New York: Routledge.

Jones, Carla (2001), *Watching Women: The Domestic Politics of Middle-Class Femininity in Late New Order Indonesia*, doctoral dissertation, University of North Carolina, Chapel Hill.

Kondo, Dorinne (1997), *About Face: Performing Race in Fashion and Theater*, London and New York: Routledge.

Lindquist, Johan (2002), *The Anxieties of Mobility: Development, Migration and Tourism in the Indonesian Borderlands*, doctoral dissertation, University of Stockholm, Sweden.

McCracken, Grant (1988), *Culture and Consumption*, Bloomington: Indiana University.

Murra, John (1989), "Cloth and Its Function in the Inka State," in Annette Weiner and Jane Schneider (eds), *Cloth and Human Experience*, Washington: Smithsonian Institution Press.

Niessen, Sandra (1993), *Batak Cloth and Clothing: A Dynamic Indonesian Tradition*, Kuala Lumpur: Oxford University Press.

Ong, Aihwa (1990), "Japanese Factories, Malay Workers: Class and Sexual Metaphors in West Malaysia," in Jane Atkinson and Shelley Errington (eds), *Power and Difference: Gender in Island Southeast Asia*, Stanford: Stanford Press.

Pemberton, John (1994), *On the Subject of "Java,"* Ithaca: Cornell University.

Pinch, Adela (1998), "Stealing Happiness: Shoplifting in Early Nineteenth-Century England," in Patricia Spyer (ed.), *Border Fetishisms: Material Objects in Unstable Spaces*, New York: Routledge.

Rutz, Henry J. and Orlove, Benjamin S. (eds) (1989), *The Social Economy of Consumption*, Lanham, MD: University Press of America.

Schein, Louisa (1997), "Gender and Internal Orientalism in China," *Modern China*, 23(1): 69–98.

—— (2000), *Minority Rules: The Miao and the Feminine in China's Cultural Politics*, Durham, NC: Duke University Press.

Schneider, Jane and Weiner, Annette (1989), "Introduction," in Annette Weiner and Jane Schneider (eds), *Cloth and Human Experience*, Washington: Smithsonian Institution Press.

Smith, Carol (1995), "Race-Class-Gender Ideology in Guatemala: Modern and Anti-Modern Forms,"*Comparative Studies in Society and History* 37(4): 723–49.

Spyer, Patricia (1998), "The Tooth of Time, or Taking a Look at the 'Look' of Clothing In Late Nineteenth-Century Aru," in Patricia Spyer (ed.), *Border Fetishisms: Material Objects in Unstable Spaces*, New York: Routledge.

Suryakusama, Julia (1996), "State Ibuism," in Laurie Jo Sears (ed.), *Fantasizing the Feminine in Indonesia*, Durham: Duke University Press.

—— (2001), "The Kebaya As Identity, Expression and Oppression," *Latitudes* 3: 71–3.

Swardson, Anne, and Sugawara, Sandra (1996), "Asian Workers Become Customers. Foreign Companies Create New Markets, Then Move On," *Washington Post*, 30 December.

Taylor, Jean Gelman (1997), "Costume and Gender in Colonial Java, in 1800–1940" in Henk Schulte Nordholt (ed.), *Outward Appearances: Dressing State and Society in Indonesia*, Leiden: KITLV Press.

Turner, Terence (1980), "The Social Skin," in Jeremy Cherfas and Roger Lewin (eds), *Not Work Alone: A Cross-cultural View of Activities Superfluous to Survival*, Beverly Hills, CA: Sage.

Van Leeuwen, Lizzy (1997), "Being Rich in Jakarta, 1994: A Mother and Two Daughters," in Henk Schulte Nordholt (ed.), *Outward Appearances: Dressing State and Society in Indonesia*, Leiden: KITLV Press.

Veblen, Thorstein (1994 [1899]), *The Theory of the Leisure Class*, New York: Dover Publications.

Wilk, Richard (1990), "Consumer Goods as Dialogue about Development," *Culture and History* 7: 79–100.

7

Fashion–Nation: A Japanese Globalization Experience and a Hong Kong Dilemma

Lise Skov

A Strategy for Asian Fashion Centers

During the course of my fieldwork in the Hong Kong fashion world I had numerous occasions to discuss whether Hong Kong was going to "make it" in international fashion and become a fashion center in its own right.[1] Fashion designers in Hong Kong are in an unusual situation because of their proximity to the large production agglomerations in South China that lend their manufacturing capacity to big international labels such as Armani, Donna Karan, and Tommy Hilfiger, as well as to an infinite number of retail chains and department stores around the world. Through their work in the export-oriented industry, local fashion designers become familiarized with fashion markets in all parts of the world, and when they set up their own labels they benefit from the industrial hinterland geared to manufacturing high-quality clothing at low prices and from the array of overseas fashion buyers who frequent the city. It is not hard to find sophisticated and ambitious designers who would like to try their luck in international markets.

However, from the point of view of the highly globalized Hong Kong garment industry, local fashion designers – even big names who successfully run a couple of boutiques and command the respect of the local fashion press – are but small potatoes in a marginal market that does not tempt further investment. When it comes to ambitious dreams of international success, these designers are "so close and yet so far" from the large-scale industrial backing that is necessary to make such dreams come true.

Nevertheless, the dream exists. In my talks with local fashion designers about whether Hong Kong could "make it," there was general agreement that the way to realize ambitions in international fashion was to "do something Chinese." For them this was the only conceivable way to turn their distance from the fashion centers into a competitive edge that could be exploited in the international marketplace. Rather than emphasizing Hong Kong's technical expertise in the manufacturing of street fashion, for example, ambitious designers felt pressured to buy into an old Orientalism strangely at odds with the culturally neutral modernism that otherwise counts as good fashion in Asia. I realized that self-exoticization was pertinent only to designers who were already well connected in the global fashion business.

In order to analyze the discursive construction of this demand for self-exoticization in non-Western fashion design, we need to dislocate the link between fashion and nation. A standard reading of fashion in terms of culture and identity, as has been applied in anthropology, cultural studies, and fashion studies, easily glosses over the complexity of the fashion-nation link. It is my contention, therefore, that an adequate analysis of the globalization of Asian fashion needs to include an examination of the highly segmented institutions of fashion production at the global level. Through such an analysis of cultural production, this chapter will expose the cracks in the exoticizing discourse, thereby bringing into focus the ambivalence of Asian designers who – just at the point when, as a professional group, they are fully at home with world fashion – are required to stage themselves as its exotic Other.

I start by tracing the self-exoticizing design strategy and its discontents back to the 1980s. In fact, the strategy has a long history, but the 1980s was the first period when non-Western fashion designers came to influence mainstream fashion, when Issey Miyake, Yohji Yamamoto, and Rei Kawakubo, along with a series of other Japanese designers, proved themselves to be the leading fashion innovators in the world. By beginning here I leave out other internationally acclaimed Japanese designers, such as Kenzo and Hanae Mori, both of whom embraced the self-exoticizing design strategy in the 1970s when Issey Miyake also started his career. The reason for this omission is that my interest here lies in the way in which the success of Japanese fashion in the 1980s increased the tension between, on the one hand, the international demand for non-Western Otherness, and on the other, Japanese designers' ability to innovate in a medium that no longer can be adequately named Western.

Various scholars have tried to uncover what it was that Japanese designers brought into international fashion (Koren 1984; Koda 1985; Coleridge 1989; Evans and Thornton 1989; Craik 1994). My argument in this chapter is different. I am less interested in the sources for their design and the innovative ways in which they put them together. Rather, I focus on the encounter between Japanese designers and Western fashion journalists who eventually were responsible for constructing the exoticizing discourse that other Asian designers today experience as an irrefutable demand.[2] I use "a Japanese globalization experience" in the title to highlight the interactive nature of the phenomenon. It marks the point in the 1980s when high fashion became multicultural in an ambivalent process in which Western supremacy was spectacularly under-mined, and yet subtly reinscribed.

In order to clarify how the exoticizing discourse of non-Western design was constructed, I introduce Barthes' distinction between image-clothing and written clothing:

> I open a fashion magazine; I see that two different garments are being dealt with here. The first is the one presented to me as photographed or drawn – it is image-clothing. The second is the same garment, but described, transformed into language . . . In principle these two garments refer to the same reality (this dress worn on this day by this woman), and yet they do not have the same structure, because they are not made of the same substances and because, consequently, these substances do not have the same relations with each other: . . . the first structure is plastic, the second is verbal. (Barthes 1983: 3)

With the Japanese trend in the 1980s, there was a stark contrast between the two garments. The image-clothing looked like clothes had never looked before, with technically novel conceptions of garments that ignored conventional dress-making techniques. They were notoriously hard to pin down, as they did not carry any overt aesthetic allusions. By contrast, the written clothing was a story of exotic Japan. It firmly placed the strange garments in the context of Western Orientalism. My point is not simply that there were two co-existing structures, but that the verbal garment dominated the plastic. How else can we make sense of collections of sophisticated minimalist deconstruction, written up as Japanese tradition and colorful Orientalism?

In the first part of this chapter I map out the way in which the Japanese collections were written up to enforce their exoticism. I move on to discuss the way in which the ensuing discourse continues to influence non-Western fashion designers. It begins with a brief outline of the historical development of global fashion production in East Asia that – it is my contention – is crucial for an analysis of how fashion works at the global level. Then I move on to an examination of the Hong Kong labels that have adopted self-exoticization as a design concept. In the opening paragraphs of this chapter I sketched out the way in which self-exoticization is experienced as an uneasy requirement by Hong Kong fashion designers who seek acknowledgement of their work abroad. I use the term "a Hong Kong dilemma" in the title to capture their ambivalence, and the chapter ends with a highly personal exploration of how the design dilemma is experienced by a young Hong Kong designer working in the global industry.

This chapter thus begins and ends with Hong Kong. The Japanese globalization experience is not inserted as a detour from the main argument, but as a
key component in the Hong Kong dilemma. The connection between the two
is established by ambitious fashion people in Hong Kong who, as elsewhere
in Asia, look to Japan and study the work of designers from the only non-
Western nation that has been recognized as a creative fashion center. The line
of thought is that "because the Japanese made it, maybe we could make it,
too, by following the same recipe." It is so integrated that my fieldwork
questions about whether Hong Kong would become a fashion center usually
were answered with an explicit comparison to Japanese designers in the 1980s.
For this reason, their story needs to be retold here.[3]

In addition, there is a critical intention in bringing the Japanese globalization
experience and the Hong Kong dilemma together. It drives home the point that
when Asian designers explore their national traditions for aesthetic input in
contemporary design, it is not simply a natural resurgence of ethnic identity.
On the contrary, it is a complex design strategy shaped by market requirements
and interpreted in the light of the Japanese globalization experience. The irony
is that Japan – instrumental in shaping the expectation that non-Western
designers can make their mark on fashion only through self-exoticization – is
also the first wedge inserted between other non-Western designers with similar
ambitions and their national cultures.

A Japanese Fashion Revolution

Recent fashion history cannot be written without reference to Issey Miyake,
Yohji Yamamoto, and Rei Kawakubo (of the label Comme des Garçons) who,
in spite of individual differences, jointly came to represent a minimalist oversize
style in dark off-colors, a style that avoided putting the female body on display
in any conventional way. They were not the first Japanese designers to appear
on the international fashion scene, and other Japanese designers were present
on the Paris fashion scene in the 1980s, including Kenzo, Hanae Mori, Kansai
Yamamoto, and Takeo Kikuchi (of the label Bigi). It was the "big three,"
however, who most radically differed from and most successfully challenged
the fashion conventions of their day.

If we borrow our theoretical framework from Bourdieu (1975) we can say
that they effected a fashion revolution. What happened in the 1980s was
similar to the 1960s fashion revolution (the point around which Bourdieu's
fashion study revolves) when the so-called Courrèges effect arose from fashion
creator André Courrèges' introduction of the miniskirt into his haute couture
collections. He presented a futuristic modernist style for youthful and sporty

women, thereby upsetting the established link between haute couture, luxury, and high class.

However, we have to add to Bourdieu's analysis that Courrèges' claim to have "invented" the mini skirt is modified by the fact that in 1965, when he first included it in his haute couture collections, the mini was already popular in London where it was sold by Mary Quant and other street fashion designers (Steele 1991: 134). Courrèges can be seen as the last fashion creator to legitimate his work solely as dictate, in the true style of haute couture, but he did so ultimately to undermine the autonomy of the field. Since then, fashion journalists have kept a keen eye on what is going on in London as well as in Paris. Fashion revolution, in other words, does not simply consist of innovation, but of bringing innovation into a particular field of cultural production.

While the Courrèges revolution was brought about by a fashion creator with accumulated capital in haute couture, the Japanese revolution was brought about by designers who – with the exception of Miyake – were unknown to the Western fashion press. Backed by Japanese industry, they came from overseas to open boutiques and present their collections in the prestigious old fashion center of Paris. They were newcomers, but nevertheless managed to make their presence noted.

Bourdieu gives us a hint as to what makes a revolution successful. While he points out that each field has its own history with its own periodization, he adds that often "a specific revolution, something that marks a 'turning-point' in a given field, is the synchronization of an internal revolution and of something outside, in the wider world" (Bourdieu 1993: 135). The minimalist style of Yohji Yamamoto, Rei Kawakubo, and Issey Miyake coincided with two important cultural changes in the 1980s: first, the budding popularity of Japanese popular culture in the West; and secondly, the theoretical appreciation of decentering and fragmentation that could be rediscovered in their clothes. The designers were thus in line with other things that were perceived as avant-garde, intellectual, and difficult at the time (Skov 1996; Kondo 1997).

However, the most extraordinary thing about the media reception of Japanese designers in the 1980s was the way in which Western fashion writers embraced the stereotypes of Japanese national culture. When journalists write about Italian fashion, for example, they may have one or two historical references, but they usually refer to the field of fashion production rather than to the opera, the Vatican, or Renaissance painting. By contrast, when writing about Japan, they presented myriad general references, eclectically jumbled together: theater, dance, religion – even the nuclear bomb was brought in! Most fashion features searched the canons of legitimate national culture for references. Historical allusions indicated that what was new in Paris was already old in Japan – in other words, that the fashion collections were a kind of national costume. In doing so fashion writers drew on the distinction between fashion and ethnic dress that tends to take on board a lingering Occidentalist dichotomy of creative Western modernity vis-à-vis mimetic Eastern tradition. Here is how one fashion editor phrased it in her comment on Comme des Garçons:

> It's ethnic, that's all. It's old National Geographic school of design. If Saint Laurent goes to Marrakesh for a long holiday you know jolly well that there'll be a few jellabas knocking about in his next collection. If he went to Tokyo instead, he'd produce a stronger Japanese collection than Rei Kawakubo. (Meredith Etherington-Smith, quoted in Coleridge 1989: 77)

The reference to Yves Saint Laurent is hardly incidental. More than any other fashion creator he has made ethnic influences the emblem of his work. A catalogue from an exhibition titled "Yves Saint Laurent – Exotismes" (Marseilles 1993) shows the creator sitting at his desk in Marrakesh. The room provides a perfect Middle Eastern setting with an arch and iron grid in front of the window, a tiled floor partially covered by a Kilim rug, a rattan desk, and chair. The fashion creator himself is dressed in *jellaba* and sandals (Figure 7.1). In the accompanying text, YSL business manager Pierre Bergé describes the creator's "genius" ability to "delve into the orientalist bric-a-brac and with the legitimacy of a magician make his own world emerge out of it" (*Yves Saint Laurent* 1993/4: 17). Here we have the setting in which legitimate fashion is created. It is marked by selective and limited immersions in exotic environments for inspiration. These can then be brought back into the fashion creators' own world where it can be converted into the currency of the field. Those who do not belong to the fashion world are automatically excluded from the privilege of creating fashion.

By an illuminating coincidence Bourdieu's article on haute couture has the subtitle "a contribution to the theory of magic" (1975). For Bourdieu, magic refers to the way in which value is infused in the designer brand. Following a classic theoretical maneuver in anthropology, Bourdieu shifts the analysis of magic from particular properties of magical operations to the way in which belief, or as he puts it "collective misrecognition," organizes social life. Hence consumers who pay the high markup for branded goods, magazine readers who closely follow the lives of their favorite designers, the editors who write about them, and the business people who devise the commercial strategies are all the believers who jointly perform the magical transformation that turns *jellabas* into Paris fashion. It is now clear what it was that Yves Saint Laurent had that the Japanese designers did not. When Pierre Bergé claims for his business partner a "magician's legitimacy," it is the kind of legitimacy that stems from his position in the field of production.

Figure 7.1 Yves Saint-Laurent in Marrakesh: "This is the setting in which legitimate fashion is created."

Bourdieu was right to stress also that the capital of one production field cannot easily be converted into that of another. When Japanese designers in the 1980s swept the Paris catwalks, fashion journalists were the reluctant believers who had to acknowledge something new in their field, but still hold on to their trump card of cultural superiority. Issey Miyake had been presenting his ready-to-wear collections in Paris since the 1970s, while Yohji Yamamoto and Rei Kawakubo had been successful in their competitive domestic market for a decade before their international breakthrough. Like the Courrèges revolution, the Japanese revolution in Paris was not so much an emergence of something new, as a recognition at a higher level in the fashion world.

The authority of Paris designers was undermined – as it was in the 1960s when London was recognized as a competing fashion center. Instead of a single fashion center, we now have a multiplicity of fashion centers, each of which has temporal significance – London in the 1960s, Tokyo in the 1980s – and regional influence – New York is a fashion center for North America, Tokyo for Asia. However, when Japanese avant-garde designers made a hit in Paris, they confirmed in the process that, in Paris, fashion is recognized for its aesthetic qualities with relative disregard for the commercial concerns that dominate fashion fairs in New York, Dusseldorf, Tokyo, and Hong Kong. Even if Western fashion people complain that Paris has been "colonized" by Japanese black austerity, we should not be blind to the fact that the Japanese fashion revolution secured for Paris its position as a truly *global* fashion center.

Written Clothing and the Field of Production

I have argued that fashion journalists have been instrumental in forging the link between fashion and nation that is the pivot of the exoticizing design discourse. It is not unusual for fashion writers to bring together contradictory concepts in purposely striking ways. Barthes describes this as the "nebulosity" of written fashion: contradictory characteristics are paradoxically united, forming "an undefined mass of concepts . . . which could be compared to a large nebula, with vague connections and contours" (Barthes 1983: 232). For Barthes, this "massive imprecision" functions to make fashion specific in terms of target groups. It distinguishes those who "get it" from those who do not.

Barthes describes the rhetoric of fashion magazines as one of pure observation. His book can be read in itself as an exercise in written fashion where the style of the analysis closely reflects the object studied. Like fashion discourse, Barthes' book presents a hermetic universe, simultaneously overly elaborate and strangely superficial. No wonder it is considered one of the most boring books on fashion ever written! Bourdieu rightly criticized Barthes for his limited focus, and suggests instead that we understand written fashion as performative statements so that the discourse is not separated from its social effects (Bourdieu 1975: 23). As we have seen above, Bourdieu's cultural production framework still provides a useful analytical entry to the study of fashion, although our interest here is more in the complex connectivity of global fashion than in the structure of any clearly delineated field of production.

Both Barthes and Bourdieu highlight the key role played by the fashion press. The designer is not alone when she delves into the "orientalist bric-a-brac." She is closely followed, and quickly overtaken, by the fashion journalist. Even when there seem to be no limits to the eclectic exoticism, statements are standardized when fashion writers quote each other. By sheer repetition their points come to appear authoritative, although the intertextual universe is often carefully staged as a series of meetings, experiences, and random findings in order to give off a sense of firsthand experience in every single article. My argument is that the tighter the intertextual net of fashion writing is woven, the weaker the information and the stronger the cliché. At this point, my critique of fashion writing is fully in line with Edward Said's critique of the high-cultural discourse of Orientalism (1978).

The following quotation gives a tongue-in-cheek recipe for how value is added under the rhetoric of simply observing and noting value. It comes from senior fashion writer Colin McDowell, commenting on John Galliano and the 1997 "Chinesey trend." He describes the work of fashion journalists in the following way:

> The most important aspect of their job is identification. They must differentiate between what is new and what is a development from previous collections, while capturing for their readers the overall cultural feeling of the show. Then they must recreate the mood in prose as purple as their editors will permit, prose that flatters the readers by assuming they have knowledge of the cultural allusions used, prose that is a clever form of self-aggrandizement for the journalist who is making the allusions. If there is a Chinese element, for example, as there has been recently in several of Galliano's collections, it is not enough merely to say so. There must be literary allusions – Pearl S. Buck, or, even better, Somerset Maugham. There must be historic references – the Boxer Rebellion is a well-worn favourite. And, to bring it down to earth so that all the readers can 'get the picture', references to Suzy Wong and even Madame Butterfly are acceptable. (McDowell 1997: 143–4)

Given such conventions of fashion writing, matched with the time pressure that characterizes the work of journalists, is it reasonable to criticize the exot-icizing discourse with which Western editors write up non-Western collections? Why not let a Chinese antiforeign militaristic movement bring us the latest in cosmopolitan fashion? Why not have sophisticated deconstructionism come in straight from the rice fields? Why not pair the prestigious rigidity of Japanese high culture with avant-garde design's deliberate disregard for conventions?

The answer to such questions lies not in a retreat to academic purism, but in an examination of what the discourse conceals. For at the same time as this kind of fashion writing recognizes Asian designers, it simplifies the conditions of their design. It is crucial, therefore, that an analysis go beyond both the written clothing and the image garment to examine the conditions of global fashion production.

Here the first point is that fashion designers are people in charge of the creative coordination of manufacturing and marketing in an industrial setting. They are not makers whose work can be understood with reference to native crafts. Market calculation is an integral part of designers' work, and although they can make fatal mistakes in this regard, there are hardly any naive designers who stumble onto the formula for international success. Or perhaps it would be more precise to say that there are many naive – and talented – designers around the world, but they are unlikely to earn the financial support required for their work to appear on a catwalk in Paris.

Designers are themselves a part of the fashion world, and they also contribute to the exoticizing discourse, acting, as Bourdieu puts it, as "their own impresarios." Therefore, it is all the more remarkable that following their breakthrough the "big three" have made it clear that they were not happy with the way in which the international fashion press portrayed them. They did not recognize any close affiliation between their collections and the official canons of Japanese national culture. Yohji Yamamoto, who in the early 1980s eloquently elaborated the link between Zen Buddhism and his designs, has now distanced himself from this. In Wim Wenders' documentary (1989), he explains that the fashion press pushed him into this position.

Issey Miyake, for his part, has repeatedly stated that his designs are based on a mixture of East and West that goes beyond not just geographical boundaries, but also the boundaries of social convention to a minimalist conception of body and cloth (for example, in Holborn 1995). This formula, which has made him one of the most influential fashion innovators in the world, underscores the fact that, although he has frequently played around with Japanese dress forms, he is certainly not a representative of Japanese particularism.

The strongest rejection of self-exoticization has come from Rei Kawakubo. For example, in an interview with anthropologist Dorinne Kondo, Kawakubo explicitly refused to enter into a discussion of key concepts in classical Japanese aesthetics, and "with some asperity" stated, "I have seen so-called 'traditional' culture maybe once in school, when I had to. Things like Kabuki, one time only, in a class for elementary school" (Kondo 1997: 67). By this she meant to demonstrate her distance from the national culture that she widely had been seen to represent.

As I close this critique of the way in which the Western fashion press wrote up the moment in an exoticizing discourse, we are beginning to discern dissident voices. Japanese fashion designers themselves object to the demand for exoticization. They speak against the dramatization of cultural difference and for a notion of culture less pure. They insist that their design developed within a popular culture that had absorbed an ongoing Western influence, and that had come to see itself as emphatically *not* traditional Japanese culture. These statements lead us to examine more closely the conditions of fashion design in Asia.

Development and Design

Again, Bourdieu provides a starting point for the analysis when – with a slight adaptation – he says:

> The sociology of [fashion] that *directly* relates works of [fashion] to the producers' or clients' position in social space (their social class) without their considering their position in the field of production (a 'reduction' which is, strictly, only valid for 'naïve' artists) sweeps aside everything that the work owes to the field and its history – that is to say precisely that which makes it a work of [fashion]. (Bourdieu 1993: 75)

What is it that the work of Asian designers owes to the field of fashion and its history, and which is swept aside in a reductive reading that directly relates it to Asian culture and identity? How does the field of global fashion production set limits for and exert pressure on the work of Asian fashion designers? I have already argued that fashion production must be seen in the context of popular culture with its unselfconscious mix of Eastern and Western influences. However, we need to go one step further and examine the globally proliferating industries that produce the garments we wear. One thing the exoticizing discourse conceals is the extent to which the global fashion business has already moved out of the West.

Since the early postwar period, East Asian textile and garment industries have been oriented towards exports to the West. The postwar economic reconstruction of Japan, for example, was boosted by imports of United States-subsidized raw cotton that was processed and re-exported first as yarn and fabrics, and later as shirts, underwear, and other relatively standardized garments. When these products entered the United States, they were considerably cheaper than locally produced items, and soon reports came in that Japanese products were flooding the market and undercutting local manufacturers. In the mid-1950s when Japan was admitted to the free-trade system of GATT, the United States simultaneously launched its first postwar textile-specific trade restriction against Japan (Dickerson 1995: 324).

A few years later, Hong Kong went through a similar trading cycle – complete with United States-subsidized import of raw material, labor-intensive manufacturing of standardized consumer goods, price undercutting in export markets, uproar from Western manufacturers and unions, and government-imposed trade restriction. The pattern was repeated by Taiwan and Korea a decade later. In 1961, a multilateral quota system was established to restrict textile and garment exports from East Asia to the West. This system was later expanded as the Multi-Fibre Arrangement, and it continues to exist in modified form in spite of several phase-out plans.

It can hardly be overemphasized that East Asian products were not admitted to Western markets because of their high-quality craftsmanship or attractive designs, but because they could take the place of domestic products. The advantages of price undercutting were reaped by Western consumers, for whom the imported product was cheaper, as well as by Western importers, Asian traders, and management, who all benefited from high markups. With some delay even the wages of Asian factory workers increased. This setup worked because any aesthetic input on the part of Asian manufacturers and workers was eliminated; to the extent that design services were required, Westerners were brought in on expatriate wage packages. Great care was taken to establish an industrial system that was geared to satisfy the overseas buyers' demand for reliable and standardized manufacturing to any given specification. In the process, local tastes and design skills were gravely devalued.

The intimate link between East Asian manufacturing industries and Western consumer markets developed under continuous protests from industries and unions in the West. The quota system has been revised numerous times due to political pressure in the United States and Europe, installing in Asian manufacturers a sense that their profitable export markets might disappear at any time. They have had a powerful incentive to ensure that their products did not flaunt their country of origin or display a style that would make them identifiable targets for boycotts. Cultural odorlessness, to use Koichi Iwabuchi's delightful phrase (1999), became official design strategy because it allowed East Asian products to fit inconspicuously into the Western markets.

One might think that accounts of economic history have little to offer on the issue of design. However, the assessment of development is closely linked to design, if not wholly determined by it. Economic theory makes a direct connection between design expertise and the progression of economic stages so that economic maturity is said to be reached when designers and managers in export industries converse freely with Western standards and Western tastes (see for example, Lau and Chan 1994). It is hardly unknown that this can be achieved only through a continuous effort to censor local tastes, inevitably followed by a certain confusion as to what is superior in quality and what is simply foreign. In East Asia, however, this process has mostly been interpreted in remarkably benevolent terms as a matter of "learning from the West."

The quota system was never intended to marginalize local tastes in East Asian fashion design; neither were such consequences foreseen when it was instituted around 1960. The main concern at the time was for the Kennedy government to contain the resistance against the free-trade regime by exempting one of the largest industrial sectors (Dickerson 1995: 228–31). In any case, the quotas were intended to be short-term measures. However, it would be a distortion to ignore the fact that – from the point of view of East Asian manufacturers – in the long term, quotas have worked to stabilize an otherwise highly volatile consumer industry. How could this be?

First, since quotas are based on so-called past performance with an allowance for a small annual growth, the system has benefited those countries that were large exporters when the quotas were first instituted. Since 1960 the global textile trade has grown much more competitive as the number of exporting countries has increased and growth of demand in importing countries has slackened. In this environment, the quota system has made it difficult for new exporters – such as Bangladesh and Indonesia (Keesing and Wolf 1980) – to enter world trade with a small quota allocation while it has ensured a stable demand for well-known exporters with large quota allocations – such as the East Asian NIEs (Newly Industrialized Economies).

Secondly, the quota system staked out the path for economic growth in East Asia. With quantitative restrictions, the only way manufacturers could increase the value of their exports has been to seek more lucrative market sectors. This has led to a continuous upgrading in terms of quality and design. The early production of standardized items such as underwear, men's shirts, and children's clothes has been replaced first by the manufacturing of private labels for department stores, and later by designer labels that eventually effected the so-called retail revolution of the 1980s when chain stores went upmarket. The process has continued with mass customization labels such as Tommy Hilfiger actually erasing the distinction between bulk and designer fashion. Such changes would not have been possible without sophisticated global production systems – operated from business centers in East Asia – to ensure that merchandise with the right look and of the right quality arrive in the retail outlets on time, often just six weeks after orders have been placed.

At this point we return to the Japanese avant-garde designers who attracted attention in Paris in the 1980s. The reason why a handful of Japanese designers had industrial backing to present their collections in the Paris ready-to-wear shows was that Japanese companies were already big players in international textile and garment production, just as Japanese were already large-scale consumers of European high fashion. The reason why other East Asian designers try to win international acclaim in a similar manner is that most Western designer brands already source their clothes through East Asian production networks. Expertise in global fashion production is already concentrated in East Asia.

East Asia's economic power has been largely underexposed in accounts of the upgrading of mainstream brand names in the West, and it is equally ignored when the Japanese trend is written up as a surprising outbreak of exoticism. It is not hard to see that any analysis of the globalization of Asian fashion that starts with cultural difference is bound to be inadequate. We can be sure that Asian designers are not knocking on high fashion's door to present rich aesthetic traditions of their very own, but because they are already peers and competitors in Western fashion markets. Even if Western and Asian designers are not creating from the same source, their fashions are of equivalent currencies.

Making the Familiar Strange in Hong Kong

The above journey across the history of global fashion production illustrates how closely fashion design in East Asia is associated not only with culturally odorless cosmopolitanism, but also with discourses of development. From this perspective, it is clear that, when East Asian designers begin to look for a way to "do something Asian," they continue a trajectory of modernism at the same time as they deviate from the discourse of convergence. Indeed, it may make good sense for ambitious Asian fashion designers to parade non-Western aesthetics because fashion has a long tradition of reveling in exoticism. However, this is a design direction adopted with a commercial overview as an essentially modernist strategy of making the familiar strange.

To clarify this discursive figure, we can bring in Anthony Giddens' (1990) formula for globalization as a dialectics of "disembedding" and "reembedding." The process works two ways: on the one hand, it is a matter of disembedding Chinese styles from everyday life and reembedding them in culturally neutral, but de facto Westernized, time and space as deliberate design. On the other hand, the process is one of disembedding fashion from its embeddedness in Westernized Hong Kong popular culture and reembedding it in abstract Orientalized time and space. The fact that Giddens' language of globalization can so easily be applied to fashion indicates the extent to which they share the same modernist premise of discursive discontinuity.

Hong Kong is a good place to examine the forged nature of the self-exoticizing design strategy. In a territory where colonial rule was only recently replaced by the shift of sovereignty to a state that equally represents a motherland and an alien regime, any appeal to national identity is complicated. Japanese designers can rather unproblematically be seen to represent Japan's tradition and aesthetics in Paris, and for some time they may believe so themselves. In

Korea where nationalist discourses already permeate popular culture, fashion designers may engage self-consciously with national aesthetics. Lao designers may dream of using Lao art in fashion, even if their clients normally adopt culturally neutral styles that they bring home from Japan.[4] Indian designers may play around with Gandhi's idea about homespun cloth in order to be representative of the nation (Tarlo 1996). Even Taiwanese designers may find their attempts to represent Chinese culture aided by the fact that the Republic of China has never given up its claim to represent China as a whole. But Hong Kong designers, what do they represent?

While the design dilemma of self-exoticization is experienced by fashion designers all over Asia, it is particularly strongly felt in Hong Kong where the giant garment industry with unrivaled global reach has been dwarfed by a fearful revival of nationalist discourse. In the current climate of political instability, a commercial embrace of Chinese aesthetics may seem more like misplaced opportunism than serious fashion.

Shanghai Tang is no doubt the Hong Kong label best known for its light-hearted implementation of the self-exoticizing design strategy. In 1995 it opened its local flagship store in central Hong Kong, followed in 1997 by a similar store in New York, both modeled on old Chinese shop interiors. The product range consists of clothing, shoes, kitchenware, and home products in simple, colorful, and explicitly Chinese styles. Garments are made with a minimum of design details. "Flat" jackets with mandarin collars and string buttons, Mao jackets with turndown collars and four pockets, and slinky made-to-measure *cheung sam* dresses are the main items. Materials consist primarily of exquisite silks, lined with bright yellows, pinks, or apple greens. The bright red label with the colonial building where the Hong Kong store is located says "Shanghai Tang: Made By Chinese" with a nationalist pastiche typical of the brand.

Behind the label we find businessman and socialite David Tang, as famous for his plummy English accent and his liking for Cuban cigars as for wearing Chinese clothes. With his polished cosmopolitanism, he is not likely to be mistaken for someone who still clings to his old-fashioned costume while the rest of the world moves on. His personal style is in itself a qualification for making the familiar strange. During the height of the Chinesey trend of 1997, a large number of Western celebrities – from Sarah Ferguson to Whoopi Goldberg – were seen wearing Shanghai Tang. In Hong Kong, Shanghai Tang also attracted celebrities and upper-class people.

Shortly after the handover in July 1997, Shanghai Tang encouraged one and all to wear Chinese clothes on a special day that the company dubbed "Dress Chinese Day." Of course, Hong Kong's reunification with China boosted the store's sales in what was widely interpreted as growing Chinese self-confidence.

Ironically, however, Dress Chinese Day equally enforced Chineseness as a carnival-like reversal of everyday life in Hong Kong. Shanghai Tang thus stages a dialectics of disembedding and reembedding primarily on the basis of the exclusive lifestyle of the people wearing the clothes. Its appeal essentially lies in a pastiche-like appreciation of the Chinese past.

It is striking that Tang's claim for original design input is modest. "We don't pretend to be a couture house from France or Italy. We do our best to explain the traditions of designs that have been around for thousands of years and worn by millions of people. They can't be that wrong," he explains in an article that adds that he was "shocked China wasn't marketed to an upscale audience before" (W, October 1997: 202). In this way, Shanghai Tang manages to balance a fairly conservative vision of China with a cosmopolitan appeal to Western and Westernized elites. This marks out the label as a schoolbook example of the self-exoticizing design strategy.

David Tang is not a fashion designer, and Shanghai Tang, like the similar Hong Kong label Blanc de Chine, is managed by businesspeople. Both labels have had a rather uneven input from designers. This may be one reason why Hong Kong fashion designers are no great fans of Shanghai Tang. Their disdain is triggered, certainly, by the way the label has been massively marketed to tourists as local fashion. This is not the first time fashion designers have found their field marginalized by the notion that what counts as local in Hong Kong is essentially the past. From their perspective local fashion must include some creative element. Modernist aesthetic convention requires that a designer embrace what Foucault (1991) has called the "author-function" and ensure that her designs carry the signs of some kind of intentional handling, however conventional the sources may be. Unlike David Tang, a fashion designer could never justify her work as simply the marketing of traditional designs.

It is worth noting also that Shanghai Tang is not a financial success. The New York store has been downscaled considerably following the inevitable wane of the Chinesey trend. Like Blanc de Chine, its continued existence depends on the transfer of funds from the owner's other business operations. This kind of financial backing is what small designer labels anywhere in the world dream of, but only few experience. Without such backing, for example, there would have been no Japanese fashion revolution in Paris. The economic rationale is that it takes some years before consumers and fashion press begin to appreciate an unusual style, but the losses of the early years may be compensated for by long-term gains. However, for a variety of reasons, including an uncertain future, Hong Kong's large garment manufacturers have proven unwilling to support local designers with long-term backing. The irony is, therefore, that Hong Kong designer labels have to be more market-oriented than a commercial label such as Shanghai Tang. In fact, most name designers struggle to keep their relatively small companies afloat through shifting economic trends.

In the last decade a small number of Hong Kong name designers have stuck to a Chinese direction in their design. These include Vivienne Tam, Flora Cheong-Leen, William Tang, and Peter Lau. No doubt, Vivienne Tam is the most successful of these. However, while her company has its production base in Hong Kong, she is operating out of New York, and it is more appropriate, therefore, to think of her as a Chinese-American than a Hong Kong designer. For example, her recently launched book *China Chic* is at the same time a memory project and an attempt at explaining Chinese culture to Western readers (Tam 2000).

If we look at the other three designers, it is clear that "doing something Chinese" has never been an easy path in Hong Kong fashion. In the early 1990s, when they first began to take their inspiration from mainland China, they were reprimanded by the organizers of Hong Kong Fashion Week for not being cosmopolitan enough in their collections. Over the years none of the three has been economically successful. In fact, they have had to subsidize their labels from other business operations, including freelance design for Chinesey labels in Europe.

Peter Lau and William Tang have developed their design over the years so that it is explicitly urban and contemporary. For example, a few months before the Hong Kong handover in 1997, William Tang presented a collection made from fabric printed over with the anticolonial graffiti seen in many parts of the city where it was written by a slightly mad old man, known as the King of Kowloon (Figure 7.2). The collection was meant to be a highly local, and somewhat ironical, comment on Hong Kong's coming reversion of sovereignty, and was generally well received. As if to underscore the logic of exoticization, the collection sold well in Germany where, even if the Chinese writing accusing the "King of England" of "stealing my ancestors' land" were understood, it would hardly be poignant. By contrast, in Hong Kong itself a minor controversy broke out about ownership of the graffiti, and whether or not artists and designers had exploited a naive artist by appropriating his work.

Six months later, William Tang presented a collection that took its inspiration from triads and the drug trade. Models paraded the catwalk with pale faces, untidy hair, and syringes stuck in their arms as a comment on drug use in the fashion world, and by implication also on the way in which illegal drug trade has contributed to a glamorous image of the city through Hong Kong gangster movies. However, unlike Shanghai Tang's triad inspiration, the collection had not been filtered through a screen of nostalgia, and it was perceived to be exceptionally provocative. Newspapers ignored the collection, expressedly for fear of the underworld it portrayed. Both collections were controversial

Figure 7.2 William Tang with his "King of Kowloon" collection: Chinese characters resonate with local meanings.

because they deliberately tried to work with local sources in a way that avoided self-exoticization.

Peter Lau has also stirred up controversy with his label China Doll, which aims at a young and punky market. In a striking design, Peter used material that looked like the Chinese flag – red with five small yellow stars surrounding a large one – for a series of short body-hugging dresses (Figure 7.3). He first did this in the January 1996 collection, and continued to do so throughout 1997. He explained to me, "I thought about what punk would look like in

Figure 7.3 Peter Lau and China Doll: Localizing punk by aid of the People's Republic of China flag.

China. I used the flag with a twist – not as something cold like dictatorship. I turned it into something very feminine like a young woman's lingerie." At the time of the handover, the flag laws were changed, and there was a good deal of anxiety in the fashion business about how allusions to national flags on the catwalk would be perceived by the new government. In the end, Peter Lau's fashion show was erased from the Trade Development Council's official video of the collections of the season.

A few months later he experienced even more direct censorship when he was invited to present two outfits at the Hong Kong Fashion Designers' Association annual show. For the occasion, he had designed lingerie outfits of flag materials, one of the flag of the People's Republic of China, the other of the Republic of China. However, the sexy meeting between mainland China and Taiwan was canceled the day before it was scheduled to take place.

By selecting Chinese sources that are urban and contemporary, both Peter Lau and William Tang have refused to accept the conventional divide between old-fashioned Chineseness and modern cosmopolitan fashion. They have deliberately staged a rupture on the catwalk by means of their unusual constellations of Chinese punks and triad trendsetters. While this represents one viable path out of the Hong Kong dilemma, it is clear from the instances of censorship that in Hong Kong it is barely acceptable to blend fashion and nation without a good dose of self-Orientalization. These designers throw David Tang's demonstrative nationalism in relief. It may be tongue-in-cheek, but it is not merely ornamental.

What is significant about these examples is not simply that they have an edge that made some people feel uncomfortable. Fashion designers elsewhere are also trying to balance a provocative freshness with the conventions of good taste, and in the process they inevitably run the risk of overstepping the line. A fashion feature from 1985, for example, presented "John Galliano's visions of Afghanistan: layers of suiting, shirting, and dried-blood tones." Even though the interest in Afghanistan was smaller then than it is today, many found the purely aesthetic color reference to war casualties distasteful. However, as Julia Emberley points out, the feature does not deviate from a standard Orientalist formula of an adventure story (1988). It upholds the perspective of the Western subject observing an aesthetically stimulating but morally ambiguous non-Western world.

By contrast, when designers like William Tang and Peter Lau begin to rework the requirement for self-exoticization, their collections potentially become critical comments in a local cultural debate. This is both the strength and the weakness of Asian designers vis-à-vis the self-exoticizing design discourse. They may find that rather than transporting them into international fashion – which was the ambition that first pushed them to engage with "something Asian" – their design strategy turns them into astute cultural commentators at home.

Leonard's Design Dilemma

This analysis of the problematic link between fashion and nation ends with a visit to an almost empty Pizza Hut in the industrial area of Kwun Tong one summer evening in 1995. This is where I met Leonard who was twenty-five and had held various different jobs as a junior designer since graduating from the School of Design the previous year. At this time of the day all the employees had left the offices, factories, and warehouses, and what in daytime was a crowded lunch restaurant was transformed into a quiet big-city escape. After each of us had ordered iced tea, we were left alone for well over three hours while Leonard told me about himself.

"It is so *embarrassing* when someone in Hong Kong tries hard to do something Chinese." This was how Leonard summarized his attitude to those Hong Kong designers and labels that try out the self-exoticizing design strategy, including those discussed above. This had a direct reference to the Japanese globalization experience: "The Japanese are very proud of their tradition, but by contrast, the Chinese are not," he said, echoing older nationalist comparisons. When I prodded him on the source of embarrassment, he explained that it was exactly Hong Kong's difference from the mainland. "We are Hong Kong people. On June 4, 1989 [the day of the Tian-An Men massacre], we felt Chinese, but in everyday life we don't feel like that."

Leonard described some experiences that had contributed to his point of view. In his second year at the School of Design, he did a project about minorities in China. While he felt that they were completely unknown to him, and therefore exciting, he also felt ambivalent about taking inspiration from mainland China. It was as if it were not legitimate for him to use this source, or as he put it himself: "I felt as if I stole it from the Chinese."

In the School of Design, Leonard had also learned that there were inflexible limits to what counted as Chinese in fashion. "I would like to respect our lecturers," he said self-consciously, "but I cannot. They are foreigners, and to them to make something Chinese means to duplicate a single detail. I wanted to use some cultural ideas in a different way. In another project I planned to make some garments that were inconspicuous on the outside and shiny on the inside because that is also part of the Chinese garment tradition. But the tutors said that this was not good design, and I was not allowed to do it." Preconceived ideas about the legitimate way in which Chineseness should be incorporated into fashion certainly did not encourage a young Hong Kong designer to play around freely with Chinese sources.

Even so, Leonard was exaggerating when he said his fashion teachers were foreigners. When he was a student, two of his four main tutors were English while the other two were Hong Kong Chinese. One of the expatriates has since been replaced by a local teacher, whereas the other has been working in Hong Kong for almost twenty years, and sees it as her main task to encourage students to use local and regional sources. In fact, she was the one to formulate the project on minorities in China that Leonard found so stimulating. So

Western fashion teachers cannot be reduced to mere instruments of cultural imperialism. However, it is true that fashion students are taught – by expatriates and locals alike – to look to the Western fashion centers "so that they can learn from the best in the world." A strong dose of Eurocentrism is inevitably a part of fashion education.

Leonard echoed a discourse of Chinese nationalism, as he pointed to the oscillation between the excitement of exploring little-known aspects of Chinese culture and disappointment at finding China reduced to conceptions that had been validated in the West. For Leonard – who came from a working-class background and who had been working in the garment industry before he was able to enter design school – the best thing about his fashion education had been aesthetic theory, which had taught him to ask the question of why anything counts as beautiful. He had accepted that, as long as he was employed in the industry, following international trends would be a condition for his work. But he had also learned to think in a way that was important to him personally. He read a lot, and had written a few critical articles about fashion for various Hong Kong magazines.

One of his articles was about the Belgian designer Martin Margiela, a key exponent of deconstruction fashion – which also includes fellow Belgians Dries van Noten, Ann Demeulemeester and Japanese Rei Kawakubo. What these designers share is a disregard for the conventions of the fashion system, and a self-conscious attempt at reworking them. They consciously try to break dressmaking conventions, for example, by placing seams on the outside of a garment and by experimenting with the way in which the cloth is cut. In addition, Margiela has questioned the value of newness by presenting a whole collection consisting only of outfits he had already presented in previous years.

I was struck by Leonard's enthusiasm for deconstruction fashion. It was not only that the term had achieved some general importance as a keyword in fashion (Gill 1998). In deconstruction, Leonard found an alternative to the self-exoticization that he found so embarrassing. Indeed, what he would have liked to take from Chinese dress was something that could question the inside–outside distinction of dressmaking conventions. His own term for this deliberate avoidance of display was the same that he used for deconstruction design: "decadence." With this he wished to emphasize the fact that even if garments *looked* simple, a lot of thought had gone into them. It is hardly a coincidence that the word "deconstruct" appeared written across the chest of a T-shirt from the label for which Leonard was working at the time (Figure 7.4).

Upon graduating from the School of Design, Leonard won a scholarship to go to Europe. For two months he traveled around and visited design schools in Italy, France, and Belgium. As a student, he had already been on a one-week study tour to London and Paris, but this was the first time he was in Europe

Figure 7.4 T-shirt from the label Leonard was working for: "Although the garment looks simple, a lot of thought has gone into it . . ."

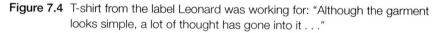

on his own for an extended length of time. This experience made him rethink the relationship between Hong Kong and Europe. "When I was a student I used to look up to European designers, but after visiting different design schools in Europe I actually think that Hong Kong fashion graduates are very good," he said.

At the same time, he had a sense of déjà vu on his trip. He felt that Europe was familiar because he already knew the famous sites. "It was like entering a world of postcards," he said. In this respect, his trip confirmed what he had already sensed – that tribal minorities in China were more exotic to a young Hong Kong designer than anything he could find in Europe. His experience reflected the fact that legitimate fashion history, like other branches of aesthetic history, is almost exclusively European. Thus most Hong Kong designers can list legitimate sources of fashion inspiration from European urban landscapes:

museums, monuments, parks, and flea markets. They may lament that such places do not exist in Hong Kong by saying, "there is no inspiration here." However, Leonard's experience was that such cultural sites are stereotypes. They become banal in the sense that they render little information (Barthes 1983: 237), and ultimately are felt to be unreal.

Leonard's important learning experience was not about Europe, but about Hong Kong's and his own position in world fashion. Before his trip, he had accepted the common view that Hong Kong fashion was lagging behind, and therefore had to keep its gaze firmly locked on the West. Now he had discovered that his own fashion sense and design skills were not inferior to those of young European fashion designers. But this budding self-confidence was not warranted in the environment of the Hong Kong export-oriented garment industry. He was particularly disappointed with his most recent job as an assistant to a Japanese senior designer. He had taken the job in the hope of learning from what he thought would be a skillful Japanese designer. Instead he found the latter's work mediocre and his own opportunities limited.

If I were to characterize Leonard's thoughts, I would point to his disillusionment with the fashion system. Leonard was disappointed with teachers who mechanically celebrated the superiority of European fashion. He was disappointed with the expatriate designer who was no better than a Hong Kong designer. Ultimately, he was disappointed with the local garment industry that keeps its attention locked on lucrative overseas markets, and thus upholds the belief that Western fashion must be superior to anything local.

At the time, Leonard had found a way of coping with his disappointments by dividing his time between work for pay and critical studies for himself. Other designers resolve their disappointment by setting up boutiques – for example, in the Beverly center in Tsim Sha Tsui where a multitude of stalls and small studios can be found. Young designers who wish to try out their ideas are attracted to the possibility of making trendy and unconventional clothes for people with elusive tastes and little money – a market segment that for the same reason puts off manufacturers who are looking to minimize the risk of their investments. In fact, many of these designer boutiques go out of business within the first year of operation.

Leonard was one of the few male students in his class. Perhaps his propensity for thinking his situation through and summarizing it in a crisp formulation can be seen as somewhat masculine, but he shares his experience of the Asian design dilemma with his women colleagues. Men are conspicuous among the most famous designers in the world. But while top levels of all industrial sectors tend to be male-dominated, the fashion business continues to offer many opportunities for women at lower levels. In the mixed economy of Hong Kong fashion where designers combine industry jobs with freelance projects and entrepreneurship, women certainly play a major part. Also, we should not overlook the fact that the men who are drawn to a field such as fashion design that is marked as both feminine and creative rarely are embodiments of conventional masculinity.

A close examination of the fashion industry therefore provides a correction to the gender-skewed image of fashion in that it supplements the fame of a few outstanding – predominantly male – designers with the numerous anonymous – predominantly female – designers who have a hand in making the clothes we wear. With Leonard's story we have traced the self-exoticizing design strategy from international high fashion to a young Asian designer whose name will probably never be known by the people who wear the clothes he designs. This journey has shown that although fashion is a highly segmented business, fashion designers share a set of discourses and dispositions wherever they are located in the global fashion system.

Conclusion: The Globalization of Asian Fashion

In recent years we have seen a number of non-Western styles and designs come to be accepted in international fashion, and we have witnessed a shift from the dominance of the West to a multicultural fashion regime. However, this chapter has questioned the idea that Asian fashion designers can best make their mark on global fashion by "doing something Asian." It has pointed to the obstacles Asian designers face vis-à-vis the self-exoticizing design strategy that requires first to break away from the modernist conventions of fashion that dominate East Asia, and secondly to disrupt the Western aesthetic Orientalism in order to carve out a meaningful subject position for themselves. Through three examples from Hong Kong I have shown that ambitious Asian designers who embark on this strategy – rather than winning international acclaim – may well end up using fashion as a critical art form which allows them to reflect on their own society.

Theoretically, I have reflected the ambivalence of the self-exoticizing design strategy through different sets of concepts. First, there is the distinction between ethnic clothes and fashion. This distinction has been employed implicitly and explicitly by Western fashion journalists and, whether intended or not, it simplifies the working conditions of contemporary Asian designers. Second, I have used Barthes' distinction between image-clothing and textual fashion to point to the ongoing interpretation of designer clothes. One of the distinctive features of fashion – in contrast to other art forms – is the openness of its meanings. While this in itself can be fascinating, this chapter has shown that it has given Asian designers a disadvantage when trying to enter the Western fashion centers. Third, I have presented Leonard's design dilemma as he – like many other Hong Kong designers – is torn between his fear of self-exoticization and his curiosity about deconstructing Chinese clothes.

With his fear of stealing something from the Chinese, Leonard is standing in the surf where the heavy signs of nationalism wash over the light signs of fashion. His dilemma pushes him to appreciate greater sophistication in design, but the question is whether a cleverly deconstructed garment can resolve this dilemma. Even as fashion designers use deconstruction techniques to stage a rupture, the fashion press may push the design back toward self-exoticization by verbally pinning the plastic garment down to well-worn cultural clichés.

By critically unpacking the link between fashion and nation, I have mapped it onto complex global economic and political structures. From this a couple of points arise. First of all, we have moved beyond a naive assumption that fashion designers and other cultural producers are unproblematic representatives of their culture. Their work needs to be situated in the context of the global fashion system that is highly segmented at the same time as its global manufacturing networks provide intimate links between East Asia and the West. Global industrial structures have to be included as an integral part of cultural analysis.

Second, I have emphasized the discursive connections within the fashion world by situating the analysis firmly in the history of the field. The chapter has drawn up lines that connect the last undisputed creators in haute couture with famous Japanese avant-garde designers; that connect the latter with Shanghai Tang, Blanc de Chine, and Hong Kong name designers; and finally that connect the big names with unknown Asian designers working in the global industry. I have shown that these designers observe one another and that they share a set of reference points and assumptions of what fashion is about. It is these kinds of connection that make up the transnational fashion world.

The chapter starts with a picture of Yves Saint-Laurent seamlessly adapting himself to a Middle Eastern setting, and it ends with an image of the understated design of a deconstruction T-shirt by a Hong Kong designer. The contrast between Western exoticism and Asian modernism is striking, and should prompt some self-critical reflections in anyone who still believes in a privileged link between modernity and the West. The modernist dialectics of disembedding and reembedding can be staged in infinite ways in fashion, and while some ways are quite conventional, others have the potential to question received notions of cultural fixity. That is why fashion design can be a critical practice.

This analysis of the globalization of Asian fashion thus also drives home the necessity go beyond the privileged link between the local and critical practice. The relation between the global and the local does not translate into a dichotomy of overarching structures, on the one hand, and agency and resistance, on the other. Fashion is part and parcel of global capitalism. Yet, if we were to limit our critical analysis to perspectives from outside capitalism, our knowledge of this complex phenomenon would be shallow and stereotypical indeed. However, as we have seen, the global highly segmented business that fashion is generates its own critical perspectives from within.

In other words, fashion emerges in a field of tension. This chapter has mapped the tensions and dilemmas that are most strongly felt by Asian fashion designers as they work to find a subject position for themselves – as Asian designers – balancing the pulls of globalization and localization in a global culture industry.

Notes

1. This chapter arises out of my doctoral dissertation, Department of Sociology, University of Hong Kong (2001). I would like to thank Sandra Niessen, Ann Marie Leshkowich and Carla Jones for their thorough and helpful editorial comments. I also thank Francine Lorimer and Brian Moeran for careful feedback.

2. My approach is similar to Dorinne Kondo's (1997) analysis of how the exoticizing discourses used by foreign fashion journalists to describe Japanese fashion in the 1980s reinscribed Orientalisms. While Kondo focuses on how these discourses have led top Japanese designers such as Rei Kawakubo to attempt counter-Orientalisms, I am concerned with how the legacy of the Japanese globalization experience has affected less well-known designers in other parts of Asia, particularly Hong Kong.

3. I have previously written about the international reception of Japanese fashion designers in Skov (1996). See also Dorinne Kondo (1997).

4. Grant Evans, personal communication.

References

Barthes, Roland (1983 [1967]), *The Fashion System*, New York: Hill and Wang.
Bergé, Pierre (1993/4), "Du côté de l'Orient," in *Yves Saint Laurent – Exotisme*, Musées de Marseille – Réunion des Musées Nationaux 17.
Bourdieu, Pierre (1975), "Le couturier et sa griffe: contribution à une théorie de la magie," *Actes de la recherche en sciences sociales*, 1: 7–36.
—— (1993), *Sociology in Question*, London: Sage.
Coleridge, Nicholas (1989), *The Fashion Conspiracy*, London: Heinemann-Mandarin.
Craik, Jennifer (1994), *The Face of Fashion: Cultural Studies in Fashion*, London and New York: Routledge.
Dickerson, Kitty G. (1995), *Textiles and Apparel in the Global Economy*, 2nd edn, Englewood Cliffs: Merrill.

Emberley, Julia (1988), "The Fashion Apparatus and the Deconstruction of Post-modern Subjectivity," in A. Kroker and M. Kroker (eds), *Body Invaders: Sexuality and the Postmodern Condition*, Basingstoke: Macmillan.

Evans, Caroline and Thornton, Minna (1989), *Women and Fashion: A New Look*, London: Quartet.

Foucault, Michel (1991), "What is an author?" In P. Rabinow (ed.), *The Foucault Reader*, London: Penguin.

Giddens, Anthony (2000 [1990]), *The Consequences of Modernity*, Cambridge: Polity.

Gill, Alison (1998), "Deconstruction Fashion: The Making of Unfinished, Decomposing and Re-assembled Clothes," in *Fashion Theory* 2(1): 25–51.

Holborn, Mark (1995), *Issey Miyake*, Cologne: Benedict Taschen.

Iwabuchi, Koichi (1999), "Return to Asia: Japan in Asian audiovisual markets," in K. Yoshino (ed.), *Consuming Ethnicity and Nationalism: Asian Experiences*, London: Curzon.

Keesing, Donald B. and Wolf, Martin (1980), *Textile Quotas Against Developing Countries*, London: Trade Policy Research Centre.

Koda, Harold (1985), "Rei Kawakubo and the Aesthetic of Poverty," *Dress* 11.

Kondo, Dorinne (1997), *About Face: Performing Race in Fashion and Theater*, New York: Routledge.

Koren, Leonard (1984), *New Fashion Japan*, Tokyo: Kodansha International.

Lau, Ho-Fuk and Chan, Chi-Fai (1994), "The Development Process of the Hong Kong Garment Industry: A Mature Industry in a Newly Industrialized Economy," in Edna Bonacich, Lucie Cheng, Norma Chinchilla, Nora Hamilton and Paul Ong (eds), *Global Production: The Apparel Industry in the Pacific Rim*, Philadelphia: Temple University Press.

McDowell, Colin (1997), *Galliano*, London: Weidenfeld & Nicolson.

Said, Edward (1994[1978]), *Orientalism*, London and New York: Vintage.

Skov, Lise (1996), "Fashion Trends, Japonisme and Postmodernism," *Theory, Culture, and Society* 13(3): 129–51.

Steele, Valerie (1991), *Women of Fashion*, New York: Rizzoli.

Tam, Vivienne (2000), *China Chic*, New York: Regan Books.

Tarlo, Emma (1996), *Clothing Matters: Dress and Identity in India*, Chicago: University of Chicago Press.

W (1997), "The Tang Dynasty," October.

Wenders, Wim (1989), *Notebook on Cities and Clothes*, Road Movie Film Production and Centre National d'Art et de Culture Georges Pompidou.

Yves Saint Laurent – Exotisme (1993/4), Musées de Marseille – Réunion des Musées Nationaux.

Afterword: Re-Orienting Fashion Theory

Sandra Niessen[1]

> . . . we remain endlessly troubled by fashion – drawn to it, yet repelled by a fear of what we might find hidden within its purposes . . .
>
> (Wilson 1985: 247)

That fashion is a global phenomenon is indisputable. We need only look at the labels in our closets to assure ourselves that this is so. That there is persistent momentum in the perception of fashion as a Western phenomenon, however, is equally indisputable. An unquestioned, popular understanding of what fashion is can be found in any fashion magazine, on the fashion page of any newspaper, on the fashion channel of any satellite package, indeed, on any city street or in any social scene anywhere in the world. And it is reflected in a century of writings by sociologists, anthropologists, art historians, and students of popular culture. It is also realized in the fashion world on haute couture runways. Fashion's presence and its forms are largely taken for granted. That fashion is a Western phenomenon is a central component in the package of assumptions about fashion. The title of this book, linking Asian dress with fashion, *should*, therefore, give pause, inspire a little discomfort.

Fashion: global but Western. A complex, ambiguous, and not just a little bit murky relationship exists between Western fashion and other clothing systems, especially non-Western, found throughout the world. Given fashion's global systems of production and marketing to which our labels testify, and given that fashion is Western, to what, then, does the relatively recent recognition of "fashion globalization" refer? What is fashion and what is not fashion? What are fashion's criteria for inclusion and exclusion? What do the criteria tell us about fashion, fashion theory, fashion theorists, and also about the social machinery that renders fashion so unquestionable a force? The seven case studies offered by this volume all address the troublesome boundaries of fashion. Selected arbitrarily from different corners of Asia, all are located at the cusp between East and West. The performance of dressing in Asia is about relations between East and West. In this Afterword, my task is to summarize and illuminate, from the perspective of fashion theory, the evidence that this volume presents – and to take stock of the theoretical implications of the findings presented in this book.

I begin with the argument that fashion's definition has long been in need of review and revision, but that this challenge has not been taken up sufficiently. As a result, the Orientalist momentum that resides in the conventional definition of fashion as a uniquely Western phenomenon has not been properly addressed, leaving both primary and concealed the power relations that I contend are central to fashion's processes.

In 1978 Polhemus and Proctor proposed the term "anti-fashion" to designate all systems of dress in the world, both Western and non-Western, that do not fall under the definition of fashion. While I argue below that this dichotomous understanding of the world's dress systems illustrates the false historicism characteristic of Orientalist thought, I also claim that, because the Orientalist understanding of fashion reifies itself throughout the world, Polhemus and Proctor's model has incipient value for understanding global fashion processes. By examining the relations of power that operate between fashion and anti-fashion – precisely that which fashion theorists have neglected on the conviction that fashion's distinctiveness is empirically founded – the dichotomous model is useful for explaining the dynamics of dress on both sides of the great divide between what is considered to be fashion and what is not. Specifically, with respect to the present volume, non-fashion refers to indigenous/local Asian dress forms.

In addition to reviewing the fashion evidence presented in this volume, therefore, I am searching for a definition of fashion that will illuminate the dusky theoretical gap between fashion and its non-fashion foil. The fashion process is about the creation of oppositions through time: that which is (conceived as) current and that which is (conceived as) past. I contend that the definition of fashion is too limited when it focuses only on one side of the process, and it must be broadened to acknowledge the systemic interdependence of the oppositions generated by the fashion process.

Europe and the People without Fashion

> . . . ideas, cultures, and histories cannot be seriously understood or studied without their force, or more precisely their configurations of power, also being studied.
>
> (Said 1979: 5)

Because the word "fashion" is accorded only to select dress phenomena, the word implies a division of the world's adornment into that which is fashionable and that which is not. Logically, the dichotomous reach of the denotation is global. Who decides, and how the decision is made, is primary to the definition of fashion, but almost invariably the definition is given exclusively in terms of the material characteristics of dress. In this section, I make the claim that fashion has been defined a priori as a Western phenomenon, and that, in this way, fashion has been a function of "the enormously systematic discipline by which European culture was able to manage – and even produce – the Orient . . ." (Said 1994 [1978]: 3). Who has, and who does not have fashion is politically determined, a function of power relations. To paraphrase Said, what was "discovered" to be *without fashion* was *what could be made* to be without fashion.

It is perhaps inevitable that temporal distinctions were invoked as the key attribute separating fashionable from non-fashionable bodily adornment. During the Enlightenment, the West prided itself on its rapid progress toward a more ennobled state. By contrast, Other societies outside the West were static. Encompassing everything from depraved to noble savages, they had in common that they possessed tradition, but not history; they were members of "cold societies" (Lévi-Strauss 1966: 233–4). The clothing of such societies was constant, stable, and unchanging; designed for "the maintenance of a particular way of life and a stable tribal identity" (Polhemus and Proctor 1978: 16). There appears to be unequivocal agreement on this point among early fashion theorists:

Fashion does not exist in tribal and classless societies. (Simmel 1904: 541)

Any area of social life that is caught in continuing change is open to the intrusion of fashion. In contrast, fashion is scarcely to be found in settled societies, such as primitive tribes, peasant societies, or caste societies, which cling to what is established and has been sanctioned through long usage. (Blumer 1968: 342)

"Fixed" costume changes slowly in time . . . "Modish" costume, on the other hand, changes very rapidly in time, this rapidity of change belonging to its very essence. (Flügel 1930: 129–30)

In custom bound cultures, such as are characteristic of the primitive world, there are slow-non-reversible changes of style rather than the often reversible forms of fashion found in modern cultures. (Sapir 1937: 141)

By contrast, the clothing in the West reflected the rapid passage of time, the constant need for improvement, the climb toward higher social echelons.

Garments that just would no longer do could be cast aside so that garments could be donned that depicted the more admirable social position to which one aspired. Social hierarchy was a second requisite to the possibility of fashion. The definition of fashion was designed and assigned within the crucible of social Darwinism by those who *could*. In addition, descriptions of the system of dress found in the West were used as the definition of fashion, a projection of "our clothing system."

The consistency in the above definitions of fashion is seductive, but its persistence is what is more remarkable. As recently as the mid-1990s, Anne Hollander wrote:

> Fashionable dress thus has a built-in contingent character quite lacking to all ethnic and folk dress, and to most clothes of the ancient world. Traditional dress, everything that I call non-fashion, works differently. It creates its visual projections primarily to illustrate the confirmation of established custom . . . All non-fashion primarily conveys an ideal of certainty, and demonstrates a link to a fixed cosmology . . . In traditional societies without our sort of uneasy self-propelling fashion, clothing may have immediately readable meaning in its forms, in its methods of wear, and in the character of adornments, all directly linked to the character of customary life, and staying relatively still to do so. (1994: 17–18)

These propositions seem to have been received without consternation or controversy. The truth appears to be self-evident, and the fashion-defining mantra has been handed down intact in academe for a century.

Furthermore, alternative uses of the word "fashion" do not seem to have inspired a review of its accepted definition. New directions of theoretical inquiry that have been launched within the study of dress have not led to a critical retrospective of the field, and a division of analytical labor in clothing studies appears to have stuck, whereby anthropologists continue to study non-Western "dress," and Western fashion remains the focus of fashion studies. A quick statistical review of the relevant library shelf reveals the strong predilection to use the word "dress" for anthropological works, and "fashion" for analyses of Western dress. Disciplinary boundaries appear to support the West/Rest fashion dichotomy even while, as a theoretical issue, the distinction of who does and who does not have fashion is no longer a burning one. But there does still appear to be a need to distinguish Western dress from the dress of other peoples. Popular fashion literature maintains the dichotomy and, as the chapters in this volume demonstrate so clearly, the central chambers of high fashion ensure that admission is limited and carefully screened.

The conventional, evolutionarily dichotomized definition of fashion seems to coexist with alternative visions, descriptions, and approaches. I pointed out, above, that the title of this book *should* inspire discomfort, but it is my greater concern that, while it flies in the face of conventional fashion definitions, no discomfort will be registered, and that acceptance of the contradiction will continue placidly! That this coexistence of different trains of thought has not been more critically evaluated is all the more remarkable given the theoretical directions taken in some partner disciplines that study fashion, as well as the diversity of findings from the study of fashion itself.

In anthropology, for example, the incorporation of a historical paradigm exposed Western, imperialist bias in the assignation of which societies have history and which do not. When anthropologists became aware that their assignation of the Other as being "without history" was a projection of a Western conceptual system, it sparked a thought revolution with much fertile energy being spent on rethinking the subject matter of the field (e.g., Wolf 1982; Hobsbawm and Ranger 1983; Dominguez 1986), changing forever the way anthropologists go about their work. The ethnographically irresponsible "lumping" of non-Western dress in undifferentiated contrast to Western clothing systems is symptomatic of the kind of false historicism with which anthropologists began to concern themselves. The characterizations of fashion cited above as exclusively Western were not constructed inductively on the evidence of exhaustive, cross-cultural study of non-Western clothing systems – only since the latter decades of the twentieth century have these begun to be a more popular (and acceptable) academic pursuit. Furthermore, the anthropologists in the first half of the twentieth century who *did* study "dress," did so in a non-Western, ethnographic setting and did not participate in the discourse about (Western) fashion. In addition, their studies of clothing were synchronic, in part due to the nature of fieldwork as a temporary drop-in affair, and in part because anthropologists accepted that they were studying societies "without history." Later twentieth-century anthropological study of systems of dress, of which several chapters in the present volume are a good illustration, approach the subject matter differently. Such study is consistent with a discipline that has been transformed by a historical paradigm (e.g. Hendrickson 1996; Kondo 1997; Tarlo 1996; Schneider 1978). Nevertheless, they have not resulted in a revision of the conventional, evolutionary, imperialist definition of fashion (Craik 1994), nor have they confronted the issue.

In a second instance, art history has been squarely confronted with the problem of what is art, by whom is it defined, and using which criteria? The pressure to accord non-Western art forms the designation "art," showed up the evolutionist intellectual framework that had dominated the field: only the West could have true art. The close company kept by fashion design(er)/analyst with art(ist)/art historian is partly to blame for the exclusively Western definition of fashion. Costume historians borrowed the parameters of their study of costume[2] from the historical study of art, with the result that the trajectory of Western costume is the same as that of Western art beginning with ancient civilization through Medieval and Renaissance Europe, and ending in industrialized Western Europe and North America. In reconsidering their subject matter in such a way as to include non-Western art and women's art, and even to throw a glance at "craft," the "new" art history that emerged from the fray was founded on a reorientation of the definition of art. They rejected the assumption that "a universal history of art . . . evolves in a linear progressive fashion and culminates in the art of Western Europe" (Phillips 1989: 5), and adopted new research strategies to approach the proliferation of art forms that had now fallen under their purview.

At first glance, fashion studies would do well to once again take a page from the field of art history. At second glance, much of the work seems to have been done already. In pointing to the need for a "model for studying dress in the modern, globally interconnected world," Baizerman et al. (1993) have conducted a critique of the costume historian's evolutionary model for its bias of Western superiority. Second, in the still relatively young journal of *Fashion Theory*, contributions to Western and non-Western dress phenomena are juxtaposed, an important step in developing a global model. Third, studies of non-Western dress systems are burgeoning, and fourth, some students of Western fashion, such as Jennifer Craik, acknowledge fashion as a "cultural technology that is purpose-built for specific locations" (Craik 1994: xi), and therefore multiple, various, and unencumbered by a West/Rest dichotomy. Fifth, the tools of analysis are available. While art historians turned to anthropological methods to approach non-Western art (Phillips 1989: 8), anthropological methods for the study of dress have never been absent. Furthermore, recent emphasis on the process of dressing above the study of dress forms (e.g., Wilson 1985; Butler 1990; Kondo 1997) facilitates global comparisons of dress phenomena.

In the world of art, one of Picasso's legacies was his recognition that Africans and other non-Western peoples produce art (Rubin 1984). Within the fashion world, such a vanguard stimulus has emerged in the person of designer Yves Saint-Laurent, known for incorporating the ethnic in haute couture. The fashion world also had its analogue to the Primitivism exhibition[3] with the "invasion" of Japanese design on European runways. And, as Parminder Bhachu points out (in Chapter 4 of this volume), the British fashionable elite now wear the South Asian salwaar-kameez. The empirical grounds on which to continue the claim that fashion is a Western phenomenon are anything but firm.

Finally, within the study of Western fashion, all has not been illusion and falsity. Sound, detailed descriptions of "the" Western fashion system abound.[4] Simmel, for example, described a hierarchical social system in which fashion forms worn by a higher class of higher means were desired by a lower class of higher aspirations, and thus appeared to "trickle down" as their wearers tried to ascend the social ladder. His work reveals the relationship between the dynamics of clothing systems and the extant social structure in his time. Roche (1994), to cite a more recent example, provided a minute analysis of the fashion system of the ancien régime in France. When fashion began appears to be as unclear as whether it might have constant features, and which they might be. Elizabeth Wilson discerns the rudiments of fashion in fourteenth-century Europe in "a proliferation of styles" and the increased means to acquire them (Wilson 1985: 16). For other scholars, fashion began when Western technological capacities allowed for mass production and expanded consumption. However, even this usage obfuscates the tremendous variety of systems of Western dress that have come into being, one succeeding the other at an accelerating rate (Crane 2000), or coexisting in different locations at the same time, since the industrial revolution. While few describe identical phenomena, the definition of the word fashion (as noted above) has persisted.

In addition, fashion has been assaulted by counter-expressions. These have been variously termed anti-fashion, oppositional fashion, and non-fashion, and are the looks of protest meant to displace the fashion elite, or to provide an ideological alternative to what fashion stands for. In the nineteenth century, for example, dress styles were developed to protest "against the artificiality and waste of fashionable attire" (Ash and Wilson 1992: xv). In the twentieth century, the dress of feminists and counterculture youth is best known for shaking the status quo. Reactions to war, and against bourgeois affluence and middle-class morality (Konig 1973), have all registered in anti-fashions.

> The Royal Family, at least in public, wear anti-fashions; my mother wears anti-fashions; Hell's Angels, hippies, punks and priests wear anti-fashions; Andy Capp and "the workers" wear anti-fashions. (Polhemus and Proctor 1978: 16)

Anti-fashion trends have become so prevalent that they are symptomatic of what is often referred to as a "crisis" in fashion (e.g., Ash and Wilson 1992). This is because they have been picked up off the street and placed on the fashion runway, thereby defusing them of their power of protest (Hebdige 1979), but also weakening fashion's elite image. The international, the ethnic, the subcultural, and the day-to-day have all paraded down Europe's most important runways. Some fashion theorists have considered whether to pronounce fashion "dead" (Polhemus and Proctor 1978: 17; Davis 1992; Konig 1973: 200). Steele is representative of the majority decision when she reassures her readers that fashion is alive and well:

As the culture of fashion has changed, so also has the fashion industry and the image of fashion. But fashion itself remains alive and well, always new, always changing. (2000: 20)

While it is reassuring that regardless of how Western clothing systems change, fashion does not die, logically it does make the issue of fashion's definition more pressing. The accuracy of Simmel's and others' time-bound sociological definitions of fashion demanded that, upon social change, the definition of fashion not just be reconsidered, but also problematized. If defined relative to a single social form, what becomes of fashion when that social form changes? Or, to approach the problem in another way, how should or may fashion be defined if it is changeable and not exclusively linked to a particular social form or forms? The problem of the unfailingly mutating, but nevertheless constantly present and always exclusively Western fashion system is particularly critical when assigning who does and who does not have fashion on a global scale. How can it be that such a proliferation of fashion forms can exist in the West but that the non-West still does not have fashion? Is there a qualitative difference in the variety of Western dress systems compared to non-Western dress systems? This problem needs to be taken up. By not doing so, fashion theorists forfeit the ability to compare fashion systems. Early fashion theorists oriented themselves entirely toward Western fashion, and the momentum of their thought persists – unconsciously, perhaps, and perhaps with subconscious intent, but certainly anachronistically. Even if evolutionary thought were no longer providing momentum to fashion studies, this would need to be addressed. A great divide between the studies of Western fashion/clothing processes and the universal phenomenon of dress/adornment still obtains. As a result, global dress events of profound implication for fashion theory are kept either hidden or barred from scrutiny.

The Globalization of Anti-Fashion

Antifashion is as much a creature of fashion as fashion itself is the means of its own undoing.

(Davis 1992: 161)

Art historians responded to the critique of evolutionist, sexist, and elitist bias in their discipline by making the definition of art more inclusive. Anthropologists, in their turn, accommodated the notion that history is universal. In dress studies, the means selected to accommodate non-fashion systems of dress within the purview of the field has been different. Rather than (for a host of reasons) molding the definition of fashion into something more inclusive, students of fashion have chosen to allow the term to continue to denote a very specific Western clothing phenomenon. In addition, they have chosen to devote more attention to clothing trends that occur outside these confines, that is, to non-fashion phenomena, especially anti-fashion, or oppositional dress. In this way the study of dress has been able both to maintain the sacred cow of fashion and to look (somewhat) more broadly at dynamic processes of clothing change.

In their important volume on *Fashion and Anti-Fashion* (1978), Ted Polhemus and Linda Proctor used the word "adornment" to recognize the universality of body decoration, and then divided up all the clothing styles found through-out the world into two categories: "fashion" and "anti-fashion." Because the authors chose to adopt the conventional definition of fashion, the bulk of the world's clothing expressions therefore belonged in their category of anti-fashion.[5] They defined anti-fashions in negative terms as being "all styles of adornment that fall outside the organized system or systems of fashion change" (1978: 16). Oppositional dress, by the time they were writing, had become one of the hallmarks of countercultural resistance to the Western establishment. A fluorescence of styles was bubbling up from the streets rather than trickling down from the runways and this demanded explanatory attention from fashion theorists. For Polhemus and Proctor, anti-fashion is a "model of time as continuity," in contrast to the "model of time as change" that fashion repre-sents (13). They used the criterion of "timeless tradition" to group "primitive," "tribal," and "peasant" clothing systems together with the anti-fashions that develop on Western streets (16). Therefore, and significantly, the scope of their anti-fashion category is universal, spilling over the boundary between the West and the non-West to encompass (by intent) all depictions of unchanging "tradition."

Oppositional structuring appears to be a fundamental characteristic of dress dynamics in general, with the production of opposites functioning at the very heart of clothing change. With every adoption of a new style, an old style results, and dressers are presented anew with the opportunity to show their affiliation with the new or with the old. In this way, fashion is said to depict the relentlessness of time. Fashion theorists would not likely suggest that "being unfashionable" by virtue of being "left behind" by fashion, or being "fashion indifferent" (Davis 1992: 162), are examples of anti-fashion. However, that a similar principle of opposition operates in purposive anti-fashion clothing statements is obvious.

Early fashion theorists noted the risk taken by potential fashion leaders in wearing something different. With appropriate savvy, and with the right conditions, the risk-taker could succeed, that is, could be recognized as having style leadership. But the path of dress history is also littered with failed design forms. It is not possible to predict the future – hence the ever-present risk in attempting fashion leadership, and hence also the ever-present risk assumed by the fashion industry.[6] Fashion leaders and industry both pose as representing dominant ideologies and stand to lose only if they back the wrong design and an alternative design steals the day as well as the profits. Fashion is successful only when it has a following. And when a dress form promises to have a following, the moment to capitalize on a trend and turn it to individual/industrial advantage has arrived. The wearer of fashion accrues social capital while the power politics of the fashion industry revolve around profits.

Fashion's success therefore depends on having an ear close to the ground to hear social trends while they are still only a whisper, and co-opting them quickly before they supersede trends promoted in fashion's establishment. Polhemus and Proctor coined the word "fashionalization" to describe the conversion from anti-fashion into fashion (17), a powerful tool of co-optation whereby the ideology and image of anti-fashion is endorsed and rendered impotent, defused by becoming mainstream and gaining the appearance of being part of the conservative, generally acceptable, establishment.

The system of fashion therefore incorporates successful material/ideological forms, as well as the potentially spurned/potentially appropriated alternatives from the ranks of non- or anti-fashion. Although only the successful forms belong in fashion's conventional definition, fashion's dynamic involves both. The consequence of dividing up Western dress into fashion and non-fashion components is that it hides the core of the fashion process from view. Appearing to be sui generis, fashion can claim all the attention, hide its vulnerability and dependence, retain its elite stature, and conceptually keep the West separate from the Rest, the rich from the poor, and the powerful from the subordinate.

I argue here that the significance of Polhemus and Proctor's work, while now twenty-five years old, is still fresh as an incipient theory of fashion globalization. In the first instance, their concepts of fashion and anti-fashion accommodate all the clothing systems of the globe. This classification is useful and accurate because Western fashion's definition is constructed on cultural alterity. I hasten to note, however, the limitations in the definitions of the terms as given by Polhemus and Proctor. They have not fully considered the power relations that inhere in the system. The same Orientalist tendency as evident in previous fashion theory has allowed them to lump the primitive/tribal/ peasant into an indiscriminate, indistinguishable mass. While their classification appears to rest on an inductive study of clothing systems, and their conclusions also assume that non-Western clothing systems have a sui generis or "discovered" anti-fashion quality, in fact the term anti-fashion is a relational term. It is a reference to anti-*Western*-fashion. Had the authors tested whether fashion and anti-fashion clothing systems are also mutually generative and derivative in non-Western contexts, they would have discovered the power relations implied in their classification. The transformation from independent dress systems to dress systems that evolve *relative to* Western fashion is an important facet of the globalization of fashion, and is the reason for the occurrence of anti-fashion outside the West. The category of anti-fashion is therefore a useful one to apply to non-Western dress, in this case Asian dress, not because of any inherent "traditional" content but rather in recognition that the power relations that obtain between fashion and anti-fashion strongly inform the direction of clothing dynamics in both. These power relations are at the core of fashion globalization.

While Polhemus and Proctor's discussion of fashionalization explores aspects of the relationship between fashion and anti-fashion, it is also true that the relations between the two are downplayed by the dichotomous model. In the previous section, I pointed out how stubbornly fashion's definition, rooted in cultural alterity, has stuck. In pointing out the mutually generative natures of fashion and anti-fashion – fashion needs anti-fashion like the West needs the East[7] – the authors show their own definition of fashion to be one-sided because it avoids recognition that anti-fashion production and inspiration are integral to fashion's processes. The dichotomy fashion/anti-fashion describes the Orientalist nature of the Western – and now global – fashion system. To serve as a theory of fashion globalization, Polhemus and Proctor's description of anti-fashion as something "found" worldwide needs to be recognized, instead, as the result of *a process of "anti-fashionalization."* The term "fashion globalization" denotes the same. The process is one in which non-Western dress systems are pulled into fashion's vortex as a result of the spread of Western fashion/political dominance.

A definition of fashion that acknowledges the relationship between fashion and anti-fashion as a universal key to understanding clothing dynamics would be truer to the facts of fashion production. As Davis has noted, "So constant an accompaniment to fashion has antifashion been that by this late date in Western dress it can fairly be said the antifashion posture has become firmly, and perhaps irrevocably, incorporated into fashion's very own institutional apparatus" (1992: 162). Fashion theorists would do well to follow the example of art historians by broadening their definition of fashion to include those clothing forms formerly considered to be outside fashion's domain. I therefore use the term fashionalization to describe both the process by which a clothing form becomes anti-fashion, and the process by which it is appropriated by fashion. I also specify, in my use of the word fashion, whether I mean the one-sided conventional, Western definition, or a broader definition that accommodates the dialectical process of the production and reintegration of fashion's opposites.

Sandra Niessen

The Fashionalization of Asian Dress

Fashion *speaks* capitalism.

(Wilson 1985: 14)

The most immediate message conveyed by this volume is that the great divide between East and West is artificial. Commodity flows have made the boundary so porous as to exist now only conceptually. The salwaar-kameez may have originally been South Asian, but Bhachu points out that its designers are now "multiply migrant," many never having lived in or even visited South Asia, and their own lives and those of their parents and children having taken place on different continents and in different cities. Design production is the result of international collaborations and influences, just as salwaar-kameez production in this age relies on fax machines, telephones, and express post to accommodate the tastes and desires of consumers who live far away from the sewers of the suit. The makers and wearers of Vietnam's ao dai are also dispersed throughout the world. Leshkowich describes a "national costume" that is a focus of collaboration and opportunity international in scope. Skov shows how designers in Hong Kong have become so cosmopolitan that the only expectation of "Chineseness" comes from outside their country. And so on. The stories written by the contributors to this volume convey the same message as the labels in our closets. The globalization of fashion is an empirical fact, is of long standing, and does not pertain just to the Western clothing industry.

Nevertheless, fashion remains a Western Orientalist construct. The contributors to this volume demonstrate that fashion and also anti-fashion are reified in the image of their Orientalist definition. Laid atop the global commodity flows that result in the clothing worn around the world today, the conceptual divide between East and West is more stubborn than the barrier put up by expanses of oceans and continents. Simply put, this conceptual boundary lines up modernity (fashion) along the Western side, and tradition (anti-fashion) along the Eastern side, providing the framework in which design, production, and marketing interactions and negotiations take place. What this volume explores is the anti-fashion roles played by Eastern clothing traditions, whether by volition or by imposition. As I point out in my chapter on Batak clothing history (Niessen, Chapter 1 of this volume), a once self-referential system increasingly takes its cues from the Western clothing system. My description of a "global fashion trajectory" is, in the theoretical terms suggested in the present chapter, about the fashionalization of non-Western clothing traditions when cast in the role of anti-fashion.

The selection of this dichotomous fashion framework for approaching the diversity of Asian dress systems theoretically places the focus on what it means to be pulled into the vortex of fashion, what it means to have anti- (Western) fashion rather than one's own clothing identity, what it is to have a dress system that is fashionalized as non-Western. Throughout Asia, the challenge has been to manage this anti-fashion fate.[8] The present theoretical focus highlights relations with the West as expressed in dress, the point of generation of new clothing forms on both sides of the divide, how the boundary between fashion and anti-fashion is maintained and how it is manipulated, shifted, and reasserted, and the advantages and disadvantages within all of that. I begin first with appearances of anti-fashion in what Skov has called "legitimate" fashion terrain. I examine initiatives taken on both sides of the conventional fashion divide, including Eastern attempts to claim legitimate participation and Western attempts to appropriate anti-fashion features. I then shift the focus to apparel types classified as "traditional" and "modern," to examine how these conceptualizations have been endorsed to construct both individual and national identity. The range of strategies recounted by the contributions to this volume is critically reviewed below to determine their significance to fashion theory, and also to test the usefulness of this dichotomous model of global fashion.

Knocking at High Fashion's Door

I begin with the case presented by Skov because, of all the descriptions offered in this collection, it best meets the popular expectation of fashion globalization. The arrival of Asian fashion on the runway gives the appearance of progress: a society once right off (written off) the fashion screen, having acquired the fashion acumen of the Western social elite. It presents the appearance of a triumphal moment in social evolution, marking the achievement of status equality with the West.[9] That competitive, indigenous designers would have their sights set on this, the highest pinnacle of fashion, seems unquestionable. Legion are the examples around the world of the disappearance of indigenous dress forms, often after a period in which they are used to express resistance against an encroaching, dominant exogenous culture. In the course of time, as resistance gives way, the indigenous dress terms become anachronistic and financially and socially nonviable. Western dress then becomes the non-Western daily norm. When, later, indigenous dress forms reemerge, modified for the international fashion market (for example, the ethnic chic parade of the late twentieth century), there has been gain and loss as well as deception. The erosion of space available to indigenous culture is dressed up in the guise of accommodation by fashion.

The appearance of openness to cultural multiplicity masks a different fashion reality. When Skov's case study is unpacked in terms of the present dichotomous fashion model, the illusory nature of the popular understanding of fashion globalization becomes evident, as does the thematic affiliation of Skov's case study with the rest of the volume. In the final analysis, such exotic arrivals on the runways are both illustrative and symptomatic of the abiding power of Western centers/definitions of fashion. The successful Asian "invasion" of the inner sanctum of haute couture on the part of a handful of Japanese designers was hailed as a shift in the boundary of the fashion/anti-fashion divide. Confusion was the result, but it was only temporary. As Skov points out, written fashion, as described by Barthes (1983), using an anti-fashion canon, ascribed "traditional" Asianness to the fashion apparel with the effect that the conceptual divide was rapidly reasserted and the Eastern "invader" transformed into a temporary, graciously received guest. Skov also describes the disappointment of designers in Hong Kong who have been able to garner little success from their creative modern designs, and much more from developing variations on stereotypical "traditional Chinese" designs. Striking here is that the *appearance* of the indigenous in (Western) fashion's forms does not, after all, imply the *acceptance* of indigenous design. To the contrary, success in fashion is sought in "a continuous effort to censor local tastes" (Skov, in Chapter 7 of this volume, p. 226). Asian fashion designers, even – or especially – the most glamorously successful ones, are shackled by an anti-fashion fate.

Indeed, the *appearance* of appropriated indigenous design forms in fashion has been received with consternation on the Other side of the fashion/anti-fashion divide. In her Chapter 2 on Vietnamese national costume, Leshkowich provides an example of this. She points out that the Vietnamese have a fear that the meaning of their national *ao dai* costume will be misinterpreted if it is embraced in the West (p. 94–98), and that this fear is founded on experience. Citing Shenon (1993), Leshkowich reminds the reader of the uptake of Vietnamese dress by Indo-chic interpretations in the 1990s, which resulted in a radical reinterpretation of meaning. "The mandarin collar and frog closures originally celebrated as the height of modesty by a conservative Confucian dynasty were now described for Western eyes as 'like erotic flash points'" (p. 95). Leshkowich's recognition of the different response, in the East, to evidence that might be interpreted in the West as an example of the globalization of fashion is important, and deserves further attention by students of fashion/dress. (Most immediately, it inspires curiosity about South Asians' responses to the marketing success of the salwaar-kameez in elite British circles as Bhachu describes in her Chapter 4 of this volume.)

Skov's study underscores that the anti-fashion designation rests upon the ascription/assumption/appearance of tradition as an indispensable concept.

The classification of dress as traditional is a tool used to preserve the boundary between fashion and anti-fashion, with the West/Rest dichotomy at stake. In this way, Western fashion both protects its position of power, and ensures the maintenance of a conceptual Other on which to rely for self-definitional purposes. The strategy illustrates what Polhemus and Proctor have referred to as the "artificial preservation" of the traditional (1978: 28) in full recognition that the "models" of time represented by fashion and anti-fashion are conceptual tools that cannot necessarily, or always, be confirmed empirically. Evidence of how fashion's anachronisms are rigorously constructed, preserved, and perpetuated is presented in this volume.

Producing Traditional Dress

Less visible to Western eyes set to view fashion globalization is the management of the traditional (anti-fashion) clothing that identifies, if not stigmatizes, its wearer as non-Western. The classification has been received ambivalently. Clothing that signifies this meaning is either shunned to demonstrate viable participation in "modernity" as defined in the image of the West (this is a motivation for knocking at fashion's door as described in the previous section), or it is endorsed to highlight an ethnic identity. In both cases, the meaning is relational, and in that sense truly constitutes anti-fashion relative to (Western) fashion.

The two sides of fashion's conventional divide appear to be complementary. A corollary of Western fashion's need to construct anti-fashion for self-definitional purposes appears to be a corresponding need among those in the indigenous (anti-fashion) domain to have conceptually traditional clothing regardless of the degree of material change that the clothing may have undergone. Leshkowich (Chapter 2), Ruhlen (Chapter 3), and I (Chapter 1) describe how conceptually traditional apparel items in Vietnam, Korea, and Indonesia, respectively – in each case, the discussion is about national costume,[10] – are coveted as models of time/ethnicity without change. To that end, logically but ironically, the traditional is continually modernized/reinvented/updated so that its meaning remains pertinent to evolving social/historical circumstances. Yet these changes are hidden conceptually. Ruhlen, for example, makes note of verbal constructions used to correctly devise the conceptual Korean outfits (a "lifestyle" hanbok rather than a "reformed" hanbok). These designations are a kind of "written anti-fashion" corollary to "written fashion" in the sense described by Barthes (1983). In Vietnam, Leshkowich notes, the Vietnamese themselves fear that they "might forget which version of the *ao dai* garment is 'authentic' and thus lose this cherished form" (p. 95). The fear is not for the loss of a material item, but for the loss of a unique, ethnic identity.

These examples illustrate one way in which fashion's Orientalist definition reifies itself both conceptually and materially in design. Fashion globalization is about the *production* of anti-fashion outside the West, not just – as Polhemus and Proctor saw it – the *labeling* of non-Western clothing as anti-fashion. It would have been more congruent with their ideas if Polhemus and Proctor had referred to non-Western dress as non-fashion, because that term does not imply the oppositional intentionality implied by the word anti-fashion. The inculcation of the concepts of traditional and modern such that they become the conceptual framework for producing and evaluating clothing designs and symbols, for producing intentional anti-fashion, is the result of fashion colonialism. Several authors in the current volume describe the self-Orientalizing inclinations of makers/wearers of "traditional" apparel. The purchase of the bifurcated model (traditional/modern) must be the original core of self-Orientalizing that is expressed equally by wearing/producing clothing in the East that belongs conceptually to either side of the fashion's conventional divide. Non-fashion ("found" rather than "intentional" anti-fashion) has no cognitive space for survival when the bifurcated model is politically and econ-omically dominant. On the two sides of fashion's conventional divide, those who protect the exclusiveness of (Western) fashions, and those who defend the purity of traditional attire, are speaking high and low dialects of the same global fashion language.

Some contributions to the present collection reveal how the image of the Asian nation has been constructed using the dichotomous terms of fashion colonialism. Eastern states need to appear modern and developed/developing, but wish to retain their own unique inherited identity. Those whose task it is to graphically depict the nation are concerned to use the appropriate dress images. Jonsson and Taylor (in Chapter 5) point out that the Vietnamese state uses indigenous dress forms of the tribal minorities, precisely those peoples whom the French colonists had deemed "primitive," in its graphic depictions of the nation. This selection flouts the colonial values from which the Viet-namese government wishes to distance itself. It symbolizes the unique path of development that the nation-state wishes to take, viz., a political entity to be taken account of internationally, but on its own unique terms. The clothing depicts resistance akin to the Karo retention of indigo-blue clothing in the colonial era (Niessen, Chapter 1 of this volume), and the Korean endorsement of their hanbok as a sign of resistance to attacks both military and economic from the West (Ruhlen, Chapter 3 of this volume), but with a significant difference. By the time of the manipulation of the indigenous dress of tribal peoples by the Vietnamese state, that dress had been fashionalized. By this I mean that while the Karo rebellion, at least initially, was a refusal to give up their own dress forms, the Vietnamese state is using the dress of its tribal peoples in an Orientalized idiom. This example is an illustration of how the bifurcated model of fashion can be complicated by social hierarchy in the East. The appropriation of tribal dress for use in an Orientalist idiom by a national elite has parallels with the appropriation of non-Western fashion by a Western fashion elite, even while the former is intended to depict resistance against an Orientalist designation of the state.

Performing Modernity

All of the contributions to the present volume describe the course of fashion colonialism whereupon men are the first to pull on suits to function in the colonial establishment and women stay behind in traditional dress to guard the home. The "dress of the home at the same time carries an ambivalent message of . . . women's exclusion from a new world, however ugly, and thus of their exclusion from modernity itself" (Wilson 1985: 14), and cannot, therefore, fully suffice. Modernity – "however ugly" – becomes a choice that women eventually make, and it is a much more dangerous choice for them than for men. Modernly dressed Asian men melt into unmarked gender terrain, while women have no recourse but to come to terms with an image of modernity that is aptly illustrated by the Korean poster that Ruhlen describes: the counterpart of the traditional "proper Korean" of "natural beauty" is a "wanna-be Westerner . . . not quite a prostitute, but . . . on that path" (p. 129). This image of modern femininity is conveyed to the Korean nation by what Ruhlen calls "patronizing and misogynistic nationalism." As a result, women's sexual identity is particularly at stake in how they perform modernity.

On the other side of the coin, images of "appropriately" modern women are propagated by the Asian state to represent national development. "Appropriately" modern styles are cued by Western trends, but the Western look is not adopted wholesale. To be fit to represent the non-Western-but-developing state, they must be modified by elements of traditional heritage. Jones conveys in Chapter 6 just how tortuous a proposition it has been for women in New Order Indonesia under President Suharto to negotiate "modernity" in order to present themselves in a way that is perceived as appropriate. Modernity is not an available commodity "off-the-shelf." It must be constructed with social intelligence, and the path of invention is anything but crystal clear. Jones notes that women's choices are dynamic and experimental. They consider options that both resist and reinforce state ideologies; judgment of their performance takes account of their class, age, social level, career, and other relevant social circumstances such as the times and the economy. They often engage the assistance of a range of more or less expensive guides, to learn how to run the gauntlet successfully, and from which they are to emerge displaying the values of the nation. The resulting blend of modernity and tradition is colored by both, but not too much by either one. Their modern-dress performance is as much in process as their performance of traditional dress.

The anti-fashion framework for modern dress appears to offers women the possibilities of either representing the state in its own, unique process of development, or selling out to the West, with women's respectability, particularly sexual respectability, hanging in the balance. While Western high fashion scrubs away Eastern design to preclude the possibility of any lingering "ethnic odor" in the fashion domain, day-to-day modern dress that is loyal to the Eastern state and to ethnic identity daubs on a splash of tradition to transform Western trends into a modernity more appropriate for Asia.

Oppositional Dress in the Anti-Fashion Domain

Antifashion assumes many forms and springs from diverse cultural sources.

(Davis 1992: 168)

Anti-fashion, by definition, offers an intentional alternative to fashion. What is called anti-fashion by Polhemus and Proctor in reference to non-Western dress is described here instead in terms of fashionalization, that is, something more akin to co-optation by Western fashion's framework than resistance to Western fashion's dominance. Nevertheless, resistance is strongly rooted in ethnic insistence on the retention/development of "traditional" dress in contradistinction to modern dress. Ruhlen writes, for example, that in Korea the "glorification of hanbok for national pride is usually tied to an indirect swipe at Westernization and the West in general" (p. 127) This kind of resistance is framed within the Orientalist fashion framework.

Beyond this, the definition of anti-fashion as a "model of time without change," functions to conceal the possibility that oppositional dress forms might be generated to oppose anti-fashion images. The classification implies that anti-fashion dynamics occur in response to Western fashion, and denotes – falsely – an undifferentiated Other as having anti-fashion in an undynamic and inescapable way. The anti-fashion scene is immensely complicated by self-Orientalizing strategies adopted by the Asian state to define itself vis-à-vis the West. Then, as described above, both traditional and modern clothing images are appropriated to depict the nation – and this is one reason why oppositional styles develop within the anti-fashion domain.

In her Chapter 7, describing East Asian attempts to participate in what she calls "legitimate" fashion, Skov brings attention to the refusal on the part of two Hong Kong designers to adopt the self-exoticizing strategy, or – in terms of the theoretical model used in this Afterword – to cater to the expectations of "tradition" as these are differently expressed on the two sides of Western fashion's divide. The designers have staged a double resistance against the binary set of possibilities offered by the fashion process, by refusing "to accept the conventional divide between old-fashioned Chineseness and modern cosmopolitan fashion" (p. 234). Instead, they select something "explicitly urban and contemporary" (p. 231). Peter Lau works with anticolonial graffiti and converts Chinese flags into sexy underwear; William Tang uses images from the drug trade. They stir up controversy and censorship because "in Hong Kong it is barely acceptable to blend fashion and nation without a good dose of self-Orientalization" (p. 234). The fashion designers become "astute cultural commentators at home." If this is not the role of fashion innovation in the West (Skov offers parallel examples), certainly it is the role of Western anti-fashion: "they have deliberately staged a rupture on the catwalk . . ." (p. 234). These vanguard oppositional fashions resist Orientalist discourse about the nation, whether that discourse takes place in the East or in the West. This important theme is unexplored in fashion studies, but its emergence in Hong Kong may well be a harbinger of future developments in global fashion.

Skov does not refer to the significance of the gender of the wearer (if any) in the anti-Orientalist message of these design creations. Nevertheless, it is clear that the burden of representing the nation is given to women because they are "creatures of fashion." In the conclusion to her Chapter 3, Ruhlen mentions her expectation of oppositional expressions developing within Korean feminism. Apparently the issues relating to women's burden of depicting the nation have "not yet" been tackled and, so far, feminists "seem willingly to accept the rules of the hanbok game" (p. 134). Feminism has been a vibrant source of anti-fashion production in the West out of reaction to fashion's preoccupation with reshaping and restricting women's bodies to conform to patriarchal notions of femininity. In Asia, the opposition to Western constructions of femininity is expressed by adhering to traditional images of the "appropriate" female – traditional dress forms serving, therefore, also as feminist anti-fashion. Indeed, Korean feminists, as described by Ruhlen, appear to place a higher value on the appearance of anti-Western, sexual propriety than on reappropriating their sexual identity: "feminist activists have to sidestep potential charges of being intellectual 'Yankee whores'" (p. 130). However, traditional images do not provide a safe haven for women in an Orientalist, nationalist discourse because these images are appropriated by the state to depict the Asian nation. In Vietnam, where these images are of tribal minority women, as Jonsson and Taylor point out in Chapter 5, the outfits are represented in greater detail than the people wearing them. Furthermore, the tribal-minority women are either objectified to typify "minorities-in-general" or are left out entirely.

That it should be a female icon that is used to represent the nation is a result not just of her associations with tradition; it is part and parcel of women's role in the capitalist fashion system.

If traditional dress represents resistance to modern images of femininity, how will resistance to the objectification of traditional images be expressed? Carla Jones notes in Chapter 6 that the performance of modernity contains elements that both resist and reinforce the feminine images promoted by the Indonesian state. In the subtle, charged process of constructing modernity, the fashion process is at play: the indomitable cycle of invention of the new, followed by the discarding of the old. It is the same process that is in evidence in the construction of tradition. Furthermore, during the process, modern and traditional elements are combined and blended in subtle and complex ways, thus increasingly blurring the distinction between fashion and anti-fashion.

This should lead the theorist to reconsider the limitations of the dichotomous model. May the production of anti-fashion be interpreted simply as a more dramatic statement of style invention? Above I have argued for a definition of fashion that takes account of process, i.e., the succession of style inventions, inclusive of even the more dramatic oppositional statements of anti-fashion. The dichotomous model is useful for understanding the unique terms by which dress is negotiated in postcolonial Asia. As the dichotomous model is complicated by innovative combinations of its oppositional terms, as the dichotomy becomes fractured and complex and the boundaries of its terms soften, we arrive full circle. The great divide between social forms and ideologies is bridged by the dialectic of fashion negotiation. Emerging ever more clearly between the terms of the no-longer-so-great divide is the global fashion process.

Conclusions

The Orient is an integral part of European *material* civilization and culture.

(Said 1994 [1978]: 2)

The studies presented in this volume require a fashion theory that takes better account of global dress phenomena. Recognizing the configurations of power that operate in fashion's global dynamic is fundamental to recognizing that fashion's conventional definition (and it mirrors fashion's industrial workings) is Orientalist. Fashion has been defined in the West without sufficient attention to who is making the judgment and how the judgment is made. Fashion theorists have pointed to temporal/historical differences when assigning who does and who does not have fashion. The false historicism to which they subscribe has been deconstructed by anthropologists, and discarded by the "new" art history so as to accommodate global systems more adequately and accurately. That it still persists in fashion studies ensures the inertia of the conventional definition of fashion, and stymies a more inclusive study of global dress phenomena.

In this Afterword, I have identified Polhemus and Proctor's 1978 model of fashion and anti-fashion as an incipient theory of fashion globalization. While global in reach, I point out that the model fails to address the configurations of power that reside at the core of the relations between fashion and anti-fashion, and also that it fails to fully deconstruct the mythical nature of fashion's temporal definition. It is by addressing these two failings that I adapt their model to accommodate the processes of fashion globalization.

Above, I have argued that a global definition of fashion needs to acknowledge the dialectical process of fashion in which anti-fashion is produced and reintegrated (fashionalized). To conceal or negate the interdependence of fashion's oppositions is to operate in fashion's ideological and economic interests, but to fail analytically. Most fashion students currently are studying what technically lies outside fashion's definitional purview. This situation is bound to persist as long as fashion is defined according to popular conventional wisdom as "what appears by that name in the media and in designers' collections in shops, after first appearing on runways . . ." (Hollander 1995: 10–11). Furthermore, the definitional restrictions will continue to limit the ability of fashion studies to fully take account of developments in global fashion dynamics.

Nevertheless, there is widespread recognition of the exchange that takes place between fashion and anti-fashion. Fashionalization is the term coined by Polhemus and Proctor to describe the appropriation of anti-fashion by fashion. Because I argue for a more inclusive definition of fashion, the process by which non-Western dress is turned into anti-fashion – i.e., the process by which it begins to function relative to Western fashion and is engaged, thereby, in a global fashion process – is, logically, then also a form of fashionalization. Eastern clothing was fashionalized as the East was "Orientalized" (Said 1994 [1978]: 5). The process by which Western fashion features are incorporated in the anti-fashion domain have not been accorded the reciprocal name of anti-fashionalization, but are accounted for in the definition of fashion globalization.

I have used the Asian dress scenarios presented by the contributors to the present volume to develop and illustrate the proposed model of fashion globalization. As independent, self-referential Asian clothing systems begin to reference Western clothing systems, the binary opposition traditional/modern begins to operate as a filtering lens through which clothing phenomena are produced and interpreted. Fashion's definition thereby reifies itself globally in clothing forms and meanings.

It has not been the goal of this Afterword to suggest that the conceptual distinction between fashion and anti-fashion is anything more than conceptual, because global commodity flows do not recognize such distinctions, nor are they clearly bounded in the dress negotiations of daily life. However, as a dominant conceptual framework, it explains some of the difficulty that Asian fashion designers have experienced in gaining any permanent entry into fashion's higher sanctum, and the passion that is ignited to protect traditional Asian dress forms from Western appropriation.

The weaknesses and limitations in the dichotomous model are evident from the complex way in which the two terms are manipulated and combined, such that binary distinctions are blurred and proliferate in new forms. The fashion cycle of style innovation, followed by the discarding of that style to make space for yet another innovation, is found in both the traditional and modern domains of anti-fashion. Furthermore, oppositional strategies to Orientalized fashion are exploring new terms on which to orient dress. The limits of the proposed dichotomous model of global fashion will be met as these efforts proceed and succeed, the evidence becoming ever more clear that fashion is a global phenomenon.

Notes

1. I am grateful to Carla Jones and Ann Marie Leshkowich for their encouragement and assistance throughout the writing of this piece.

2. The history of dress was once referred to as the history of costume. Today historians of dress tend to reserve the word "costume" for more specific dress forms such as for theater or disguise.

3. The Primitivism exhibition was staged in the Museum of Modern Art in New York, until then an unlikely venue for non-Western art in which to make an appearance (Rubin 1984).

4. I have used the singular here to be consistent with the notion of a single fashion system in contrast to non-fashion elsewhere. However, to be consistent with the argument that I develop in this Afterword, the word should be in the plural to acknowledge the diverse forms that fashion can take.

5. The authors also recognized the category "unfashionable" – i.e., "those who can't keep up with fashion change but would like to" (1978: 16) – but it plays an unimportant role for their theory. It underscores the narrowness of their definition of fashion when even "discarded fashion" falls outside.

6. There is a tendency to perceive fashion as beyond any control. As Polhemus and Proctor note (1978: 16), "The introduction of any fashion innovation must respect and relate to the fashion changes which have come before. In this sense, neither designers nor the fashionable are in charge and in control of fashion change. Fashion

is to a large extent running its own show, and one can only choose to get on or get off the fashion merry-go-round – if, indeed, even this is really a matter of personal choice."

7. "The Orient has helped to define Europe (or the West) as its contrasting image, idea, personality, experience" (Said 1979: 1–2).

8. This constitutes another parallel with the world of art. Michael Ames (1987) has described the frustration experienced by North American Northwest Coast indigenous artists expected to continually produce within the restricted design canons expected of Northwest Coast Indians by the exogenous consumer market. They operate within a different set of exogenous imposed expectations than their counterparts who are members of the dominant culture, and they are expected to exhibit their works in ethnological museums rather than art galleries.

9. It is no wonder that when post-Mao China opened its doors to Western fashion, the event was politically significant and supported by top levels of government. "Fashion is implicated in the state project of modernization precisely because of its signification of change, and its identification with Western fashion centers, high lifestyles, and most importantly, an exuberant modern society that China is striving to become. It satiates a genuine desire for annihilating China's status as a 'Third World' country" (Li 1998: 87).

10. Elizabeth Wilson describes national outfits as "sartorial lies" because they are "newly created" rather than "authentic" as they seem (1985: 23).

References

Ames, Michael (1987), "'Free Indians from Their Ethnological Fate': The Emergence of the Indian Point of View in Exhibitions of Indians," *Muse. Journal of the Canadian Museums Association* 5(2): 14–25.

Ash, Juliet and Wilson, Elizabeth (eds) (1992), *Chic Thrills: A Fashion Reader*, London: Pandora.

Baizerman, Suzanne, Cerny, Catherine and Eicher, Joanne B. (1993), "Eurocentrism in the Study of Ethnic Dress," *Dress* 20: 19–32.

Barthes, Roland (1983 [1967]), *The Fashion System*, New York: Hill and Wang.

Blumer, Herbert (1968), "Fashion," in David Sills (ed.), *International Encyclopedia of the Social Sciences* 5: 341–5.

Butler, Judith (1990), *Gender Trouble: Feminism and the Subversion of Identity*, New York: Routledge.

Craik, Jennifer (1994), *The Face of Fashion: Cultural Studies in Fashion*, London and New York: Routledge.

Crane, Diana (2000), *Fashion and its Social Agendas: Class, Gender, and Identity in Clothing*, Chicago and London: University of Chicago Press.

Davis, Fred (1992), *Fashion, Culture, and Identity*, Chicago and London: University of Chicago Press.

Dominguez, Virginia (1986), "The Marketing of Heritage," *American Ethnologist* 13(3): 546–55.

Flügel, J.C. (1930), *The Psychology of Clothes*, London: Hogarth Press.

Hebdige, Dick (1979), *Subculture: The Meaning of Style*, London and New York: Routledge.

Hendrickson, Hildi (ed.) (1996), *Clothing and Difference: Embodied Identities in Colonial and Post-Colonial Africa*, Durham, NC and Londong: Duke University Press.

Hobsbawm, Eric and Ranger, Terence (eds) (1983), *The Invention of Tradition*, Cambridge and New York: Cambridge University Press.

Hollander, Anne (1995 [1994]), *Sex and Suits*, New York: Kodansha International.

Kondo, Dorinne (1997), *About Face: Performing Race in Fashion and Theater*, New York and London: Routledge.

Konig, René (1973), *The Restless Image: A Sociology of Fashion*, London: George Allen & Unwin Ltd.

Lévi-Strauss, Claude (1966 [1962]), *The Savage Mind*, Chicago: University of Chicago Press.

Li, Xiaoping (1998), "Fashioning the Body in Post-Mao China," in Anne Brydon and Sandra Niessen (eds), *Consuming Fashion: Adorning the Transnational Body*, Oxford: Berg.

Phillips, Ruth B. (1989), "Native American Art and the New Art History," *Museum Anthropology* 13(4): 5–13.

Polhemus, Ted and Proctor, Lynne (eds) (1978), *Fashion and Anti-Fashion*, London: Thames & Hudson.

Roche, Daniel (1994), *Dress and Fashion in the "Ancien Regime,"* Cambridge: Cambridge University Press.

Rubin, William (ed.) (1984),*"Primitivism" in 20th Century Art: Affinity of the Tribal and the Modern*, 2 vols, New York: Museum of Modern Art.

Said, Edward (1994 [1978]), *Orientalism*, London and New York: Vintage.

Sapir, Edward (1937), "Fashion," *Encyclopedia of the Social Sciences*, The McMillan Co.

Schneider, Jane (1978) "Peacocks and Penguins: The Political Economy of European Cloth and Colors," *American Ethnologist* 5(3): 413–47.

Shenon, Philip (1993), "The Mist off Perfume River," *New York Times*, 21 November.

Simmel, Georg (1957 [1904]), "Fashion," *The Journal of American Sociology* LXII (6): 541–58.

Steele, Valerie (2000), "Fashion: Yesterday, Today & Tomorrow," in N. White and I. Griffiths (eds), *The Fashion Business: Theory, Practice, Image*. Oxford: Berg.

Tarlo, Emma (1996), *Clothing Matters: Dress and Identity in India*, Chicago: University of Chicago Press.

Wilson, Elizabeth (1985), *Adorned in Dreams: Fashion and Modernity*, London: Virago.

Wolf, Eric R. (1982), *Europe and the People without History*, Berkeley: University of California Press.

Index

British Asians, 142, 155
cultural, 81, 85–86, 225
dress practices, 2, 7–8, 62–3
essentialized, 16, 20–2, 25, 33–4, 81,
  86
ethnic, 155, 218, 226, 257, 260
Hong Kong, 228–9
Indonesian, 186, 192–3
men, 208n10
national, 26–8, 34–5, 110n8,
  119–20, 228, 258–9
performance of, 22–6, 36–7, 133
personal, 201
political, 118, 130
Vietnamese, 88–9, 164, 167, 170,
  179–80
  ao dai, 92–4, 98, 105
  dress practices, 181n3
  ethnic, 165, 167–8
  national, 166, 172–3, 179–80
  women, 189, 198
ideology
  anti-fashion, 252
  Confucianism, 28, 89–90, 129, 160
  gender, 15–16, 20, 203
  globalization, 14, 85–7
  state, Indonesia, 193–4, 207
  Western feminist, 122, 129, 133
illiteracy, Vietnam, 172–3
image
  Asia, 17–19
    nation, 258
  clothing *see* clothing
  ethnic minorities, 159, 161–2,
    165–7, 170–6, 179–81
  Japan, 28–9
  women, 21, 38, 40n10, 200, 259,
    261–2
    Korea, 128–30
    Vietnam, 162–6, 170
imitation, 11–13, 20, 35, 56, 186, 199,
  208n4
  see also mimicry
immigrants

Batam island (Indonesia), 209n11
British Asians, 140, 142–3
  see also migrants, multiple
imports, textiles, 53, 59, 65, 74n11,
  226
independence
  Indonesia, 52, 62
  Vietnam, 172–4
India
  colonialism, 9–12, 39n7, 39n9
  national identity, 110n8
Indian subcontinent, 142
  designers, 149, 151
  production, 145, 148–9
indigenous design, in Western fashion,
  256
indigenous dress, 49–50, 255
  ao dai, 96–7
  Batak, 56, 58, 63, 71
indigenous textiles
  Batak, 51–3, 66
  history, 72
Indo-chic, 1, 94–5, 105–6, 256
Indochina *see* Vietnam
Indonesia, 35, 49–75 passim, 185–210
  passim
  dress practices, 1, 4–5, 52–65 passim,
    187, 192–3, 200–2, 208n8–208n9
  modernity, 259, 262
industry
  clothing, 19, 210n21
    exports, 197, 215, 225–7, 238
    Hong Kong, 215–16, 225–6, 229,
      230, 238
    Korea, 125–7
  fashion, 19–21, 208n4, 215–16, 252
  textiles and clothing
    East Asia, 225–8
    Indonesia, 197
    Vietnam, 81, 104
influence
  Asia, on the West, 1–2, 5, 7
  Asians
    in Europe, 155, 227–8